WYATT & BAT
EARP MASTERSON

WYATT EARP & BAT MASTERSON

LAWMEN
OF THE
LEGENDARY WEST

BILL MARKLEY

TWODOT®

Helena, Montana
Guilford, Connecticut

A · T W O D O T® · B O O K

An imprint and registered trademark of The Rowman & Littlefield Publishing Group, Inc.
4501 Forbes Blvd., Ste. 200
Lanham, MD 20706
www.rowman.com

Distributed by NATIONAL BOOK NETWORK

British Library Cataloguing in Publication Information available

Library of Congress Cataloging-in-Publication Data available

ISBN 978-1-4930-3567-0 (paperback)
ISBN 978-1-4930-3568-7 (e-book)

CONTENTS

ILLUSTRATIONS LIST

Dedicated to my parents, Bill and Gloria Markley,
who instilled in me a love of the West.

HATZELL '18

It is not the critic who counts; not the man who points out how the strong man stumbles, or where the doer of deeds could have done them better. The credit belongs to the man who is actually in the arena, whose face is marred by dust and sweat and blood; who strives valiantly; who errs, who comes short again and again, because there is no effort without error and shortcoming; but who does actually strive to do the deeds; who knows great enthusiasms, the great devotions; who spends himself in a worthy cause; who at the best knows in the end the triumph of high achievement, and who at the worst, if he fails, at least fails while daring greatly, so that his place shall never be with those cold and timid souls who neither know victory nor defeat.

THEODORE ROOSEVELT,
"THE MAN IN THE ARENA,"
EXCERPT FROM THE SPEECH
"CITIZENSHIP IN A REPUBLIC"
DELIVERED AT THE SORBONNE,
IN PARIS, FRANCE, ON 23 APRIL, 1910

INTRODUCTION

A solitary marshal steps into the deserted street of an Old West town to confront three desperados hell-bent on terrorizing the townsfolk. After a moment sizing up each other, they all draw their six-shooters and blast away. As the gun smoke clears, the marshal stands unscathed as the bad hombres, riddled with holes, lie dead in the dusty street. Even though most gunfights didn't happen this way, it's the typical outcome of many Western movies.

Think of Old West lawmen you have read about or seen on screen; many are fictional: James Arness as Marshal Matt Dillon in the *Gunsmoke* television series (1955–1975), Gary Cooper as Marshal Will Kane in *High Noon* (1952), or John Wayne as US Marshal Rooster Cogburn in *True Grit* (1969). If you ask people to name real-life Old West lawmen, most would probably answer Wyatt Earp, maybe even Bat Masterson. A few might throw in Wild Bill Hickok or Bill Tilghman.

Wyatt Earp and Bat Masterson are the best-known lawmen. Neither of them was a saint. At times their actions were not in compliance with the law, and they only served as peace officers for limited portions of their lives. What sets them apart from the thousands of sheriffs and marshals who served on America's frontier? Did they make more arrests than others? Did they kill large numbers of men? Did they lead adventurous lives? Was it their character? Was there just the right ring to their names that led people to remember them? Did they get the right publicity at the right time? Did they just outlive all the others? Or was it a combination of these factors?

Masterson and Earp did receive national publicity, and they did outlive most other lawmen. In this book, I'll explore the lives of Wyatt Earp and Bat Masterson side by side, focusing on their actions when the frontier was wild and woolly. In the end, I'll give my opinion as to who I believe was the best lawman of the two, but you may come to a different conclusion.

Bat Masterson, in later life, became a sports reporter and journalist. The editor of *Human Life Magazine* asked Bat to write about Western gunfighters he had known. Bat said there were three characteristics separating a good gunfighter from a bad one or, worse yet, a dead gunfighter:

1. *Courage*
2. *Proficiency in the use of firearms*
3. *Deliberation*

Bat went on to tell several tales of gunfighters who had courage and knew how to shoot but became excited and did not take the time to aim their weapon, paying the ultimate price.[1]

Wyatt Earp told his biographer, Stuart N. Lake, something similar: "The most important lesson I learned from those proficient gunfighters was that the winner of a gunplay usually was the man who took his time. The second was that, if I hoped to live long on the frontier, I would shun flashy trick shooting—grandstand play—as I would poison."[2]

Both Wyatt and Bat shared these attributes and lived to tell their stories, whereas others did not heed this advice and did not live to tell their tales.

Neither Wyatt nor Bat was continuously employed as a lawman. Just like most everyone on the frontier, they were out to make a buck. So, they worked at all types of jobs: buffalo hunting and skinning, driving wagons, dealing cards, and acting as bouncers. The only activity they both avoided was farming, having had enough of that while growing up.

Much more has been written about Wyatt than Bat. Bat spent more time writing about other Western characters than he did of his own exploits. Many historians discount Lake's biography, *Wyatt Earp: Frontier Marshal*, but, in writing this book, I rely on his version of Wyatt if there is no conflicting evidence. Loren

D. Estleman, recipient of Western Writers of America's lifetime achievement Owen Wister Award, contributed the foreword to the Pocket Books 1994 printing of Lake's biography of Wyatt. Estleman wrote, "*Wyatt Earp: Frontier Marshal* is exceedingly well written and contains a vast amount of authentic information braided in among the tall tales. Its account of Wyatt's early life has seldom been questioned, and it fills the gap plausibly where no witnesses have come forward to dispute the version attributed to Wyatt."[3] However, Wyatt went to great lengths to hide some of his activities such as working in houses of ill repute. Neither Wyatt nor Bat liked to dwell on their improper actions. Who does?

Where does the legend end and the truth begin? I found those who write about these two men pick and choose what they think is real. I, too, have chosen what I believe to have a basis in truth. I do believe many stories are true but embellished. For example, Wyatt's arrest of Ben Thompson in Ellsworth, Kansas, is discounted by most historians. Maybe it did happen, but not to the extent Stuart Lake and Wyatt glorified it. Or what about the gunfight between Corporal Melvin King and Bat—which of several plausible stories do you pick?

Wyatt and Bat met on the plains of Kansas in the early 1870s and remained best friends for the rest of their lives. Wyatt was taciturn and rarely expressed any humor, while Bat was outgoing and loved a good joke. Wyatt usually drank coffee but on occasion would drink a little alcohol while Bat was ready to belly up to the bar. One thing they had in common was their loyalty to each other and to their friends; they truly had each other's back.

This book compares Bat and Wyatt side by side through each chapter. Wyatt was five years older than Bat, so the first chapter is heavily weighted toward Wyatt. Through his illustrations, Jim Hatzell has done a masterful job recreating how major events in Wyatt and Bat's lives might have appeared.

So, are you ready? Let's enter the frontier world of Wyatt Earp and Bat Masterson to determine who was the best lawman.

CHAPTER 1
EARLY YEARS

The Frontier—ever since Europeans founded the first colonies on North America's East Coast, the frontier has held the promise of independence, freedom, and potential wealth for the common folk. In Europe, it was almost impossible for a peasant to get ahead; the aristocracy controlled the land. People were judged by what social class they were born into, not by what they could make of themselves. However, in America after the Revolution, the kings and lords were sent packing. The common folk could own their own land in America—a novel idea. People flocked to the frontier where they could develop virgin land, sell it for a profit, move on to new land, and then do it all over again. This quest for new land and new opportunities exemplified the basis of the Declaration of Independence—life, liberty, and the pursuit of happiness.

Wyatt Berry Stapp Earp was born on March 19, 1848, at Monmouth, Illinois, into such a pioneering family, Nicholas and Virginia Earp. Nicholas named the boy after his cavalry regiment commander, whom he served under during the Mexican-American War in 1846.[1] Wyatt had four brothers, three sisters, and one older half-brother by Nicholas's deceased first wife.

The Earp family had recently migrated from Kentucky to Illinois. They were pioneers acquiring virgin land, developing it into farmland, selling it at a profit, moving on to new undeveloped land, and repeating the process. Nicholas had not only a passion for developing farmland but also a fondness for animals, especially horses. He passed down that love of animals to his children. Nicholas and Virginia were regular church attenders belonging to the Methodist Church. They instilled a strong sense of right and wrong as well as a respect for the law in the children. They insisted the children attend school and supplemented that by additional lessons at home.[2]

When Wyatt was two years old, Nicholas moved the family to Pella, Iowa, where he developed new farmland.[3] In the early 1850s, Nicholas left the family to make the overland trek to California. Scouting for potential farmland, he liked what he saw in San Bernardino County. He returned to the family in Iowa, planning someday to take them to California.[4]

Bartholomew Masterson was born November 26, 1853, to Thomas and Catherine Masterson in Henryville, Quebec, Canada. The boy must not have liked his name as he only used it on a few occasions during his lifetime. He called himself William Barclay and, later in life, signed documents as W. B. Masterson or Bat Masterson. As to why people called him Bat, many believed it was because he carried a cane, at times whacking opponents with it, but more than likely it was a contraction for Bartholomew.[5] Bat had one older brother, three younger brothers, and two younger sisters. The Masterson family were farming pioneers similar to the Earps. Probably around 1861, they moved from Canada to farm in upstate New York.

Tragedy struck the Earp family in May 1856 when ten-year-old Martha died after a long, unspecified illness.[6] Wyatt learned farm chores and hunting skills, becoming the best hunter in the family. He shot prairie chickens, rabbits, squirrels, and deer around their home. Nicholas later gave Wyatt his first muzzleloader, a combination rifled barrel on top and shotgun barrel below, with which he became proficient.[7]

For years, trouble had been brewing between North and South over slavery. With the election of abolitionist and Republican Abraham Lincoln, on December 20, 1860, South Carolina was the first among eleven states to secede from the Union. A national civil war broke out with the Confederate bombardment of Fort Sumter on April 12, 1861.

Nicholas and Virginia had Southern roots, but they opposed secession. Nicholas believed slavery should continue in the states where it had always existed but that it should not spread into new states. With his military experience, Nicholas became a Union army recruiter and trainer. Wyatt's older half-brother, Newton, enlisted in the Union army, followed by Wyatt's older brothers, James and Virgil. Wyatt wanted to join the action, but his parents forbade it, telling him he was too young. He was more useful if he stayed home tending their eighty-acre cornfield with the help of his two younger brothers, Morgan and Warren.[8]

Wyatt was determined to join the Union army. One morning while his father was away, he left home heading west to Ottumwa where he planned to enlist. Much to his disappointment, he ran into his father, who promptly took him home. Wyatt was made to promise he would not enlist without his mother's permission.[9]

In the spring of 1864, Wyatt was now sixteen years old. James had returned home from the war in the summer of 1863 after being shot in the left shoulder. Nicholas did not like the direction the Union war effort was heading and decided to move the family to California to start a new life. The Earps joined with other Iowans to form a forty-vehicle wagon train. Since Nicholas had already been to California, the wagon train members elected him captain. The Earps took along three wagons and forty head of horses, oxen, and other livestock including Taylor, Virginia's thoroughbred gelding.[10]

Upon reaching the outskirts of Omaha, Nebraska, Nicholas sent his hired hand Charles Copeley and Wyatt to town to buy supplies. While in town, they witnessed a gunfight between two men in the street. The men fired several shots at each other, and both died.[11]

On his return to camp, Wyatt told his father about the gunfight. He remembered Nicholas's advice for the rest of his life. Nicholas told Wyatt he should always give someone the benefit of the doubt except when it was apparent the person was vicious with no regard for human rights and decency. He said lawlessness was humanity's greatest enemy. Nicholas said that when fighting a vicious person, hit first, and hit to kill.[12]

The wagon train rumbled west following the North Platte River through Nebraska. Wyatt provided meat for the family riding off alone hunting prairie chickens and antelope. Taking his turn at guarding the livestock, he twice helped defend the wagon train as Indians attempted to steal their animals.[13]

Wyatt and thirteen-year-old Morgan were guarding the Earp animals when the first attack took place. Sioux warriors galloped toward the herd to stampede the animals. Morgan and Wyatt were able to control the family's animals while other wagon train members lost twenty head of livestock. Virginia ran to her thoroughbred and held on to him even though she stood directly in the path of the racing warriors.[14]

On the second occasion, Wyatt was guarding the herd when he spotted Sioux warriors sneaking between the camp and the herd to cut them off and drive away the animals. Wyatt fired his shotgun barrel to warn the camp and stampede the herd in the camp's direction. The warriors scrambled out of the way of the charging animals, giving the alerted men in camp time to mount a counterattack and drive off the would-be thieves.[15]

The wagon train rested and replenished at Fort Bridger where Wyatt met the famous fur trapper and scout Jim Bridger, who took young Wyatt fishing.[16]

Nicholas had a temper and was sometimes dictatorial on the trip. Sarah Jane Rousseau, one of the wagon train members, recorded on November 24, "This evening Mr. Earp had another rippet with Warren [Earp] fighting with Jimmy Hatten. And then he commenced about all the children. Used very profane language and swore if the children's parents did not correct their children he would whip every last one of them."[17]

After seven months on the trail, the Earps arrived in San Bernardino, California, December 17, 1864, and soon began developing their ranch.[18] Wyatt had no desire to be a farmer and soon found jobs working for freighting outfits hauling loads to Salt Lake City, Utah, and Prescott, Arizona.[19] Wyatt's youngest sister, Adelia, said Wyatt worked alongside older brother Virgil, and, on one occasion when they reached Prescott, the Earps went along with the other teamsters to celebrate in one of the saloons. Wyatt drank too much and passed out. He became so sick, he was determined never to let that happen again.[20]

Nicholas Earp decided to return east, taking the family with him in the spring of 1868. The Union Pacific Railroad was laying track from Omaha westward in its race with the Central Pacific Railroad, building from the west, to complete the first transcontinental railroad. When the Earp family reached the Union Pacific Railroad's railhead in Wyoming, twenty-year-old Wyatt found a job with Charles Chrisman, who had a railroad grading contract. Wyatt had freighted for Chrisman before, and Chrisman, impressed with Wyatt's knowledge and care of horses, put Wyatt in charge of his work horses and mules plowing the prairie ahead of the tracks being laid.[21]

The railroad grading camps were rough-and-tumble portable towns ahead of the railhead. Gambling was one of the major pastimes for the railroad graders. It was while working on the railroad Wyatt most likely learned to play cards and other games of chance. He had probably already learned to fight with his fists growing up with his brothers and taking care of himself during his freighting experiences. Wyatt participated in bare-knuckle boxing, one of the many forms of entertainment every Sunday morning. Chrisman, impressed with Wyatt's knowledge of the rules and his fairness, arranged for him to referee the fights. Wyatt's interest in refereeing prizefights would remain with him into later life.[22]

The main boxing event that summer was a Fourth of July prizefight between Mike Donovan, a professional boxer, and John Shanssey, an up-and-coming fighter. Wyatt and the other graders traveled to Cheyenne to watch the fight. Wyatt interviewed both fighters the night before the match and recommended the graders pool their bets on Donovan. They followed Wyatt's advice. Donovan beat Shanssey, and Wyatt and the graders won their bets.[23]

Chrisman completed his contract with the railroad late that fall. Wyatt sold the livestock he had accumulated and traveled east to visit his grandfather in Monmouth.[24]

Wyatt was in Beardstown, Illinois, the summer of 1869. Beardstown was experiencing a boom as a railroad line was being constructed through town. Wyatt was at John T. Walton's hotel, actually a brothel. A railroad brakeman, Thomas D. Pinard, mocked Wyatt, calling him "the California boy." They fought, and Wyatt threw Pinard into the street. Pinard drew a gun and shot at Wyatt as he pulled his gun and shot Pinard in the hip.[25]

In 1869, Nicholas Earp sold his Pella, Iowa, property and moved the family to Lamar, Missouri. Wyatt made his way from Beardstown to join them in Lamar. That November, Nicholas became justice of the peace, and Wyatt was appointed town constable.[26]

No information is available on how Wyatt met Aurilla (also known as Urilla) Sutherland, or how long they courted, but they were married January 16, 1870. On August 28, they bought a house next door to his half-brother, Newton, and two doors away from Wyatt's parents.[27]

In November 1870, Wyatt ran for his office against Newton and won. This would be the only time Wyatt would run for office.[28]

A life-changing event overshadowed Wyatt's election. Aurilla died possibly in a typhoid epidemic or during childbirth, no one knows for sure.[29] Although Wyatt rarely mentioned it, his love and loyalty to Aurilla ran deeply throughout his life.[30] Then for no recorded reason, Wyatt and brothers James, Virgil, and Morgan brawled in the streets with Aurilla's two brothers and their three friends the Brummett boys.[31] At some point after all this, Wyatt decided to leave Lamar.

Unresolved allegations arose after Wyatt's departure. On March 14, 1871, Barton County filed a lawsuit against Wyatt for two hundred dollars. The lawsuit alleged that as town constable, Wyatt had collected school fund license fees but had never turned over the money to the county. The action was later dismissed, probably because Wyatt had left the area. It may never be known if this complaint was true.[32] Then James Cromwell accused Wyatt of changing the dollar amount on a court document Wyatt served on Cromwell, implying Wyatt pocketed twenty dollars; however, two others involved in the case were found not guilty, and nothing ever came of it.[33]

Thomas Masterson's family had been on the move leaving upstate New York to farm in several different locations in Illinois. The 1870 US Census shows the Masterson family living in St. Claire County, Illinois, east of St. Louis, Missouri. The census listed Bat as a seventeen-year-old farm laborer living on his parents' farm.[34]

Like Wyatt, Bat would have learned how to clear the land, do farm chores, and hunt with a gun in the woods. There is no record of his schooling of any kind, but he did know the three Rs and made good use of them throughout his life, being a voracious reader, a gambler weighing the odds, and a newspaper reporter.

Wyatt worked as a hunter for a government surveying party after leaving Lamar for Indian Territory (modern-day Oklahoma).[35] Trouble with the law continued to follow him. He, along with Edward Kennedy and John Shown, was accused of stealing two horses from Jim Keys on March 28, 1871. They were arraigned on April 14, 1871. Kennedy was tried and found not guilty. Wyatt never stood trial, and the authorities never followed up on his case.[36]

Wyatt turned up at the Market Square in Kansas City, Missouri, where he mingled with hunters, freighters, and gunmen while listening to them spin tales of hunting, gunfights, and other adventures. Here, he claimed he met Wild Bill Hickok and witnessed his marksmanship exhibitions.[37] Wyatt began to formulate where he would head to make his way in the world.

On June 6, 1871, Thomas Masterson settled his family on an eighty-acre tract of land in Sedgwick County, Kansas, fourteen miles northeast of Wichita.[38] During that summer, Bat and his older brother, Ed, helped their father break the prairie sod to plant crops and build a house. The Mastersons were on the frontier's edge. As Bat later described the Masterson property, "It was only a few miles west of the Arkansas River to the buffalo range. . . . It was also right in the center of the Indian range."[39]

COMMERCIAL BUFFALO HUNTING

Immense bison herds had roamed the North American continent ever since the Ice Age. Bison, also known as buffalo, may have numbered more than seventy million animals before Europeans arrived. Vast herds migrated in a seasonal pattern across the plains from north to south and back. Indians hunted buffalo on foot, driving or luring them over cliffs as well as impounding and killing them in natural cul-de-sacs. With the European introduction of horses, metal spear and arrow points, and firearms, Indians became efficient buffalo hunters. White frontiersmen increased hunting pressure on buffalo herds so that by 1832 buffalo were extinct east of the Mississippi River. Buffalo robes became popular as lap blankets in the East, and buffalo tongues were sought after as a delicacy. Railroad companies advancing westward across the plains contracted with hunters such as Buffalo Bill Cody to shoot buffalo to feed their railroad workers.[40]

By 1870, German and then American tanneries developed processes to turn buffalo hides into good leather for industrial purposes.[41] Industrial demand for buffalo hides was limitless, and the price per hide skyrocketed by 1871. Men formed professional hunting parties advancing onto buffalo grazing ranges to kill as many buffalo as they were able. A typical party consisted of a hunter, hide skinners, and others to care for the camp, depending on how much the hunter could afford to pay. Hunters used a wide variety of firearms with varying calibers and weights including Springfield rifles and Remington Rolling Block sporting rifles. One of the more popular firearms was the Sharps rifle, modified to hunt specifically buffalo. In some models its weight was increased to sixteen pounds and shot a .50 caliber slug. Buffalo hunters nicknamed it the Big 50.[42] An experienced hunter would advance on foot downwind to within two hundred yards of a small herd; if he believed he could get closer without spooking the herd, he would do so.[43] He used a forked stick to prop up the gun's barrel and either sat or lay prone to shoot. His first shots were to pick off the leaders. If he could accomplish this, the herd would remain in place through most of the killing before running away.

The efficient slaughter of the herds led to the bisons' near extinction. By the end of the nineteenth century, only about fifteen hundred buffalo remained. Through the efforts of men such as South Dakotans Fred Dupree and James "Scotty" Philip, and Texan Charles Goodnight, the buffalo were saved.[44] According to the National Bison Association, in 2017 the North American bison herds were at 385,000 animals.[45]

CHAPTER 2

HUNTING BUFFALO AND CROSSING PATHS

Everyone believed the number of American bison was limitless. Massive herds stretched across the prairies as far as the eye could see. The latest in tannery technology made it possible to use strips of buffalo hide for durable industrial belts. The industrial East and Europe now wanted all the buffalo hides they could obtain. The price of hides rose, creating profits for hunters and skinners. The herds' spring and autumn migration routes crossed Kansas, a prime area to hunt buffalo and make money.

In autumn 1871, nineteen-year-old Ed and seventeen-year-old Bat Masterson finished helping their father harvest the crops at the new Kansas homestead. The boys were ready for adventure and old enough to set out on their own to seek their fortunes. One sure way to make money for anyone willing to work hard and who didn't mind getting his hands dirty was to join a buffalo hunting outfit. Ed and Bat rode south from their father's farm to Stone's Store, the site of future Caldwell, Kansas. Buffalo hunters, skinners, and hide buyers rendezvoused at Stone's Store. The boys found work as skinners and stock tenders with a buffalo hunting outfit. The hunter and leader of the outfit took them west crossing the Medicine Lodge River to Nescatunga Creek, a tributary to the Arkansas River's Salt Fork, where they set up camp and built a dugout.[1]

The buffalo herds migrating through Kansas were immense, and the slaughter commenced. Each day, the hunter for Ed and Bat's party would pick a small herd close to camp, ride to a point downwind, dismount, and walk to no more than one hundred yards from the buffalo. He would find a stable position, prop up his rifle barrel, and begin shooting. He first shot the lead animal, reloaded, shot the next animal, and repeated the process. The herd usually stood still. If an animal started to walk away, the hunter shot it. After the hunter dropped thirty to forty animals, he waved for Bat, Ed, and the other skinners to drive up the wagon and begin the skinning. The hunter rode to the next herd where he made his next stand and began the slaughter again.[2]

The skinners took over the field of carnage. First, they propped the buffalo carcass on its back and kept it in place with a three-foot-long stick driven into the ground; a large nail on the stick pierced the buffalo, keeping it in place. Next, they made an incision from the jaw across the belly to the tail as well as down the inside length of each leg. A circular cut was made around the circumference of the neck. The carcass was flipped on its stomach. The skinner then tied a rope to the loosened skin around the carcass's neck and the rope's other end hitched to a horse. The horse was coaxed forward, stripping the buffalo hide off the carcass from neck to tail. The skinners loaded the hide, weighing from eighty to one hundred pounds, onto the wagon and repeated the process with the next carcass.[3]

Once a skinner had a wagonload, he drove it back to camp where he unloaded the hides. Sprinkling arsenic on each hide to kill insects, he laid them on the ground hair side down. The skinner inserted stakes through slits made in the hide's outside edges and then pounded the stakes into the ground to keep the hide taut as it dried over the course of three to five days. The hide was then flipped to dry the hair side. The skinners loaded the cured hides into the wagon and drove them to the nearest buying station, or buyers might arrive in camp and buy them direct.[4]

Ed and Bat did this backbreaking, dirty work day after day as autumn slipped into winter. Flies and other annoying insects were replaced with finger-numbing cold; but the killing, skinning, and hide curing continued. Work was occasionally interrupted with visits from members of other buffalo camps or whiskey peddlers. Drinking, card playing, and gambling were the major pastimes at the buffalo hunting camps, and Bat learned to gamble and drink with the best of them.

Back in late August 1871, Wyatt Earp roamed Kansas City's Market Square listening to buffalo hunters tell how they were making good money selling buffalo hides. He decided to get in on the action and rode to Stone's Store where he got a firsthand look at the buffalo hide business. Wyatt determined he did not want to hire on with a hunting party; he wanted to hunt on his own. He had enough money to purchase supplies, a wagon, and a four-up team of horses in addition to his saddle horse. He partnered with an experienced skinner to share in the work and share equally in all the profits.[5]

Heading west across the Medicine Lodge River, Wyatt and the skinner saw massive buffalo herds. Arriving at the Salt Fork of the Arkansas River, they set up their permanent camp.[6]

Wyatt's method of hunting was different from the large hunting outfits. In the larger parties, the hunter only hunted and took no part in skinning or menial camp chores. Wyatt partnered with only one skinner and equally shared in the work with him. The large outfits had multiple wagons whereas Wyatt had one. His plan was to kill only the number of animals he and the skinner could handle in a day. Wyatt said the least amount he killed was eighteen in a day and the most was twenty-seven.[7]

His method of hunting was to use a shotgun.[8] He would advance on foot to within fifty yards of a herd and begin shooting the lead animals. When Wyatt was finished shooting all the animals he and the skinner could handle, he would stand, wave his coat, and shout at the remaining buffalo, which usually moved away.[9]

Wyatt and his skinner camped along the Salt Fork, and so did Ed and Bat Masterson's outfit. It's not recorded how or on what day the Mastersons and Wyatt met, but they did and grew to like each other. Bat and Wyatt would remain best friends for the rest of their lives.[10]

Winters on the plains could be bitter with high winds, subzero temperatures, and snow creating deadly arctic conditions. During the night of November 15, 1871, a blizzard blew out of the north sending the thermometer to twenty below zero. Eight woodchoppers were traveling north to Hayes City, Kansas, when they were caught in the blizzard six miles from town. All but one froze to death.[11] It's not recorded if Ed and Bat stayed at Salt Fork working through the winter or not. Wyatt left for warmer surroundings.

Wyatt and younger brother Morgan Earp moved to Peoria, Illinois. Wyatt was living at Jane Haspel's house on Washington Street and working with her at a business on Hamilton Street. Jane's profession? Madam of a house of ill repute. On February 24, 1872, four women, Wyatt, and Morgan, along with another man, were arrested for keeping and being found in a "House of Ill-Fame." Then again on May 9, 1872, Wyatt and Morgan were arrested in the McClellan Institute, "that hotbed of iniquity." They could not or would not pay their fines of $44.55 each and were thrown in the calaboose.[12] Although there is no record, at some time during his stay in Peoria, Wyatt married sixteen-year-old Sarah (aka Sally) Haspel, Jane's daughter.[13] Wyatt had nothing to say about his arrests or his marriage to Sally. In Stuart Lake's biography, Wyatt claimed he hunted buffalo through the winter until April 1872 when he returned to Stone's Store, sold his hides, and made a profit of twenty-five hundred dollars, which he split with his skinner.[14]

The Santa Fe Trail, originating at Franklin, Missouri, and crossing the Kansas plains to Santa Fe, New Mexico, was one of the major trade and emigrant routes west. Attacks from roving bands of Indians were constant concerns. In 1864, to help deter attacks, the army first established a camp and then built Fort Dodge in April 1865 along the Arkansas River in southeastern Kansas. H. L. Stitler built a sod house five miles west and upriver from the fort in 1871. Tent saloons popped up near Stitler's soddy. The site was popular with off-duty soldiers who were prohibited from drinking at the fort. Buffalo hunters and hide buyers began rendezvousing there to buy and sell and go on drinking sprees. Everyone began calling the tent town Buffalo City.[15]

The Atchison, Topeka, and Santa Fe Railroad was laying track from east to west roughly following the Santa Fe Trail. The railroad, then known as the Santa Fe, had ended construction in 1871, north of Wichita, creating the boomtown of Newton, Kansas. The first passenger train had arrived there July 17, 1871, but the Santa Fe was under the gun. The federal government was giving it land grants to help pay for construction. Part of the ten-year deal was that to get its total land grant, the Santa Fe needed to have its rails laid to the Colorado Territory border by the end of 1872. The Santa Fe had one year to construct 350 miles of track, which ran through Buffalo City.[16]

In the spring of 1872, the Santa Fe's route was abuzz with railroad contractors and workers. The Santa Fe was paying top dollar to get the tracks laid in time. A member of a work gang could make two dollars a day, which was good pay in those days. The gangs were averaging more than a mile a day of track laid.[17]

Bat and Ed, along with family friend Theodore Raymond, were looking for work. The Santa Fe contracted with a Topeka business, Wiley & Cutter, to grade the railroad track bed. Wiley & Cutter subcontracted with Raymond Ritter for some of the grading. Ritter offered Bat, Ed, and Theodore good pay to grade a five-mile section of track bed from Fort Dodge to Buffalo City. They accepted the offer, and, starting at Fort Dodge, they worked long hours through the spring and summer until they reached Buffalo City in July, finishing their job.[18]

The town was booming when they got there. A. A. Robinson, the Santa Fe's chief engineer, was laying out the town's streets, and its name was changed from Buffalo City to Dodge City.[19] The town was right in the heart of prime buffalo hunting territory, and now that trains could reach it, hides could be quickly transported east. The first train to town experienced a two-hour delay due to a three-miles wide and ten-miles long buffalo herd crossing the tracks. Not only did the trains haul buffalo hides east, but they also brought west saloonkeepers, gamblers, and sporting gals. Soon Dodge City acquired additional names—"Hell on the Plains" and "The Wickedest Town in America."[20]

Raymond Ritter met Bat, Ed, and Theodore in Dodge, paying them a small amount of the money he owed them for their efforts. He told them he needed to get the balance of three hundred dollars from Wiley & Cutter. Ritter headed east promising he would return shortly with the cash. Bat, Ed, and Theodore, low on cash, realized after several weeks that Ritter had duped them.[21]

Back in Peoria, Wyatt teamed up with his old Beardstown brothel-owner acquaintance, John T. Walton. Attempting to circumvent Peoria's anti-prostitution ordinances, Walton operated a fifty-foot keelboat with a deckhouse consisting of a dance hall, saloon, and eight bedrooms. Locally known as "the gunboat," his pleasure craft plied the Illinois River. Walton employed Wyatt as bartender, and Wyatt's wife, Sarah, came along for the ride as well as five other women. On the night of September 7, 1872, the gunboat was moored three miles downriver from Peoria. As the occupants and guests danced to a fiddler, imbibed at the bar, and frolicked in the bedrooms, the police raided the party, arresting seven men and six women. Wyatt and Walton were each fined $43.15. Walton later said Wyatt and Sarah left town for "deep water on the Mississippi, where they don't fine decent people, sleeping in their beds at night."[22]

Short on cash due to Raymond Ritter's dishonesty, Bat and Ed Masterson, along with Theodore Raymond, needed to earn a livelihood. They left Dodge, returning to the buffalo range. Riding southeast to Kiowa Creek, they joined hunting partners Tom Nixon and Jim White's large and experienced buffalo hunting camp.[23] Later in November 1872, Jim Masterson, Ed and Bat's younger brother, and Henry Raymond, Theodore's younger brother, joined them.[24] Henry kept a journal for 1872 and 1873, recording events in and around Dodge.

Ed and Bat had now graduated from skinners to buffalo hunters while the Raymond brothers and Jim worked mainly as skinners. Not only did they skin the buffalo for their hides, but they also butchered the carcasses and sold the meat in Dodge. Bat met and became friends with frontiersman and buffalo hunter Billy Dixon, who later described Bat, "He was a chunk of steel and anything that struck him in those days always drew fire."[25]

Henry Raymond's journal entries are sparse, but interesting. Here are a few:

Saturday, November 30, 1872: "Ed and Bat and me killed and butchered 17 buffalos. [sic] Jim pegged."[26]

Wednesday, December 11, 1872: "Bat, Abe, Ed, Jim, Rigny and me went to Indian camp to trade."[27]

Friday, December 20, 1872: "very cold day. Shook snow off hides. The[odore] and Bat went to Big Johns. Started to town. 4 bull whackers here to spend eve. Sang songs and played violin. Snowed."[28]

Wednesday, December 25, 1872: "Christmas day. Shot at a mark to see whos [sic] treat. Ed and me best."[29]

The buffalo disappeared from around Kiowa Creek. Tom Nixon headed back to his wife and ranch on the outskirts of Dodge. Bat, Ed, and the others decided to follow his example and rode back to town on January 1, 1873. The Raymond boys, Ed, and Jim all boarded the train for home; but Bat stayed in Dodge.[30] On nice winter days, he rode out buffalo hunting with Tom Nixon and Jim White. In the spring, he resumed full-time buffalo hunting. Henry Raymond and Ed Masterson returned to Dodge toward the end of February. Henry continued buffalo hunting and skinning, but Ed found a job in town working at Jim "Dog" Kelley's Alhambra Saloon.[31] Kelley's nickname was "Dog" because he was known for his pack of racing greyhounds.[32]

After the Santa Fe railroad came through Dodge City on its way to the Colorado territorial line, the town boomed. It rose from a tent city servicing off-duty soldiers to more permanent frame buildings serving as a booming marketplace where buffalo hunters sold their hides to be loaded onto freight cars and shipped east. The hunters bought supplies and ammunition. They spent their money on drinking sprees, gambling, and women. Within a year of its existence, fifteen men had been killed and buried in the new Boot Hill cemetery.[33] Residents formed a vigilance committee arbitrarily dispensing justice as they saw fit. Henry Raymond, still journaling and writing detailed letters, witnessed killings sanctioned by the vigilance committee and murders committed in the open. For instance, on Thursday, March 13, 1873, hearing gunshots, Henry ran into the street to see a crowd gathering around Charles Burns, who had been shot and was trying to crawl away from Tom Sherman. While holding a large-caliber revolver, Sherman ran after Burns, caught him, and stood over him, saying to the crowd, "I'd better shoot him again hadn't I boys?" Sherman shot Burns in the head, blowing out his brains. Henry wrote in a letter, "All I could learn was that Sherman had killed a friend of Burns and thought it would be safer to have him out of the way."[34] Dodge City would remain a wide open lawless town. It would not be incorporated until November 5, 1875.[35]

Where was Wyatt Earp? According to Stuart Lake, in September 1872, Wyatt and his skinner headed west again onto the Kansas plains. This time, they had to hunt less-frequented areas as there were fewer buffalo and more buffalo hunters. Wyatt and his skinner stayed out on the prairie until April 1873, when they returned to civilization to sell their hides and split their profits. Wyatt now had several thousand dollars to invest.[36] Where was his wife, Sarah, and what was she doing all that time?

A friend of Bat's arrived in Dodge from Granada, Colorado, the Santa Fe's current end of the line. He told Bat that Raymond Ritter, the contractor who never paid Theodore, Ed, and Bat for grading the railroad bed, was in Granada but would be leaving with three thousand dollars in cash. He was expected to be on the next eastbound train and that train would be making a stop in Dodge. The news spread through town that the man who stiffed the Masterson boys and Theodore Raymond would be passing through. Everyone wondered what the Mastersons would do.[37]

On Tuesday, April 15, 1873, the eastbound train pulled into town. A crowd gathered, watching Bat as he boarded the train searching the passenger cars. The crowd saw Ritter emerge onto the platform of one of the cars. Bat then walked onto the platform. Bat's six-shooter was cocked and leveled on Ritter as he demanded the three hundred dollars Ritter owed them. Ritter appealed to the crowd that he was being robbed, but no one came to his defense. Bat told Ritter he was not leaving town alive if he didn't hand over what he owed them. Ritter said the money was in his valise inside the car. Bat called to Henry Raymond in the crowd to fetch Ritter's valise. Bat asked Henry to hand Ritter the valise and then told Ritter to count out three hundred dollars and give it to him. After Ritter complied with Bat's order, Bat allowed him back into the railroad car with the remainder of his money. The jovial crowd cheered as Bat led them to the Alhambra Saloon, where Ed worked and bought them a round of drinks.[38]

After distributing their share of the money to Ed and Theodore, Bat teamed up with George Mitchell in May and left Dodge
on a long buffalo hunt.[39]

Beef cattle had become big business after the Civil War. If Texas
cattlemen could get their longhorn cattle to Eastern markets, they
could make substantial profits, and so began the large cattle drives
from Texas to railheads that could transport the cattle. Cowboys
herded the longhorns from Texas to Sedalia, Missouri, and Baxter
Springs, Kansas. Problems arose. Tick-infested longhorns carried
Texas fever. The longhorns were immune to the disease, but it was
fatal to northern cattle. Local governments established quarantine
lines forbidding the entry of Texas cattle, so cowboys drove the
cattle beyond the quarantined areas to board cattle cars at railroad
towns farther west in Kansas.[40] In 1873, Ellsworth, Kansas, was
one of those towns. When trail-weary, ready to whoop-it-up cowboys hit town, anything could happen.

Wyatt was touring Kansas towns during the spring and summer of
1873, trying to figure out where he should invest his buffalo hunting profits in the cattle industry. While visiting Abilene, Kansas,
he heard that another Kansas railroad town named Ellsworth was
the place to invest money in cattle. In August, he traveled to Ellsworth to investigate.[41]

Among the Texans in town were Ben and Billy Thompson. Both
the older Ben and younger Billy were men not to be trifled. Originally from England, they had settled in Texas. Ben fought for the
Confederacy during the Civil War and fought for Emperor Maxi-
milian's army against Mexican revolutionaries. He had a temper and
on multiple occasions threatened and shot people. He had arrived in
Ellsworth in June as a professional gambler.[42] Brother Billy had also
fought for the Confederacy and was just as bad, if not worse, than

Ben. In 1868, he killed a soldier in Austin, Texas, but fled, escaping punishment. Billy arrived in Ellsworth a few days after Ben, joining in gambling and drinking sprees. On June 11, both brothers were fined for discharging their weapons in the street.[43]

On August 15, 1873, Wyatt was minding his own business sitting in the afternoon shade under the awning of Beebe's General Store next to Joe Brennan's saloon.[44] Inside the saloon, Ben Thompson and his drunken brother Billy were playing a high-stakes card game with gambler John Sterling and others. Deputy Marshal "Happy Jack" Morco, a shady character wanted for murder in Oregon, was present. A wide variety of accounts make it hard to find the truth of what happened next, but a fight broke out over the game with the Thompsons on one side and Sterling and Morco on the other. The fight emptied into the street. Each side went to get guns. Ben and Billy retrieved their firearms from the Grand Central Hotel and stood together in the street. Billy brandished a double-barreled shotgun, both hammers pulled back at full cock. Sterling and Morco had disappeared.[45] Deputy Marshal Ed Hogue had also joined in the action against the Thompson brothers. According to Ben, Hogue and Morco were "my inveterate enemies."[46]

Ellsworth County Sheriff Chauncey Whitney walked up to the Thompsons to calm them down, promising to protect them. The Thompsons relaxed, and Whitney invited them for a drink back in Brennan's. As they walked toward the saloon, Morco suddenly appeared with a six-gun in each hand. Ben fired at Morco and missed as Morco ducked from sight. Billy fired too, but the shotgun blast hit Whitney, fatally wounding him. Ben convinced Billy to mount his horse and ride out of town while Ben stood his ground covering Billy's getaway. A mob of armed Texas cowboys stood in the street backing Ben. Mayor James Miller approached Ben ordering him to surrender his guns, but he refused.[47] Ellsworth's police force consisted of three men: Marshal "Brocky Jack" Norton and deputies Happy Jack Morco and Ed Hogue, who was also a deputy sheriff.[48] They were slow to head out and arrest Ben. In frustration, Mayor Miller fired them.[49]

According to Stuart Lake, Mayor Miller turned to Wyatt to defuse the situation and temporarily appointed him to the police force. On one side stood the armed Ben Thompson backed by Texas cowboys and on the other side were the still-armed former city policemen and irate Ellsworth citizens. Wyatt, a neutral outsider, was in a position to negotiate between both sides. After a short, tense conversation, Wyatt convinced Ben to lay down his guns in the street.[50]

Hogue, acting in his capacity as deputy sheriff, "received" Ben's guns, and Ben "surrendered" after Mayor Miller guaranteed his safety and the former city police were disarmed. So, it is plausible that drifter, buffalo hunter, and pimp Wyatt Earp acted as intermediary between Ben and the mayor to take Ben's guns, give them to Deputy Sheriff Hogue, and have Ben surrender to him. However, Wyatt is not mentioned in the newspaper account of the event, court proceedings, or Ben Thompson's memoirs. Everyone had something to hide—the city with its corrupt and ineffective police force and Ben Thompson trying to spin the killing of Sheriff Whitney as an accident to save face.[51]

Wyatt did not care to stay in Ellsworth. By September, he was heading back to the buffalo ranges, but buffalo were becoming harder to find. The mass slaughter of the herds was taking its toll on the Kansas ranges.[52]

CHAPTER 3

IN AND OUT OF TROUBLE

Bat continued to hunt buffalo through the summer and fall of 1873 and into the winter of 1874. Late in 1873, Bat and his buffalo hunting party were camped along the Medicine Lodge River.

One December day, Bat was out hunting alone. He shot a buffalo and was skinning it when he was suddenly surrounded by five Cheyenne men from Bear Shields's band. Bat was distracted by one of them picking up his Sharps rifle while another came from behind and seized his revolver. As Bat turned on the man who took his revolver, the man holding his Sharps rifle whacked Bat on the head with its barrel, opening a bloody gash. The Cheyenne pointed his own weapons at him. Through gestures and strong language, they made it quite clear for him to leave immediately. Bat ran the half mile to camp and told his partners what had happened. Bat wanted to go back and recover his weapons, horse, and hides, but the others were apprehensive about doing that. They told Bat no, struck camp, and all returned to Dodge.[1]

Bat was out for revenge. He persuaded fellow buffalo hunter Jim Harvey to go with him on a raid of Bear Shields's camp on the Medicine Lodge River. Christmas night, the two of them ran off 150 head of horses from Bear Shields's camp and started herding them back to Dodge. Later Bat learned that forty of Bear Shields's warriors had followed them, but a snowstorm struck, forcing the warriors to turn back. Bat and Jim sold the horses in Dodge for twelve hundred dollars.[2]

Wyatt hunted buffalo through the winter of 1873–1874. By early spring, he was finished with buffalo hunting. There just weren't enough buffalo left in Kansas to make it profitable. He sold his hides, wagon, horses, and everything else, except his guns, and began searching Kansas cowtowns for the best place to make a living.[3]

Dodge City buffalo hunters searched for more herds to hunt. Most hunters were wary of heading south into the dangerous Indian Territory, "No Man's Land,"[4] and Texas Panhandle. However, back in July 1873, J. Wright Mooar and John Webb had ridden from Dodge through No Man's Land to the panhandle. Wright talked about what they had seen there: "Buffalo. A solid herd as far as we could see, all day they opened up before us and came together behind us." Mooar returned to Dodge and took a hunting party back down to the panhandle in September, hunting through the winter.[5]

A few other outfits followed Mooar into the panhandle, but there were no nearby markets to sell their hides. Dodge was the closest market over 150 miles north; and it was a dangerous journey. The Comanches, Kiowas, and Cheyenne were not pleased with the buffalo hunters' encroachment on the southern buffalo herds.

During January and February of 1874, Dodge City buffalo hunters discussed their options. Town merchants Charlie Myers and Fredrick Leonard made a proposal to the hunters. They would set up a store in the panhandle, buy the hunters' hides, and charge Dodge City prices if the hunters would haul their goods in their hide wagons to the panhandle for a reasonable rate. Enough hunters agreed to the proposal to make it profitable for Myers and Leonard.[6]

In March 1874, a wagon train of more than a hundred wagons left Dodge heading south for the panhandle. One of the hunters riding along was Bat Masterson. Crossing No Man's Land into the panhandle, the wagon train camped along the Canadian River on the sixth day.

One tenderfoot new to the buffalo hunting business was eager to shoot Indians. Bat and a few others decided to play a practical joke on him. A flock of turkeys roosted in a grove of cottonwood trees near camp. Bat and two other men secretly entered the grove and built a small campfire. Bat returned to camp while the others hid in the trees near the fire. Bat invited the tenderfoot to go shoot a few turkeys. Charlie Myers, who was in on the joke, went along. Reaching the campfire, Bat said he was sure Comanche had built it. The hidden men fired a few shots. Bat and Charlie fired their weapons, yelling for the tenderfoot to run for his life. He ran back to camp yelling that the trees were full of Indians who had killed Bat and Charlie. By now the whole camp was in on the joke. One man ripped the back of the tenderfoot's shirt as another quickly poured hot coffee on his bare back, convincing him he was wounded. He was ready to head straight back to Dodge. When the tenderfoot realized he was the butt of their joke, he was furious.[7]

The next day, the wagon train headed downriver along the north bank of the Canadian River to some old ruins called Adobe Walls. William Bent had built a trading post there in 1840, but soon abandoned it due to hostile Comanche and Kiowa. In 1864, troops led by Colonel Kit Carson fought Comanche, Kiowa, and Kiowa-Apache there and were forced to withdraw.[8]

One mile north of the Adobe Walls ruins, Charlie Myers and Fredrick Leonard enlisted the aid of the buffalo hunters to build their store, a stable, and a combination mess hall and kitchen. A corral with three picket bastions enclosed the buildings, which everyone called Adobe Walls. In May, Dodge City merchants Charlie Rath, Robert Wright, and James Langdon sent a party to Adobe Walls to build their trading post alongside Myers and Leonard's. This was followed by Jim Hanrahan's saloon and Thomas O'Keefe's blacksmith shop.[9]

While waiting for the massive southern buffalo herds to arrive on their spring migration from the south, the hunters spent their time scouting the territory, hunting the small local herds, drinking, gambling, holding shooting matches, or racing horses. Billy Dixon and Bat usually won the rifle shoots.[10]

In late May, the plains echoed the thundering arrival of the southern buffalo herds. The hunters and skinners went to work with a passion. The hides began to stack up around Adobe Walls. Bat worked for Billy Dixon and at other times for Myers and Leonard. Bat said about the amount of cured buffalo hides at Rath's trading post: "[Hides were] in piles of 40 and fifty . . . piled up all around the store, from 30 to 100 feet."[11]

Buffalo hides were used as money at the trading posts. Hunters exchanged them for supplies, food, and liquor. Rath's trading post was paying $2.00 per bull hide and $1.10 per cow hide.[12]

As the days passed into June, hunting outfits were killing and skinning thousands of buffalo; merchant wagons loaded with buffalo hides were rolling from Adobe Walls to Dodge then back again loaded with provisions and ammunition. Life was good. Everyone was making money.

A railroad spur line was built from the Santa Fe main line to Wichita, Kansas, transforming it into a booming cowtown terminus for cattle drives.[13] Wichita was located on the east bank of the Arkansas River. Across the river arose Delano, a collection of saloons and brothels technically off limits to the Wichita police. Delano's raucous, anything-goes atmosphere catered to liquor-and-woman-deprived cowboys arriving off the hot, dusty trail. Delano was ready to separate the cowboy from his cash; and he was ready to spend it on anything Delano had to offer.

Wyatt arrived in Wichita in May 1874. His wife, Sarah, was already living there as well as Wyatt's older brother James and his wife, Bessie. Sarah and Bessie had been working together running a brothel since at least January 1874. In early May, they were fined eight dollars each for prostitution.[14]

Wyatt also found himself in trouble after just the second morning in town. Wyatt and a few other men rushed to a commotion behind Doc Black's corral. Black, a large man, was beating a boy half his size. As Wyatt and the other men pulled Black off the boy, Black took a wild swing hitting Wyatt in the face. Wyatt punched Black in the eye, knocking him to the ground. Black filed charges against Wyatt, who was arrested and temporarily housed in a shed. Drunken Texas cowboys learned he was being detained in the shed. A rumor was floating that Wyatt had killed two Texas cowboys the previous summer in Ellsworth. Approaching the shed, the angry cowboys were ready to do the same to Wyatt. He told them he had not killed anyone in Ellsworth. Knowing Ben Thompson was in town, Wyatt told the mob to check with Ben to verify his story. The drunks drifted away, and Wyatt was soon released.[15]

Besides drinking and loose women, gambling was a major form of entertainment in Wichita and other cowtowns. During his stay in Wichita, Wyatt must have continued honing his card playing skills, which would last him a lifetime.

On May 26, Charley Sanders, a black brick carrier, came home from work to find two Texas cowboys bothering his wife. Sanders beat the Texans and tossed them out of his house. The Texans returned to their cow camp outside of town and told the rest of the outfit what had happened. The cowboys were furious and out for revenge. They chose Shorty Ramsey to kill Sanders. The next day, as Sanders was working at a downtown construction site, Ramsey walked up to him and shot him in the head and chest—killing him. Ramsey jumped on his horse and dashed down the street yelling and waving his pistol followed by cowboys who rode with him until he crossed the Arkansas River bridge and escaped. Other cowboys pulled their revolvers covering Marshal Bill Smith, so he could take no action. Wyatt saw Ramsey's escape and was disappointed with the lack of police action. In response to Sanders's murder, *The Wichita Eagle*, the town's newspaper, called for a reorganization of the police force.[16]

On June 3, Sarah and Bessie were arrested again, this time on a complaint by Samuel Martin that they were keeping a brothel north of Douglas Avenue near the Arkansas River bridge. They pled guilty and were locked up until they could make their $250 bail.[17]

Most likely due to the newspaper's call to reorganize the police force, on June 17, 1874, Wichita Marshal Bill Smith hired Wyatt Earp as a policeman. He would serve in that capacity through most of 1874.[18]

Buffalo hunting had been good in the Texas Panhandle. Hunters were selling hides to the Adobe Walls merchants. The merchants sent wagons loaded with hides north to Dodge where they were reloaded with ammunition and goods and driven back to Adobe Walls, but trouble was brewing. By mid-June, Indians had attacked several buffalo hunting outfits. Four white men had been killed in two separate attacks. An army scout, Amos Chapman, who was half Cheyenne, stopped at Adobe Walls warning the merchants that a large war party was rumored to be gathering to attack Adobe Walls. Many buffalo hunters, skinners, teamsters, and merchants heeded the warnings and headed north to Dodge. Bat Masterson was one of twenty-eight men and one woman who decided to stay at Adobe Walls.[19]

The sod roof on Hanrahan's saloon was not good at keeping out the rain, so on Saturday, June 26, 1874, Hanrahan had his employees add more sod to the roof. Around 2:00 a.m., on June 27, a loud crack sounding like a rifle shot woke many. Hanrahan shouted he thought the saloon's ridge pole was breaking. Some men ran out of the building, but others were too tired or intoxicated to leave their bedrolls. Hanrahan ordered his employees to immediately remove the added sod from the roof while some of the men found a timber to prop up the ridgepole. Hanrahan provided free drinks for all who helped in the repair. Some of the men decided they might as well stay up and not go back to bed.[20]

Billy Dixon was one who did not go back to sleep, preparing to head out hunting. In the predawn light, Dixon saw "a large body of objects" advancing on the horse herd. As the sun broke over the eastern horizon behind the objects, he saw they were Indians mounted on horseback. With a single, thunderous war whoop, hundreds of Indians raced their horses toward the buildings. Thinking the Indians were only going to run off the horse herd, Dixon securely tied his saddle horse to a wagon. Then realizing they were charging the buildings, Dixon raised his gun, took a shot, and raced to the saloon.[21]

Because the buildings were hot and stuffy, most everyone was sleeping outside under the stars. Fred Leonard and Bat were sleeping in their bedrolls inside the Myers and Leonard store corral. Gunshots coming from the direction of Hanrahan's saloon woke them. Bat ran to the saloon while Leonard ran into his store.[22]

Everyone made it to the buildings except for brothers Shorty and Ike Scheider. They and their Newfoundland dog slept in their wagon out beyond corral. Surrounded by warriors, they were killed and scalped. The dog valiantly defended their bodies, but he too was killed, a strip of hide removed from his side.[23]

The Indians made repeated charges against the buildings. According to Bat, they were close enough to stick their guns through the windows and fire in while Bat and the other defenders shot them at close range. Some tried to batter down the door by backing their horses into it while the hunters pushed back on the other side to hold it closed.[24]

Bat learned that his friend Billy Tyler had been shot through the lungs at Myers and Leonard's store. As the Indians continued to attack, he ran to the store to see about his friend, who would later die.[25] Billy Dixon said, "'Bat' Masterson should be

remembered for the valor that marked his conduct. He was a good shot, and not afraid."[26] By midafternoon the massed attacks had stopped. Hundreds of warriors remained on the ridges shooting at the buildings. The buffalo hunters began picking off warriors at long range using their Big 50s. The hunters were well practiced at long-distance shooting due to hunting and holding regular shooting matches against each other. They could hit targets three hundred to a thousand yards away. They forced the Indians to move out of range.[27]

Although Plains Indians rarely attacked at night, the Adobe Walls defenders didn't get much sleep. The next day, the Indians continued to take potshots at the hunters and merchants. The men ventured out of the buildings to bury Billy Tyler and the Scheider brothers. That evening, Henry Lease rode out after dark toward Dodge to get help. Over the next few days, additional hunters began arriving at Adobe Walls, making it through surrounding Indians as their numbers began decreasing.[28]

One of the new hunters to arrive at Adobe Walls was nineteen-year-old Bill Tilghman, a crack shot. He and Bat became friends for life. Tilghman said about meeting Bat that he was "a handsome young fellow . . . with a reckless devil-may-care look. He was already an experienced plainsman and noted shot."[29]

On day three, Billy Dixon made a legendary shot. Fifteen mounted Indians appeared on a bluff about seven-eighths of a mile to the east. Dixon said, "Some of the boys suggested I try the big '50' on them. . . . I took careful aim and pulled the trigger. We saw an Indian fall from his horse."[30]

Unknown to the defenders, Lease had made it to Dodge, and a rescue party was on its way. The men broke into two groups, those who were headed back to Dodge and those who wanted to stay. Hanrahan was heading back, and Dixon and Bat agreed to go along to help protect the wagon train. They would be leaving on day seven after the attack.[31]

Bat had borrowed a Big 50 from Hannah Olds, whose husband, Bill, killed himself in a gun accident on day five. The evening before the wagon train was to leave, Mrs. Olds worried that Bat would leave with the gun. Bat was in the saloon at the time, and through an intermediary she asked for the gun. He told the man he wanted to keep it through the night and to assure her he would return it the next morning before he left. She didn't believe him and sent a man named Brown to get it from Bat. Brown used some rough words with Hanrahan, who had vouched that Bat would return the gun in the morning. Hanrahan threw Brown out of the saloon and pulled his gun on him until cooler heads disarmed Hanrahan. Bat returned the gun to Mrs. Olds the following morning as he had promised.[32]

Bat and the others made it to Dodge without incident. Eager to hear tales of the battle, the town turned out to greet them. It was time for a little carousing, and Bat was a willing participant.

During the summer of 1874, the Wichita police force and Wyatt had multiple encounters with wild Texas cowboys. Carrying a firearm in town was against city ordinances, but that didn't stop the Texans. *The Wichita Eagle* reported on the evening of July 6 that Policeman Sam Botts had disarmed a man and was in the process of arresting him when twelve men pulled their weapons on him. The city's triangle alarm rang notifying the vigilance committee to assemble. Over fifty men came in support of the police officers, and the "roughs" were arrested.[33]

Stuart Lake and Wyatt may have elaborated on and embellished this incident as the Abel "Shanghai" Pierce incident. Abel "Shanghai" Pierce, one of the big Texas cattle bosses, was in town. Pierce, who was a rough character when intoxicated, sat in a chair in the middle of the sidewalk on Main Street. He was drunk and armed. Botts attempted to get Pierce to return to the saloon where he could check his weapons along with the other cowboys, but Pierce refused to do so. Wyatt arrived on the scene and helped Botts disarm Pierce, manhandling him off the sidewalk and into a saloon. The Texas cowboys, incensed at how Botts and Wyatt had handled Pierce, formed an angry mob, which Wyatt and the other policemen, with the help of additional townsmen, faced down.[34]

Shortly after this incident, a large Texan drunkard named George Peshaur verbally harassed Wyatt on several occasions. One day, Wyatt found Peshaur sober and invited him to fight. They entered a store where Wyatt placed his badge and guns on the counter. The two men entered a large, empty backroom where Wyatt fought Peshaur, beating him with his fists until Peshaur could not stand. Wyatt returned to the front where he recovered his badge and guns.[35]

Wichita Deputy Sheriff Jimmy Cairns told of another confrontation with Texas cowboys that happened later that summer. The Texans, led by cattleman Mannen Clements, were determined to take over the town and run things their way. About fifty of them gathered in Delano. The Wichita police and vigilance committee got wind of the plot. About fifty armed townsmen took positions around the east end of the Arkansas River bridge. With guns drawn, Clements and the Texans began to cross the bridge. Seeing the defenders on the other side, the mob halted within speaking distance. Wyatt, who was in the middle and a little in front of the defenders, spoke to Clements, "Manning, [sic] put up those guns." Clements did not respond. Wyatt said again, "Manning, [sic] put up those guns and go home." Clements hesitated then holstered his guns and led the mob back across the river.[36]

Stuart Lake tells that after the Mannen Clements incident George Peshaur approached a young Texan who had been drinking and fancied himself a gunfighter. Peshaur convinced the boy that if he shot Wyatt, he and other Texans would back his getaway. The boy got the drop on Wyatt as he was making his rounds. Peshaur and other Texans stood by waiting for the boy to shoot, but Wyatt was fast pulling his pistol out and shooting the gun out of the kid's hand.[37] There are no other sources for this story.

In October 1874, Officer John Behrens and Wyatt tracked down a cattle outfit that had left town without paying its bills. Wyatt and Behrens caught the Texans just before they reached the Indian Territory border. Leveling a shotgun and six-shooter on the cowboys, they recovered $146 owed the town merchants.[38]

Sometime during this period, brothers Virgil and Morgan joined Wyatt and Jim in Wichita, but Wyatt would soon be leaving town for a different job.

After the Adobe Walls fight, many of the Southern Plains Tribes were on the warpath indiscriminately attacking whites wherever they found them. On July 27, 1874, Colonel Nelson A. Miles began organizing a force at Fort Dodge, Kansas, to take military action against the hostile tribes. Miles assigned Lieutenant Frank Baldwin to organize a detachment of scouts. On August 1, Billy Dixon signed up as a scout, and Bat joined him five days later.

Many of the scouts were buffalo hunters who were good shots and knew the territory.[39]

On August 11, the army marched south. Lieutenant Baldwin was ordered to lead a detachment of cavalry and scouts totaling forty-nine men, including Dixon and Bat, to Adobe Walls to check on the situation there. At Crooked Creek they discovered the mutilated bodies of a five-man survey crew.[40]

Baldwin sent Dixon and Bat ahead of the detachment to inform the buffalo hunters at Adobe Walls not to shoot when the main body rode up. The buffalo hunters were happy to see their old acquaintances. Everyone but twelve men had left. The Indians had kept them penned up in the buildings. The rest of the detachment arrived about 9:00 p.m. that night.[41]

The next day, the buffalo hunters were feeling secure with the detachment's arrival. Tobe Robinson and George Huffman rode down the valley toward the Canadian River to pick wild plums. They were jumped by ten Indians who raced after them at a full gallop. One warrior got close enough to run his lance through Huffman and seize the riderless horse. Seeing the troops ahead, the warriors spun around their horses and galloped away. The detachment gave chase, but the Indians were long gone. They buried Huffman beside the other four Adobe Walls casualties.[42]

The next day, August 20, the detachment and the remaining buffalo hunters left Adobe Walls heading east down the Canadian River to intersect Miles's column. They saw plenty of Indian signs and jumped two warriors, killing one, while the other got away. Baldwin sent scouts McGinty and Masterson ahead to Miles with dispatches explaining the situation and telling him that the Indians were in the vicinity. Upon receiving the dispatches, Miles changed direction and joined with Baldwin on August 24, near the Antelope Hills.[43]

For days, Miles's troops pursued a large body of Indians to the southwest. The march was grueling with temperatures climbing to 110°F and with little drinkable water. On the morning of

August 30, the scouts were two miles ahead of the column as they followed the Indian trail into hills bordering the desolate Staked Plains. The Indians ambushed the scouts as they entered a narrow pass through the hills. The scouts withstood the attack until the cavalry joined them followed by a Gatling gun battery. The warriors retreated onto the Staked Plains fighting rearguard actions until Miles called off the attack when he saw his troops were exhausted and his supply train was far to the rear.[44]

Miles set up a base camp on the Sweetwater Creek and sent out patrols searching for Indians. Bat participated in scouting missions and carried army dispatches back and forth to Camp Supply in Indian Territory until October 12 when his employment as a scout officially ended.[45] However, Bat must have accompanied a military detachment led by Major Charles Compton that returned to Adobe Walls on October 20, 1874. Bat stated later in a deposition, "The last time I was there in October 1874, everything was destroyed, all the buildings etc., at Adobe Walls, and all the stockades had been burned down."[46]

On November 2, 1874, Bat was hired as a teamster to transport supplies from Fort Dodge to Camp Supply. According to author Robert K. DeArment, sources stated on November 8, 1874, Bat was with a detachment of scouts and troops who attacked the Cheyenne village of Gray Beard. Forcing the Indians to retreat to the Staked Plains, they rescued two white captives, nine-year-old Julia German and her seven-year-old sister, Adelaide.[47] Henry Raymond wrote in a letter dated December 18, 1874, "I hear that Bat has got a job at camp supply, of counting mules, night and morning."[48] During the winter of 1875, Bat continued to work off and on as a teamster for the army. The Kansas state census listed Bat as a teamster out of Dodge City on March 1, 1875.[49]

In September 1874, a dispute called the Polecat War erupted over the ownership of a herd of eight hundred head of cattle. Two competing interests claimed ownership of the herd that "Shanghai" Pierce and other cattlemen had driven from Texas into Kansas. A Springfield, Illinois, banker, E. R. Ulrich, held a debtor's claim against the herd. Deputy US marshals seized the herd for Ulrich and had it driven to and held at Polecat Creek in Indian Territory.[50]

Wyatt was hired in late November to help guard the herd while the disputing parties battled it out in court. Not waiting for the court to resolve the issue, Pierce and his cattlemen partners sent twelve men to take the herd in February 1875. The marshals, Wyatt, and other gunmen were prepared to fight the Texas cowboys who backed down but camped nearby biding their time. On April 14, 1875, the Texas cowboys, along with the Sumner County Vigilance Committee from Kansas, must have had legal standing and peacefully took the herd from the deputy US marshals, ending the Polecat War and Wyatt's employment.[51]

Wichita's city election found Marshal Bill Smith in a three-way race against Assistant Marshal Dan Parks and former marshal Mike Meagher, who would win the election.[52] Wyatt returned to Wichita and was reappointed to the police force on April 21.[53]

In May, Wyatt went into action identifying and arresting W. W. Compton, who was wanted for stealing two horses and a mule. When confronted by Wyatt, Compton tried to run away into the night until Wyatt fired a warning shot bringing him to a stop.[54]

Sergeant Melvin King, whose real name was Anthony Cook, was in town during July on furlough. Drunk, he stood in the street wearing new-bought civilian clothes and brandishing a pistol in his right hand with a second pistol stuck in his belt. Knowingly violating the city firearms ordinance, King loudly boasted to a large crowd of cowboys that he would take on Wyatt Earp. Wyatt was walking his beat and, turning the corner, heard and saw King. Figuring King was bluffing, Wyatt walked right up and disarmed King while he was still wielding his gun. Wyatt led King off to jail.[55]

That December, Wyatt found a drunk with a bankroll of five hundred dollars passed out in the street. Wyatt took the drunk to jail to spend the night and handed him back his cash the next morning. *The Wichita Beacon* proclaimed: "There are few other places where that $500 roll would ever been heard from. The integrity of our police force had never been seriously questioned."[56]

Embarrassing accidents happen. On January 9, 1876, *The Wichita Beacon* reported Wyatt and several others were sitting in the back room of the Custom House Saloon. Wyatt had the hammer of his pistol resting on the cap of a fully loaded chamber. The pistol slipped from its holster. As the pistol fell, its hammer hit Wyatt's chair causing the pistol to fire. The bullet shot through Wyatt's coat, ricocheted off the wall, and sailed through the ceiling. The party stampeded out of the room, thinking someone shot at them through the window.[57]

The Southern Plains tribes found little game to hunt during the brutal winter of 1875. By spring, most of them had surrendered. The army decided to maintain a presence in the Texas Panhandle to control the tribes, so it began to improve the camp or cantonment on Sweetwater Creek. In February 1876, the army would name the cantonment Fort Elliott.[58]

Believing it safe, buffalo hunters returned to the panhandle. Charlie Rath and his Dodge City partners established a buffalo hide buying station on Sweetwater Creek five miles from the cantonment. During the winter of 1875–1876, Rath would buy one hundred thousand buffalo hides and ship them two hundred miles to Dodge. Other merchants began building stores, hotels, restaurants, and saloons. The little settlement first called Sweetwater would later be renamed Mobeetie.[59]

Here Henry Fleming and Billy Thompson owned and operated the Lady Gay, a combination saloon and dance hall. This was the same Billy Thompson who had killed Sheriff Whitney in Ellsworth, Kansas. His brother Ben had arrived in town and was dealing faro at the Lady Gay. Billy's girl, Mollie Brennan, was in town working at Charlie Norton's saloon along with a woman named Kate Elder and five other dancers all known together as The Seven Jolly Sisters.[60]

Stationed at the cantonment on the Sweetwater was Melvin King, the same Melvin King whom Wyatt Earp confronted in Wichita back in July 1874. King, still a bully and braggart, was now listed as a corporal with Company H, Fourth US Cavalry.[61] King was infatuated with Mollie and considered Mollie his girl.[62]

Sometime after March 1875, twenty-one-year-old Bat Masterson was no longer employed as a teamster. He returned to buffalo hunting in the panhandle and was a regular customer at the Sweetwater establishments where Bat met Mollie and was friendly with her.[63] It was also at Sweetwater that Bat began a lifelong friendship with the Thompson brothers.

There are several versions as to what happened in Sweetwater the night of January 24, 1876. Here's one:

It was a lively night at the Lady Gay filled with buffalo hunters, including Bat; soldiers, including a drunken, jealous Corporal King; and Mollie, with some of the women from Norton's saloon, which was closed for the night.[64]

After midnight, Charlie Norton, Mollie, and Bat walked over to Charlie's saloon, which he opened for them. Charlie stood behind the bar and Bat and Mollie had sat at a table when there was pounding at the door. Bat walked to the door and opened it. King burst in shouting and waving a gun. He fired the pistol, hitting Bat in the hip. Mollie threw herself between them just as King again fired, killing Mollie. As Bat fell to the floor, he pulled his six-shooter and fired a shot into King's chest.[65]

The people inside the Lady Gay rushed to Norton's saloon. King's friends were incensed and were going to finish off Bat, but, with revolvers drawn, Ben Thompson held them at bay.[66]

Mollie was dead, King died the next day, and everyone thought Bat would follow them to the grave; but he pulled through and would walk with a limp for the rest of his life. However the gunfight went down, Bat now had the lifelong reputation as a gunfighter.

It was spring of 1876 and time for another Wichita city election. Former marshal Bill Smith was running against current marshal Mike Meagher. Bad words must have been exchanged between Smith and Wyatt. Smith was claiming that if Meagher won reelection he would place Wyatt's brothers on the police force. For some reason, this infuriated Wyatt. Meagher ordered him to stay away from Smith, but he did not heed his boss's orders. On Sunday night, April 2, 1876, two days before the election, Wyatt caught Smith and began beating him. Meagher had to pull Wyatt off Smith and arrest him for disturbing "the peace and order of the city." The next day Wyatt was fined thirty dollars and dismissed from the police force. Meagher allowed Wyatt to continue his police duties for two weeks afterwards, and an attempt was made to reinstate him. The city council voted, and the reinstatement failed by one vote.[67]

The *Wichita Weekly Beacon* stated after reporting on Wyatt's attack and dismissal, "It is but justice to Erp [sic] to say he has made an excellent officer, and hitherto his conduct has been unexceptional [without flaw or fault]."[68] Wichita Deputy Marshal Jimmy Cairns, who served with Wyatt, said, "Wyatt Earp was a wonderful officer. He was game to the last ditch and apparently afraid of nothing. The cowmen all respected him and seemed to respect his superiority and authority at such times as he had to use it."[69]

THE INDIAN SIDE OF THE ADOBE WALLS FIGHT

White hunters were slaughtering the buffalo, and the federal government was doing nothing about it. Provisions in treaties allowed tribes to hunt buffalo on ranges outside the reservation limits so long as there were buffalo. Most white people believed if the buffalo were eliminated, the Southern Plains tribes would peacefully settle down on their reservations in Indian Territory. But all was not well in Indian Territory. The tribes were furious not only over the wanton destruction of the buffalo herds but also over the inferior and infrequent food and supplies the government had promised. Whiskey peddlers were wrecking lives. To add insult to injury, white horse thieves were raiding their herds driving the horses to Texas and Dodge City, Kansas, to sell at auction. The Indians had had enough.[70]

In the spring of 1874, a Comanche prophet, Isatai, promised his fellow tribesmen they would be invincible against the white buffalo hunters and that he could stop their bullets in midair. Quanah Parker, a young Comanche war chief, was ready for war. His goal was to wipe out the buffalo hunter outpost at Adobe Walls. Along with the Comanche, the Cheyenne, Kiowa, and Arapaho warriors also believed Isatai. A war party of seven hundred men rode west from Elk Creek to Adobe Walls. Isatai told them along the way that his medicine would stop the white man's guns and they would wipe them out when they charged.[71]

Just before sunrise on June 27, the war party charged Adobe Walls. In their path, they found two white men in a wagon. The warriors shot and scalped them. Some of the buffalo hunters were awake and had time to grab their guns and repulse the charge. Trying to get the hunters to waste their ammunition, the warriors rode circling the buildings and charging in and out. Quanah and another Comanche poked holes in the roof of one building and shot into it. The white hunters' long-range buffalo guns were taking a toll. Fifteen warriors were killed and many wounded by early afternoon. Quanah had a horse shot from under him and was wounded in the shoulder as he took cover and was later rescued. The warriors were angry and began whipping Isatai until Quanah stopped them saying that Isatai's disgrace was punishment enough. The war party began to disband. Some warriors determined to stay and pick off any white hunters they could; some men returned to their reservations while others continued on the warpath looking for easier targets.[72]

CHAPTER 4

IN AND OUT OF DODGE

odge City's surrounding countryside was becoming more settled. Kansas Governor Thomas Osborn declared Ford County organized on April 5, 1873, and the Ford County voters selected Dodge City as county seat on June 5.[1] However, Dodge City did not become incorporated until November 1875.[2]

Texas cattlemen brought 180,000 head of longhorn cattle to Dodge in 1875 and liked what they saw.[3] The 1876 cattle season promised to be even bigger, making Dodge the most important cattle shipping town in Kansas, earning the title "Queen of the Cowtowns."[4]

Cowboys endured months of hard work on the hot and dusty trails. Dirty and sore, deprived of liquor and female companionship, they dreamed of finding it all and more in Dodge. When they hit town, they were ready to cut loose in its saloons, brothels, gambling establishments, and dance halls. Dodge soon earned more nicknames: "Cowboy Capital" and "Wickedest Little City in America."[5]

Dodge City's population was growing. In 1877, it would reach twelve hundred people, not counting transient cowboys and buffalo hunters. The Santa Fe railroad tracks ran through town from east to west. Paralleling the tracks was bustling Front Street, the north side of which was packed with saloons, restaurants, hotels, and shops. The city passed an ordinance that no one was allowed to wear or carry guns north of the railroad tracks. This was the "deadline." South of the tracks was wide open for anything goes.[6]

In April 1876, Dodge City voters elected wholesale liquor dealer and law and order faction champion George Hoover as mayor. His opponents, the Dodge City Gang, advocated leniency with saloons, gambling, dance halls, and, unofficially, brothels. Hoover appointed three-hundred-pound Larry Deger as marshal, and Deger hired a noted gunman, Jack Allen, as the chief deputy marshal and three additional deputy marshals.[7]

"Hurrahing" a cowtown was one of the Texas cowboys' favorite pastimes. Racing their horses back and forth on the town's main street, the cowboys relished firing their six-guns in the air as they whooped and hollered. Of course, it was the city police's responsibility to prevent or stop the "hurrah" before someone got hurt.[8]

One day early in May 1876, rowdy cowboys were hollering and firing their six-shooters as they galloped their horses down the street hurrahing Dodge. Deputy Marshal Allen tried to stop their frolic, but instead they chased him off the street and down an alley. He walked to the train station and boarded the next westbound train. Dodge had a job opening for a new deputy marshal. Several former residents from Wichita told Mayor Hoover that Wyatt Earp would be a good man to have on the police force. He could handle the Texas cowboys.[9]

It was mid-April 1876, and Wyatt was unemployed. Now what was he going to do? Stay in Wichita? Move to a new town and start over?

What about Wyatt's wife, Sarah? She and Bessie Earp were in business in Wichita until at least April 1876.[10] Wyatt and Sarah may have parted ways when Wyatt lost his police job or maybe before that. At some point, Sarah headed east. She was listed as living in Kansas City, Missouri, in 1883.[11]

In May, Wyatt received a letter from Dodge City Mayor George Hoover offering him a job as deputy marshal. The mayor sent Wyatt a follow-up telegram again offering the job. Wyatt accepted and arrived in Dodge the morning of May 17, 1876. By noon, he was appointed deputy marshal.[12]

Dodge City had three additional deputy marshal positions at the time. Joe Mason held one position. Bat Masterson's younger brother, Jim, held another position, leaving one open. Not long after Wyatt's appointment to the Dodge City police force, Bat arrived in town. He was hired as the third deputy marshal but was still convalescing from his fight with King in Sweetwater. Bat walked with a cane until his gunshot wound healed. The cane also came in handy for whacking rowdy cowboys over the head.[13]

Dodge City's police force did a good job tamping down the Texas cowboys' exuberance. They attempted any method other than gunplay to keep the cowboys in line. After all, the town businessmen wanted the cowboys' cash, not their bodies planted on Boot Hill. When gunplay was necessary, the police officers shot to wound, not to kill. Wyatt had always been good with his fists. He fought three fistfights with cowboys that their outfits put up as champions and won all three. Two of those fights were back-to-back.[14]

Wyatt was proficient at another form of subduing cowboys—buffaloing. Buffaloing was using a revolver's barrel to whack a person on top of or alongside the head, stunning them. Just to emphasize, they used the gun's barrel, not the butt of the gun. Flipping the gun to grip it by the barrel would take too long; it could also end the officer's life if the person to be whacked grabbed the hammer and pulled the trigger.[15]

Using these methods, the Dodge City police force kept it relatively peaceful to the north of the deadline; but on the south side, they pretty much allowed anything.[16]

Back in the summer of 1874, Lieutenant Colonel George Armstrong Custer led a military expedition into the Black Hills of Dakota Territory. Custer had invited along two professional miners who confirmed enough gold in paying quantities to set off a gold rush. The only problem was that the Black Hills were part of the Great Sioux Reservation, and, according to the 1868 Fort Laramie Treaty, white people were excluded from the Black Hills. However, the argonauts didn't care, and the government made half-hearted attempts to kick them out. It finally resulted in the Great Sioux War and the death of Custer and his 7th Cavalry command. By the summer of 1876, Deadwood was the major gold camp in the northern Black Hills. The gold bug was hitting every-one, and they were heading for the Hills.

Wyatt's younger brother Morgan arrived in Dodge with plans to prospect for gold in the Black Hills. Wyatt and Bat both came down with gold fever, but Wyatt promised Mayor Hoover he would stay until the end of the cattle-shipping season. Bat, who made no such promise, resigned in July and prepared to get out of Dodge and head for the Hills. Morgan was hired to take Bat's deputy marshal position.[17]

Bat rode the rails to Cheyenne, Wyoming Territory, one of the jumping off points for the Black Hills. He would have to figure out his own transportation from Cheyenne to Deadwood. There was no stage line yet to Deadwood, so he would need to buy a horse and supplies to travel over 260 miles. He also needed to join a party for mutual protection from Indians and road agents.

After exploring Cheyenne's saloons, dance halls, gambling houses, theaters, and more, Bat decided to spend a few days play-ing games of chance in the "Magic City of the Plains." He had a winning streak at the faro tables—increasing his cash. A few days turned into five weeks. By the end of that time, Bat had heard enough hard-luck stories from returning Black Hills prospectors that he decided to forget the Black Hills and return to Dodge with his winnings. He rode the rails eastward, getting off at Sidney, Nebraska, to tour the town.[18]

Back in Dodge, Wyatt and Morgan still had gold fever. At the end of the cattle-shipping season, they left the police force, bought a wagon and a team of four horses, and drove north out of Dodge on September 9.[19]

They arrived at Sidney, Nebraska, another jumping off location for Deadwood. There they ran into Bat, who told them he was headed back to Dodge because he had heard from returning prospectors that all the good claims in the Hills were taken. Wyatt and Morgan were still determined to see for themselves and drove their team northwest out of town to follow the trail to Deadwood.[20]

Wyatt and Morgan arrived in Deadwood to find that Bat was right, all the good claims had been taken. Wyatt was determined to stay and figure out a way to make money.[21] Morgan had other plans and left with a pack train headed to Montana.[22]

As autumn progressed into winter, Wyatt made a deal with a claim owner outside of town who had cut and stockpiled firewood. He bought the firewood from the man, hauled it to town in his wagon, and sold it there for a higher price. This arrangement kept him busy throughout the winter and made him a nice profit.[23]

Meanwhile back in Dodge, Bat could now get around without using a cane, but he would have a slight limp for the rest of his life. Teaming up with fellow veteran hunters Bill Tilghman and Neil Brown in the fall of 1876, they went buffalo hunting. They hired as skinner a young boy, Fred Sutton, from Tilghman's hometown, Atchison, Kansas. Sutton was impressed with Bat's skill at trick shooting. "I saw him kill many a rabbit by simply pointing, without sighting, the six-shooter no higher than his hip." Tilghman had praise for Bat's skill with a gun: "I've seen Bat shoot at a tin cup thrown in the air, with his six-shooter, at twenty-five cents a shot, and make money at it."[24]

With the 1877 spring thaw, Deadwood's demand for firewood died out. Wyatt explored the Black Hills creeks prospecting for gold; but other placer miners had already claimed all the locations with promising pay dirt. Not seeing any further opportunity to make money, he sold his team of horses and wagon and decided to take the next stagecoach out of Deadwood for Cheyenne.[25]

The Cheyenne and Black Hills Stage and Express operated the stage line between Cheyenne and Deadwood. Law enforcement along the trail between Deadwood and Cheyenne did not exist. There were plenty of locations where road agents could stop and rob a stagecoach. Throughout the spring of 1877, road agent activity increased.

After learning of another stagecoach robbery on the night of June 1, superintendent and part owner Luke Voorhees telegraphed a message from Cheyenne to his Deadwood agent, Isaac H. Gray. Voorhees told Gray to send two shotgun messengers with every gold shipment. They had orders to shoot any armed man who approached the coach day or night.[26] Even so, multiple holdups continued throughout June.

Wyatt went to buy a ticket for the next stage out of Deadwood. Instead of selling Wyatt a ticket, Gray hired him to ride along as a shotgun messenger on the next gold shipment. The stagecoach left the next Monday morning. Wyatt said about ten miles out of Deadwood, two groups of four riders rode parallel to the stagecoach. He fired his rifle at one group and that ended the pursuit. The rest of the trip to Cheyenne was completed without incident.[27]

Jim "Dog" Kelley, owner of the Alhambra Saloon, had been elected mayor of Dodge in April 1877.[28] Kelley sent a telegram to Wyatt in Cheyenne offering him a law enforcement job. Kelley needed him to get to Dodge in time to help manage the cowboys during the Fourth of July festivities. Wyatt accepted, but he wouldn't make town until the morning after the celebrations when he was immediately reappointed to the city police force.[29]

During the spring of 1877, Bat had returned to Dodge from buffalo hunting. He was a backer of the Dodge City Gang, which was in favor of looser law enforcement. The gang's candidate for mayor, "Dog" Kelley, won the election. Kelley had kept Larry Deger as marshal and the rest of the police force intact including Ed Masterson.[30]

Bat invested his money partnering with Ben Springer in the operation of the Lone Star Dance Hall, one of the largest entertainment facilities in Dodge, popular with the Texas cowboys and located on the south side, where anything goes. Not only did the dance hall have a dance floor and girls to dance with their customers, but also a small stage for a band and the occasional show, a bar, and games of chance: faro, roulette, poker, monte, and chuck-a-luck. The dance hall girls' rooms were on the second floor where they could be alone with their customers.[31]

On the morning of June 6, Bobby Gill, a small man who had consumed too much alcohol, was standing on a south side street making fun of Marshal Deger. A small crowd, including Bat, gathered round, amused at Bobby's humorous harangue. Marshal Deger came along and arrested Gill, putting an end to his oration.[32]

Gill was not moving fast enough so Deger kicked him in the butt a few times. Bat jumped in and wrapped his arms around the marshal's neck, allowing Gill to escape. Deger and Bat grappled as Deger yelled for the bystanders to take Bat's gun and help arrest him. Deputy Sheriff Joe Mason arrived and took Bat's gun. Half a dozen Texans pulled Bat off Deger, who drew his pistol and buffaloed Bat as Bat flailed and kicked with his blood splattering Mason. Bat fought every inch of the way to the jail until they threw him in a cell.[33]

That afternoon, brother Ed tracked down Bobby Gill and threw him in the cell with brother Bat. The next day, Bat appeared before the judge, pled guilty to disturbing the peace, and was fined twenty-five dollars. A month later Mayor Kelley and the city council remitted ten dollars of his fine. Bat held a grudge against Marshal Deger for years after the Bobby Gill incident.[34]

Charlie Siringo, a Texas cowboy, recounted the 1877 Fourth of July celebration that started out in Bat's dance hall: "This celebration came near to costing me my life in a free-for-all fight in the Lone Star dance hall. . . . The hall was jammed full of free-and-easy girls, long-haired buffalo hunters, and wild and woolly cowboys." Charlie told how one of his friends started a fight with the buffalo hunters to prove cowboys were tougher. His friend was severely stabbed, but that didn't stop the cowboys. He continued, "After mounting our ponies, Joe Mason, a town marshal, tried to arrest us, but we ran him to cover in an alley, then went out of town yelling and shooting off our pistols."[35]

Too bad Wyatt arrived in town a day late.

CHAPTER 5

BAT GETS A LAWMAN'S JOB, AND WYATT WANDERS

Wyatt arrived in Dodge the morning of July 5, 1877.[1] The July 7, 1877, edition of the *Dodge City Times* endorsed his return to the police force: "Wyatt Earp, who was on our city police force last summer, is in town again. We hope he will accept a position on the police force once more." The article went on to say, "[Wyatt] had a quiet way of taking the most desperate character into custody which invariably gave one the impression that the city was able to enforce her mandates and preserve her dignity. It wasn't considered policy to draw a gun on Wyatt unless you got the drop and meant to burn powder without any preliminary talk."[2] Wyatt was given his old job again and went to work.

The Dodge City police force must have done a good job keeping the peace the rest of that summer as no killings or major incidents were reported in the newspapers. However, there was an altercation between Miss Frankie Bell and Wyatt reported in the July 21, 1877, edition of the *Dodge City Times*. Miss Bell, one of the ladies of the night, "heaped epithets on the unoffending head of Mr. Earp to such an extent as to provoke a slap from the ex-officer." She spent the night in jail and the next day was fined twenty dollars. Wyatt was fined "the lowest limit of the law, one dollar."[3] It is interesting to note that the *Times* referred to Wyatt as an "ex-officer." Was he not on the police force at that time? Did the newspaper make a mistake?

As for the end of the cattle-shipping season, Wyatt Earp said in Stuart Lake's biography, "The closing weeks . . . were fairly quiet. We had the run of South Side fracases and heaved the daily grist into the calaboose. We made a few arrests north of the Dead Line and knocked over an occasional gun-totter, but there were no major affrays that I remember."[4]

Charlie Bassett had been Ford County sheriff since the county was organized in 1873. His second term would end in January 1878. The Kansas State Constitution stated elected officials could not hold office for three consecutive terms. In July 1877, Charlie appointed Bat Masterson as undersheriff, his second in command, viewing Bat as his successor to run for his position in the November election.[5]

That same month, Dodge City promoted Bat's older brother, Ed, to the assistant city marshal position. Ed was already on the police force.[6] On July 20, Ed had to quell a disturbance between Mayor Kelley and Marshal Deger. At 2:00 a.m., Deger jailed gambler Charlie Ronan, who was a friend of Kelley's and a member of the Dodge City Gang. Kelley ordered Deger to release Ronan. Deger refused. Kelley demanded Deger hand in his badge. Deger refused. Kelley ordered Ed and Officer Joe Mason to arrest Deger. Deger pulled his revolver and warned Ed and Joe not to try to arrest him. Ed defused the showdown by getting both men to agree that Deger would submit to arrest but be released under his own recognizance until police court later in the morning. Ed also arrested Kelley for interfering with a police officer in the discharge of his duty with the same conditions as Deger's. At the police court, all charges were dropped, and the *Dodge City Times* reported, "The municipal machinery is now running smoothly."[7]

Dodge City politics continued to be interesting. Not only was Larry Deger Dodge City's marshal but also at the same time was a

Ford County deputy sheriff. Bat fired him from the sheriff's office on August 4.[8] Then on September 17, Bat joined his two brothers on the city police force. Mayor Kelley appointed him a special city policeman serving under Marshal Deger for ten days.[9]

September was busy for Bat. He was still involved in running the Lone Star as well as his city police and undersheriff duties. The September 8 edition of the *Times* reported his capture of a horse thief, and, on September 17, he was involved in the capture of three buffalo hunters turned con artists and thieves.[10] A week later, it was night in the plaza, north of the deadline as Texas cowboy A. C. Jackson hurrahed the town, racing his horse as he fired his six-shooters into the air. Ed and Bat ran to the plaza shouting at Jackson to stop. Jackson waved his hat in defiance as he galloped toward the Arkansas River bridge and freedom. The Mastersons opened fire on Jackson's horse, killing it and forcing Jackson to walk back to camp.[11]

The next day, news of a Union Pacific train robbery at Big Springs, Nebraska, reached Dodge. The gang of five bandits were thought to be heading south and would have to cross the Santa Fe tracks at some point. Sheriff Bassett, Josh Webb, and Bat took the morning train west to Larkin, Kansas, and back, but saw no sign of the robbers. Then they received another report saying the bandits had crossed the Santa Fe tracks thirty miles west of Dodge. The three saddled their horses and cut cross-country to attempt to intercept the robbers but found no sign of them. It was later learned the robbers were the Sam Bass gang out of Texas.[12]

Another Texas gang led by Dave Rudabaugh and Mike Rourke had been plaguing the Santa Fe Railroad. The Santa Fe asked Wyatt to track down and capture the gang. He agreed, claiming he also had the authority to do so as a deputy US marshal.[13] As with the Polecat War, there is no official documentation Wyatt was a deputy US marshal although he may have been field commissioned.[14]

The rumor was Rudabaugh and his gang had returned to Texas, so Wyatt left Dodge on October 1, to track them down.[15]

Bat announced he was a candidate for Ford County sheriff in the October 13, 1877, issue of the *Dodge City Times*. Part of his announcement read, "I have no pledges to make, as pledges are usually considered before election to be mere clap-trap. . . . Should I be elected [I] will put forth my best efforts to so discharge the duties of the office that those voting for me shall have no occasion to regret having done so."[16] The *Times* followed up his announcement with the endorsement: "'Bat' is well known as a young man of nerve and coolness in cases of danger. He has served on the police force of this city, and also as under-sheriff, and knows just how to gather in the sinners. He is qualified to fill the office, and if elected will never shrink from danger."[17] Bat also announced he relinquished his share in the Lone Star Dance Hall.[18] Most of the Dodge City Gang backed Bat. Marshal Larry Deger announced he was also running for sheriff. Former Mayor George Hoover and other anti-gang townsmen backed Deger.[19]

Monday afternoon, November 5, 1877, the day before the election, trouble erupted in the Lone Star Dance Hall. Bob Shaw accused Texas Dick Moore of robbing him of forty dollars. The situation looked bad, and someone ran to find Assistant City Marshal Ed Masterson. When Ed entered the Lone Star, he saw Shaw standing at the bar with his six-gun leveled at Texas Dick. Ed ordered Shaw to put down the gun. Shouting at Ed to keep away, Shaw shot at Texas Dick, hitting him in the groin. Ed slugged Shaw over the head with his gun. Shaw swiveled, shooting Ed in the right chest, paralyzing his right arm. As Ed fell to the floor, he flipped his gun from right hand to left and pumped a slug into Shaw's left arm and another into his left leg. A stray shot hit a bystander. Everyone survived the gunfight, and Ed left Dodge to recuperate at his parents' farm.[20]

The election was held November 6, the day after Ed was shot. Bat won by three votes. Deger contested the election but withdrew two months later.[21]

Wyatt learned the robber Dave Rudabaugh was in Fort Griffin, Texas. He left Dodge following the cattle trails south four hundred miles, through Indian Territory, entered Texas at Doan's Crossing on the Red River, and then proceeded to Fort Griffin on the Brazos River.[22]

The army had constructed Fort Griffin in 1867 to protect settlers from Indian attacks. A small community catering to soldiers and buffalo hunters grew nearby. Its saloons and dance halls became a favorite stop for Texas cowboys driving their herds along the Western Trail to Dodge City. It also became a hangout for riffraff, many on the run from the law. The town was so wicked it earned the nickname "Babylon on the Brazos."[23]

It was likely mid-November 1877 when Wyatt rode into Fort Griffin.[24] He learned Mike Shanssey was operating a combination dance hall, bar, gambling hall, and eatery. Wyatt knew Shanssey from Cheyenne, Wyoming, when on the Fourth of July, Shanssey fought and lost to the professional boxer Mike Donovan. When Wyatt asked Shanssey about the whereabouts of Rudabaugh and his gang, he said they had been in town but were now gone. He had no idea where they were headed but if anyone knew it would be Doc Holliday. Shanssey said Holliday owed him a few favors, and he was sure Holliday would help Wyatt. Shanssey introduced them and told Holliday that Wyatt needed information on the whereabouts of Rudabaugh. Holliday said to give him some time and he would see what he could find.[25]

John Henry Holliday was born in 1851 in Griffin, Georgia, to a well-to-do family. He was well educated and studied dentistry. He developed tuberculosis and headed west to Dallas, Texas, in 1873, hoping the drier climate would prolong his life.[26]

Doc started out in dentistry, but business fell off. Who wanted their teeth worked on by someone with a hacking cough? He found his true calling—gambling. He was cold, calculating, and fearless. What did he care? He was going to die soon anyway. Physically he was sickly and frail, but he was proficient with a six-gun, practicing often, and he was handy with a knife. Doc was reputed to consume two quarts of whiskey a day and known to have a mean disposition. He was witty with a sarcastic sense of humor, but at times could be kindhearted. He had a strong sense of loyalty to his few friends.[27]

Rumors floated that back in Georgia he had shot some black boys over a swimming hole dispute, or maybe he just shot at them. Then people gossiped he had to leave Dallas because he killed a man. They said he was involved in multiple killings and gunfights across the West.[28] Rumors if left alone can grow into a reputation. A reputation as a cold-blooded killer can add to a gambler's position when in the game.

By the Fourth of July 1877, Doc was living in Breckenridge, Texas, and playing poker with gambler Henry Kahn. An argument erupted between them, and Doc repeatedly whacked Kahn with a walking stick. They were both arrested, fined, and released. Later that day, they met and resumed their argument. Kahn shot Doc. The wound was so bad the July 7, 1877, edition of the *Dallas Weekly Herald* reported him killed. He recovered and moved to Fort Griffin, where he met the dance hall girl Big Nose Kate Elder, whose real name was Mary Katherine Haroney. They would have a notorious love-hate relationship for the rest of Doc's life. Doc, with Kate by his side, was at the faro table in Shanssey's saloon every evening.[29] This is where Wyatt would have met them.

In less than a week, Doc learned where Rudabaugh was headed. Doc told Wyatt that Rudabaugh had traveled five hundred miles southwest to Fort Davis, Texas. Wyatt pursued Rudabaugh, but the man was always on the move, always one step ahead of Wyatt. From Fort Davis, Wyatt followed Rudabaugh to Fort Clark, then on to Fort Concho, onward to Fort McKavett, and finally back to Fort Griffin.[30] It was a circuit through western Texas over a thousand miles in distance.

Arriving in Fort Griffin on January 20, 1878, Wyatt discovered once again the wily Rudabaugh had eluded him. He also learned Doc and Kate had skipped town. Wyatt said it was due to Doc killing a gambler, Ed Bailey, over a poker game. Shanssey had a message from Doc to Wyatt that he would see him in Dodge.[31] There is no collaborating evidence that Doc killed Ed Bailey.

The Dodge City Council had had enough of Marshal Larry Deger and removed him from office on December 5, 1877. They replaced him with Ed Masterson, who had recently returned to Dodge after recuperating on his parents' farm.[32]

On January 14, 1878, twenty-five-year-old Bat Masterson was sworn in as Ford County sheriff. His first act was to appoint former sheriff Charlie Bassett as undersheriff. Not only was the Ford County sheriff responsible for his own county, but he was also responsible for law enforcement in Kansas's southwestern, unorganized territory, an area encompassing ninety-five hundred square miles.[33]

News reached Bat on January 17 that a gang of robbers had attempted two back-to-back train robberies at Kinsley, thirty-seven miles to the east in neighboring Edwards County. The robbers had disappeared into the sand hills country south of the Arkansas River. Three separate Edwards County posses searched for them without success.[34]

Money shipped on the Santa Fe railroad was under the care of the Adams Express Company, which had an office in Dodge City. The local company representative asked Bat to join the search for the bandits. Bat agreed, formed a posse of former buffalo hunters, and rode into the sand hills on January 29.[35]

They rode through a snowstorm for three days until they came to Harvey Lovell's lonely ranch. Lovell told Bat he had seen no suspicious characters. Bat had a hunch that if the gang was in the area, they would try to seek shelter from the storm at Lovell's. Late the next day, four riders approached the ranch while the posse hid in the ranch buildings. As they got close, Lovell identified two of the riders as his cowhands. Bat recognized the other two as Ed West and Dave Rudabaugh. The posse got the drop on them as Bat warned, "Throw up your hands!" Rudabaugh went to draw his pistol but stopped when he heard posse member Josh Webb's six-gun hammer click behind him. After the posse members disarmed the pair, Bat noticed a bulge under Rudabaugh's coat. Opening the coat, Bat found a gun stuck in Rudabaugh's waistband. As Bat pulled it out, Rudabaugh grabbed for the gun, but in the struggle Bat held on to it.[36]

February was turning out to be even busier than January. The posse returned to Dodge with their prisoners on February 1. Bat had to arrest his buffalo hunting friend Bill Tilghman, who was accused of being an accomplice to the attempted train robberies. Fortunately for Tilghman, the case against him was dropped several days later due to lack of evidence.[37] On February 5, Bat traveled by train to Las Animas, Colorado, and arrested James McDuff for stealing horses. The *Dodge City Times* reported Bat "promptly arrested him, having searched for his man under the bed in a dancehall." [38]

Bat learned that what was left of Rudabaugh's gang were hiding out on the Staked Plains. He formed a posse to go after them, riding south out of Dodge on February 10.[39] Reaching Lovell's ranch again, they learned Mike Rourke and another gang member, Dan Webster, had been there three hours earlier. The posse took off dogging the gang's trail, but when the trail led out onto the Staked Plains, they lost them. The posse returned to Dodge empty-handed after riding six hundred miles over thirteen days during midwinter.[40]

Then on the night of March 15, Bat learned two of the train robbers, Tom Gott and J. D. Green, were spotted in Dodge's south side. Bat took Charlie Bassett and brother Ed along to make the arrest. With a full moon shining, it was easy to spot Gott and Green south of Anderson's stable. The two robbers saw they had been spotted and started to run. The three officers gave chase and caught them. Gott and Green tried to resist drawing their guns, but the three officers overpowered them. Gott and Green revealed that Mike Rourke and another gang member named Lafeu had been in town with them. The lawmen scoured the town, but Rourke and Lafeu were long gone.[41] The next morning, Bat led a posse made up of Charlie Bassett, Josh Webb, and brother Jim. They scoured the countryside for three days but found no sign of Rourke and Lafeu.[42]

Meanwhile back at Fort Griffin, Texas, Wyatt received word from Dodge that Mike Rourke was still on the loose and he was to track him down. By April 1, Wyatt tracked Rourke to San Antonio only to find he was two days behind the bandit. He learned Rourke planned to visit his hometown of Joplin, Missouri, so Wyatt traveled there to hunt him down.[43]

Dodge City had two newspapers by March 1878, the *Times* and the *Globe*. Both papers were concerned about an increase in the "boys" carrying weapons in the streets contrary to city ordinances and of increased robberies at night. On March 26, the *Globe* reported, "Our police force were kept jumping till three o'clock yesterday morning, corraling [sic] disturbers of the peace. The result was a full calaboose of soldiers for police court yesterday."[44]

Tuesday, April 9, 1878, 10:00 p.m., was like any other night on the south side of Dodge. Cowboys were in town whooping it up, and the businesses that catered to them were in full swing. Ed Masterson along with Assistant Marshal Nat Haywood walked into the Lady Gay Saloon. Trail boss Alf Walker and five of his cowboys were having an alcohol-fueled, rip-roaring good time.[45]

Ed spotted one of the cowboys, Jack Wagner, openly displaying a six-gun in a shoulder holster. Ed told Wagner it was against city ordinances to wear a gun in town. Without an argument, Wagner handed Ed his gun. Ed gave it to Walker telling him to check it with the bartender. Walker agreed, and Ed and Haywood left the Lady Gay.[46]

No sooner had they left the building than they saw Walker and Wagner step out of the saloon. Wagner's six-gun was back in his shoulder holster. Ed tried to disarm Wagner, and a scuffle ensued. The Lady Gay's clientele stepped out to watch the struggle. Wagner pulled his pistol as Ed tried to grab it. Pressing the six-shooter's muzzle against Ed's abdomen, Wagner pulled the trigger, blowing a hole through Ed and setting his clothes on fire. At the same time, Walker pulled a pistol on Haywood as Haywood reached for his gun. Walker pointed the muzzle at Haywood's face, pulled back the hammer, and squeezed the trigger—a misfire. People panicked, running in every which direction.[47]

Hearing the shot, Bat raced to the scene and saw Ed staggering with his clothes on fire, Wagner with his gun pointed at Ed, and Walker with his gun pointed in Haywood's face. Bat fired his six-gun, hitting Wagner in the abdomen. Walker swung his gun toward Bat as Bat fired three times, hitting Walker once in the chest and twice in the right arm.[48]

Wagner staggered into A. J. Peacock's saloon, collapsed in the arms of Ham Bell, then slid to the floor. Walker followed Wagner into the saloon, dropped his gun, walked out the back door, and fell to the ground. With a large hole through his body and his clothes still smoldering, Ed walked north two hundred yards across the railroad tracks to George Hoover's saloon where he collapsed on the floor. He was carried upstairs to his room. There was

no chance he would survive. Bat sat with Ed until he died forty minutes later.[49]

Bat served warrants and arrested the four cowboys who had been with Wagner and Walker, but they were soon released. Before Wagner died the next day, he admitted he was responsible for Ed's death. Walker's father came for him and took him back to Texas. Ed was buried at the cemetery at Fort Dodge on April 10. The next day, Bat, with his friend Mike Sutton, left town to tell his parents the sad news.[50]

The city council passed a resolution concerning Ed's death, part of which read: "RESOLVED by the Council of the City of Dodge City, that in his death, the city has lost an officer who was not afraid to do his duty, who never shrank from its faithful performance, a worthy servant and upright citizen."[51]

BROTHERS-IN-LAW

Wyatt Earp and Bat Masterson were not the only family members involved in law enforcement. They each had brothers who served as peace officers.

Virgil Earp, five years older than Wyatt, was elected as one of two constables for Prescott, Arizona Territory, in 1878. In 1879, he was appointed deputy US marshal for Pima County and later Cochise County, Arizona.[52] He served most notably as marshal of Tombstone, Arizona, during the infamous October 26, 1881, gunfight near the O.K. Corral. On December 28, 1881, he was ambushed, being hit by a shotgun blast, on the streets of Tombstone. He survived to open a detective agency and be elected the first city marshal for Colton, California.[53] Morgan, three years younger than Wyatt, served as a peace officer in Butte, Montana, and then joined his brothers in Tombstone as a deputy city marshal participating in the gunfight near the O.K. Corral. Morgan was assassinated March 18, 1882, in Tombstone.[54] Warren, seven years younger than Wyatt, was a deputy city marshal in Tombstone. He missed the action near the O.K. Corral, but, after Morgan's assassination, he participated in the posse ride to track down Morgan's killers. In 1900, Warren was shot and killed in a Willcox, Arizona, saloon fight.[55]

Ed Masterson, a year older than Bat, was first a deputy marshal in Dodge City and later city marshal. Drunken cowboys gunned him down in the street when he tried to disarm them.[56] Jim Masterson, two years younger than Bat, served in dual roles as a Ford County deputy sheriff and Dodge City deputy marshal; later he was appointed Dodge City marshal for two years. He served as a Logan County deputy sheriff out of Guthrie, Oklahoma, as well as a deputy US marshal.[57] The Masterson brothers' sister Nellie, four years younger than Bat, married James Cairns, who served as city marshal in Wichita, Kansas, for many years.[58]

CHAPTER 6

DODGE CITY ON EDGE

ith Ed Masterson's murder on the night of April 9, 1878, Dodge City needed to fill the vacant marshal position. The city council met the next day and appointed Charlie Bassett marshal while he kept his undersheriff position with Ford County.[1] Assistant Marshal Nat Haywood, who cheated death when Alf Walker's six-gun misfired, resigned according to the April 20 edition of the *Dodge City Times*, "preferring to follow other vocations."[2]

After traveling to his parents' home in Sedgwick County to tell them the horrible news of Ed's death, Bat was back in Dodge on April 17 and went right to work tracking stolen horses and their thieves. He found the horses there in town and arrested the two suspected thieves, one of whom was Bat's good friend Bill Tilghman. This made the second time Bat had to arrest Tilghman within three months. Tilghman must have had a good alibi. After reviewing the evidence, the judge had the one man jailed and Tilghman released.[3]

The 1878 cattle-shipping season promised to be the biggest yet. Later estimates tallied 265,000 longhorns herded by 1,300 cowhands passed through Dodge. Cowboys were usually paid off at the end of the drive so an influx of gamblers, dance hall gals, entertainers, and sharps of all types converged on Dodge.

To help manage this temporary population increase, the town needed more police officers. Wyatt was in Joplin, Missouri, waiting to nab Mike Rourke when he received a message from Mayor "Dog" Kelley asking him to return to Dodge.[4] Wyatt arrived there on May 8, and the city council immediately appointed him assistant marshal. The May 14, 1878, edition of the *Ford County Globe* praised Wyatt as "one of the most efficient officers Dodge ever had."[5] Another police officer resigned, and Bat's younger brother Jim was hired June 1.[6]

Professional gamblers were flooding Dodge, including Luke Short and the Thompson brothers Ben and Billy. By June 8, Doc Holliday and Kate Elder were in town. Most likely he went right to work gambling with Kate by his side, but he also reverted to his old profession. He ran an advertisement in the June 8, 1878 edition of the *Times*:

DENTISTRY.

J. H. Holliday, dentist, very respectfully offers his professional services to the citizens of Dodge City and surrounding country during the summer. Office at room No. 24, Dodge House. Where satisfaction is not given money will be refunded.[7]

When Wyatt arrived in Dodge he most likely brought along his third wife, Celia Ann "Mattie" Blaylock. Not much is known about their early relationship. There is nothing about when or where they met, nor documentation of their marriage. In her memoirs, Kate Elder wrote that Doc and she "first met Wyatt Earp and Mrs. Earp in Griffin, Texas."[8]

Little is known about Bat's romantic affairs in Dodge, but the June 8, 1878, edition of the *Times* reported on the Summit House opening in nearby Spearville. An orchestra played as the guests danced and partook of a "sumptuous board." The paper reported on the Dodge City attendees including "Sheriff Masterson and lady."[9]

The local businesses brought in entertainers such as the popular husband and wife team Dick Brown and Fannie Garrettson as well as Dora Hand, whose stage name was Fannie Keenan. It was said her physical beauty had provoked gunfights and her singing voice brought hard cases to the point of tears.[10]

In July, the comedy team of Jim Thompson and Eddie Foy arrived in town on the train from the east. Foy said the whole town turned out to meet the train. Thompson and he were introduced to many Dodge City citizens including the mayor, the marshal, Wyatt Earp—"one of the city police and a famous gunfighter"—Luke Short, Doc Holliday, and Sheriff Bat Masterson. Foy described Bat as "a trim, good-looking young man with a pleasant face and carefully barbered mustache, well-tailored clothes, hat with a rakish tilt and two big silver-mounted, ivory-handled pistols in a heavy belt. Masterson and I soon took a liking to each other and were friends thenceforward."[11]

Jim Thompson and Eddie Foy's show was a hit with most everyone in Dodge except possibly Ben Thompson. One evening between acts, Foy was backstage putting on makeup as he sat by a table and lamp. A drunken Ben Thompson wandered in. Seeing Foy, he drew his gun and demanded "Getcher head outa the way! I wanta shoot out that light." Foy's head was in Thompson's direct line of fire to shoot the lamp. Not moving, Foy turned and stared at Thompson. Still pointing his gun at him, Thompson yelled, "Getcher head outa the way, I told you! I'm gonna shoot out that light. If you want it through yer head, too, all right!" Foy said he couldn't move, hypnotized by his own stubbornness. Bat burst in, threw up the muzzle of Thompson's gun, and forced him out. Foy said his hands shook so that he couldn't finish putting on the makeup and was limp for the rest of the evening.[12]

Death could come unexpectedly and at any time in Dodge. The Long Branch Saloon still had a crowd in it at 4:00 a.m. on July 13, 1878. Deputy US Marshal Harry "Mack" McCarty stood at the bar having a drink and conversing with another man. A group of cowboys working for the Shiner Brothers were ridiculing their cook, "Limping" Tom Roach, known as a mean drunk. Furious at their jokes at his expense, Roach rushed up behind McCarty and snatched the pistol out of his holster. McCarty turned from the bar to see who had taken his gun. Roach brandished the gun and shot McCarty in the groin. McCarty staggered toward the door and fell. A bystander shot Roach in the head, but just grazed him. Roach's bullet had severed McCarty's femoral artery, and he was dead within an hour. Roach was later tried and sentenced to the state penitentiary for twelve years and three months.[13] Ford County was now without a deputy US marshal.

Years later in 1883, Andy Adams was a young cowboy on a cattle drive about to enter Dodge City. An old cattleman by the name of McNulta gave the cowboys advice about Dodge:

> *I've been in Dodge every summer since '77, and I can give you boys some points. . . . The buffalo hunters and range men have protested against the iron rule of Dodge's peace officers, and nearly every protest has cost human life. Don't ever get the impression that you can ride your horses into a saloon, or shoot out the lights in Dodge; it may go somewhere else, but it don't go there. So I want to warn you to behave yourselves. . . . don't ride out shooting; omit that. Most cowboys think it's an infringement on their rights to give up shooting in town . . . [but] your six-shooters are no match for Winchesters and buckshot; and Dodge's officers are as game a set of men as ever faced danger.*[14]

Eddie Foy was performing in the Comique Hall to a packed house at 3:00 a.m. on July 26, 1878. Bat and Doc were there sitting at a gaming table playing Spanish Monte. The Comique was a popular house of entertainment in Dodge City's south side near the Arkansas River bridge. On the far side of the river were the cowboy camps. Jim Masterson and Wyatt were outside on the night beat. They were loitering alongside the Comique to hear Foy's routine through the building's thin walls.[15]

Three cowboys rode by on their way to cross the bridge. Suddenly, one of the riders wheeled his horse and raced back at a gallop. As he passed where Wyatt stood, the rider shot his six-gun

three times. The bullets passed through the wall. Fortunately, no one inside was hurt as everyone hit the floor.[16]

Jim and Wyatt drew their revolvers and began firing at the cowboy, his horse rearing. He reined it around and came galloping back, firing two more shots. Wyatt and Jim continued to fire as bystanders joined in trying to hit the cowboy. The rider raced past them heading toward the bridge. Wyatt squatted to silhouette the rider against the night sky, aimed, and fired.[17]

Shot in the arm, the rider fell from his horse on the far side of the bridge. No one really knew who hit him. More than twenty shots had been fired in the exchange with the cowboy, who they later learned was named George Hoy from Texas.[18]

Why did Hoy shoot up Comique Hall? Eddie Foy thought Hoy shot at the building because of an argument Hoy had with the Comique's owner. Wyatt claimed his enemies had placed a thousand-dollar bounty on his head, and Hoy was trying to collect. Bat thought Hoy might not have even seen Wyatt standing by the building when he started shooting.[19] Hoy's arm was badly mangled, and the local doctor cared for him in town.

Plenty of cowboys arriving in Dodge chose to ignore the ordinances forbidding the carrying of guns and wound up in the calaboose. One such cowboy was young Jim "Spike" Kenedy. On July 29, Wyatt hauled him into police court where Kenedy was fined for carrying a pistol in town.[20]

Spike Kenedy was the son of Captain Mifflin Kenedy, a wealthy and respected Texas cattleman. Spike was wild, and with abundant wealth he thought he could get away with anything, including drinking to excess and cavorting in brothels. In 1872, he was in an Ellsworth, Kansas, saloon playing cards and losing money to Texas cattleman I. P. "Print" Olive. Kenedy accused Olive of cheating. Later that day, Spike found Olive again playing cards in another saloon. Spike shot him in the hand, groin, and thigh and was stopped only when Jim Kelly, one of Olive's black cowhands, burst into the saloon and shot Spike in the leg. Spike was arrested, but friends helped him escape that night. He laid low in Texas for the next few years managing his father's ranch.[21]

Bat was busy in June and July capturing horse thieves and a fugitive from justice. He confronted shady operators of games of chance and returned the money to the people who had been swindled. However, something was wrong with Bat's health. The weather had been stifling hot. Bat suffered from vertigo and was confined to bed during the attacks. On August 1, he left on the train for Hot Springs, Arkansas, hoping the thermal baths would restore his health. He was expected to be gone three to four weeks.[22]

The August 6, 1878, *Ford County Globe* reported, "Clay Allison, one of the Allison Bros., from the Cimarron, [New Mexico], south of Las Animas, Colorado, stopped off at Dodge last week on his way home from St. Louis. We are glad to say that Clay has about recovered from the effects of the East St. Louis scrimmage."[23] Allison was a well-known bad hombre. Born in Tennessee in 1840, he served in a variety of Confederate units during the Civil War. After the war, he moved to Texas then later to New Mexico. He worked as a cowhand herding cattle to Kansas cowtowns and eventually built up his own herd. Allison was a heavy drinker and a killer.[24] By the time Allison was mentioned by the *Globe* as being in Dodge, he was known to have killed four men and was suspected of two additional murders.[25] Apparently, he had been in a well-publicized fistfight in Missouri and had stopped off in Dodge on his return home.[26] Cowhand Pink Simms was a friend of Allison's and said that Allison and George Hoy were friends. It's quite likely Allison would have heard about the shooting of Hoy and visited him while he was convalescing in Dodge.[27] Hoy claimed he was not the one who had done the shooting.[28] He probably told Allison his side of the story if Allison visited him.

By August 12, Bat was back in Dodge. On that day, Deputy Sheriff William Duffy and Bat apprehended suspected horse thief James Smith three and a half miles outside of town.[29]

Marshal Charlie Bassett hauled Spike Kenedy into police court on Saturday, August 17; this time Kenedy was fined for disorderly conduct. Kenedy found Mayor Dog Kelley in his Alhambra Saloon. Kenedy told Kelley he did not appreciate the actions of the Dodge City police force. Kelley replied they were working under his orders and Kenedy needed to behave or face even worse treatment. Enraged, Kenedy leaped at Kelley. Kelley beat Kenedy and threw him into the street. Kenedy was furious as he found his horse and rode out of Dodge.[30]

That same Saturday night, an intoxicated cowboy tried to take over the bar at the crowded Comique Hall. The barkeeper objected, and a fight ensued. The cowboy's friends jumped into the fight as the city police entered the fray, buffaloing cowboys alongside the head. Shots were fired, but fortunately no one was hurt. The *Globe* only stated that "Our policemen interfered and had some difficulty handling their man." On that date, the police force consisted of Charlie Bassett, Jim Masterson, and Wyatt Earp, so two or all of them were involved in the "broil."[31]

George Hoy's shot-up arm was not healing. Gangrene set in and the doctors had to remove it. Hoy did not improve. Slipping into a coma, he died on August 21.[32] The August 27 edition of the *Globe* reported, "He had many friends and no enemies among the Texas men who knew him. George was nothing but a poor cow boy, [sic] but his brother cow-boys [sic] permitted him to want for nothing during his illness, and buried him in grand style when dead, which was very creditable to them."[33]

The September 10, 1878, issue of the *Ford County Globe* stated Clay Allison visited Dodge on September 5, passing through on his way east.[34] Many people have told a variety of versions of Allison's visit to Dodge and the confrontations between him and Wyatt and him and Bat. Wyatt claimed Allison wanted to collect on that thousand-dollar bounty placed on his head.[35] Cowboy Charlie Siringo claimed the entire police force was in hiding when Allison and an army of cowboys "treed" the town.[36] If there had been any confrontation with Allison, the newspapers would have printed it. Allison was big news. Just by Allison passing through town in early August and stopping there on September 5, the newspapers printed about those events.

Years later, Pink Simms, who as a boy was friends with the older Clay Allison, wrote about what he heard had happened in Dodge. Allison stopped there because of the death of his friend George Hoy. He wanted to meet with Bat, but Allison was armed, drinking heavily, and may or may not have threatened to kill Wyatt, so Bat waited to meet with him after he sobered up. During the meeting, Allison registered a protest with Bat against the Dodge City police and the needless killing of George Hoy, and that was it.[37]

Dodge City was experiencing an influx of confidence men attempting to con people out of money. The September 14, 1878, issue of the *Times* reported that on September 10, Harry Bell and the "Kid" cheated E. Markel, "an illiterate gentleman from some backwoods." They gave Markel a twenty-dollar gold piece in exchange for his twenty dollars in greenbacks. Markel later realized the coin was base metal and did not even resemble a gold coin. Bat arrested the two men and placed them in the charge of Deputy Sheriff William Duffy. They promised they would not try to escape and asked Duffy not to put them in jail. Duffy had been on duty the previous night and needed to sleep, so he turned them over to an "incompetent guard," who fell asleep while guarding the men. Seeing their opportunity, the two men "lit out" on the 5:00 a.m. westbound train.[38] Dodge City citizens were irate and held a public meeting to discuss the confidence men problem and to criticize the sheriff and his deputies. Both newspapers printed critical editorials.

The citizens of Dodge soon had lots more to worry about than a drunken killer and slippery confidence men. On the night of September 9, 1878, Chiefs Dull Knife and Little Wolf led nearly three hundred Northern Cheyenne in a breakout from their reservation in Indian Territory heading toward their homeland in

Montana and Wyoming Territories. Dodge City lay directly in their path.[39]

The Cheyenne were heading home peacefully until the army attacked them along the Cimarron River on September 13. After that, Cheyenne warriors began raiding and killing. On September 16, a war party struck at Meade City, Kansas, about forty miles southwest of Dodge, killing Washington O'Conner, a mail carrier. Other war parties looted two ranches eighteen miles outside of Dodge.[40]

Not scheduled to return until September 24, Sheriff Bat Masterson, Marshal Charlie Bassett, and other Dodge City notables were in Kansas City for a week.[41] Wyatt Earp was the chief law enforcement officer in Dodge. The *Times* reported that on Wednesday, September 18, riders were arriving in town with reports of Indian depredations throughout the countryside. Some were spotted within a few miles of the city. At 2:00 p.m., Dodge City's fire bell rang. It was rumored that Indians had set Harrison Berry's house on fire. People in town could see the flames four miles west of town. The volunteer fire company assembled under the leadership of Wyatt and others, boarded a locomotive that transported them to the scene of the fire, and extinguished it.[42] The Northern Cheyenne kept moving north. The excitement they caused soon died down, and it was business as usual again in Dodge.

On the night of September 19, 1878, Texas cowboys who had been out chasing Indians were carousing in Dodge.[43] One of them was Tobe Driskill, an influential Texas cattleman. The previous year, he had celebrated his cattle sale by getting drunk and firing his six-shooters into the air as he stood on Front Street outside the Alhambra Saloon shouting obscenities at Mayor Kelley. Wyatt had run across the plaza, buffaloed Driskill, and hauled him off to the calaboose.[44] He still held a grudge against Wyatt. Ed Morrison was along. He had been involved in the "Shanghai" Pierce affair in Wichita and had no love for Wyatt.[45] Another cowboy who may have been in the group and could have had a beef with Wyatt was

Joe Day, a good friend of George Hoy. Day stayed with Hoy and cared for him until he died.[46]

As Wyatt was making his rounds, he ran into Driskill, Morrison, and over twenty liquored-up and armed cowboys in front of the Long Branch Saloon. Wyatt did not have his weapons in his hands. Driskill and the mob had the advantage and were either going to beat him severely or kill him. At the moment they began to surround him, Doc Holliday burst out of the Long Branch, six-shooters in each hand. Now with backup, Wyatt drew his revolvers. One individual fired a shot and Holliday returned fire, hitting the shooter in the leg. With that, the cowboys stood down, and the incident ended.[47] Years later in Tombstone, under oath, Wyatt would state in his prepared statement, "I am a friend of Doc Holliday's because when I was city marshal of Dodge City, Kansas, he came to my rescue and saved my life when I was surrounded by desperadoes."[48]

By September 24, Charlie Bassett and Bat had returned from Kansas City. The Indian scare had died down, and Dodge had returned to business as usual—separating cowboys from their money.

One of the most popular entertainers in Dodge, if not the entire Midwest, was Dora Hand, who usually played to a packed house. Her voice enraptured audiences, and her admirers dubbed her "the Nightingale of the Frontier." At thirty-four years of age, she was stunning. Newspapers claimed her beauty "caused more gunfights than any other woman in all the West." Not only did she have a beautiful voice, but she spent her off hours helping the poor in town.[49]

The night of October 3, 1878, Dora entertained a standing-room-only crowd in Mayor Dog Kelley's Alhambra Saloon. After her performance, she walked to Kelley's small house behind the Great Western Hotel. She was staying there with her good friend and fellow entertainer Fannie Garrettson.[50] Fannie occupied the front bedroom, and Dora had the back bedroom. Kelley was gone. He had been ill for two or three weeks and had left on Monday for the hospital at Fort Dodge, which had the best physician in the countryside.[51]

Spike Kenedy arrived back in town and was out for revenge. He planned to kill Dog Kelley for beating and humiliating him. Kenedy had brought along a beautiful racehorse he had purchased in Kansas City. His plan was to use the horse to make a quick getaway once he killed Kelley. He had cased Kelley's two-room house, learning Kelley's bedroom was in the front.[52] Not completing his homework, he never asked anyone if Kelley was in town.

Late that night, Kenedy and a friend were drinking in the only saloon still open. Around 4:00 a.m., fortified with liquid courage, Kenedy saddled his horse and rode close to the front of Kelley's house. Drawing his six-shooter, he rapidly fired four shots, two of them through the door into Kelley's bedroom, and then raced away.[53]

Fortunately for Fannie, neither bullet hit her. She checked on Dora in the back bedroom. Dora moved her head side to side, gave several gasps, and died. A bullet had struck Dora, penetrating her chest.[54]

Jim Masterson and Wyatt ran to the sound of the gunshots and found Fannie sobbing in the street. Entering Kelley's house, they found Dora dead.[55] At first, they couldn't understand why anyone would want to try to kill the two women. They walked toward the saloon, which was still open, to question the occupants on what they might know of the shooting.[56]

Kenedy had returned to the saloon, joining his friend. When the two officers entered, Kenedy quietly slipped out, mounted his horse, and raced west. Jim and Wyatt learned Kenedy had been in the saloon but was now gone. It was pointed out Kenedy's friend was still there. They arrested the man and took him to jail where he told them he believed Kenedy did the shooting.[57] Others claimed they saw Kenedy riding out of town.

With that information in hand, Bat started forming a posse as R. G. Cook, justice of the peace and acting coroner, held an inquest on Dora's murder. The jury found in its opinion Dora had died from a gunshot wound "produced by a bullet discharged from a gun in the hands of one James Kennedy [sic]."[58]

At 2:00 p.m., Sheriff Bat Masterson led the posse west following the route Kenedy had taken. The posse consisted of Charlie Bassett, town marshal and deputy sheriff; Deputy Sheriff Bill Tilghman, who had been accused of train robbery and stealing horses; Deputy Sheriff Bill Duffy, who had turned con men over to an incompetent guard allowing them to escape; and Assistant Marshal Wyatt Earp. They were all seasoned plainsmen. The *Times* called them "the most intrepid posse as ever pulled a trigger."[59]

Kenedy had told people he had friends in Cheyenne, Wyoming, and it was thought he might head in that direction, but the posse decided he would most likely head for home by taking the Texas Trail to Tascosa in the Texas Panhandle, so they headed cross-country to the trail's ford over the Cimarron River.[60]

The posse was unaware that they were being tailed by twenty Texas cowboys led by Kenedy's good friend Dr. Henry Hoyt. Their mission—to intercept the posse and delay it long enough for Kenedy to escape.[61]

By evening the weather changed for the worst, as dark clouds rolled in with thunder and lightning. Strong winds blew as freezing rain changed to pelting hail that hit Kenedy, the posse, and the cowboy pursuers. Kenedy found an outcropping along a hill to hunker down as best he could until the storm passed. The posse found a high, overhanging stream bank under which to huddle.[62] Hoyt decided to change plans and led the Texans back south as fast as they could to inform Kenedy's wealthy father, Mifflin, what had happened to his son. He would know what to do.[63]

The weather cleared, and the posse reached a ranch outside of Meade City, where they believed Kenedy would have to pass. They unsaddled the horses and allowed them to graze, giving the appearance they were not a posse.[64]

Their hunch and ruse paid off. At 4:00 p.m., a rider appeared in the distance and cautiously approached. The rider stopped before reaching camp. It was Kenedy. They invited him in, but he sensed danger. He raised his quirt to strike his horse to flee when the posse opened fire on him.[65] Bat shot Kenedy in the left shoulder. Still mounted, he urged his horse to run, and Wyatt shot three bullets, killing the horse. They had to pull Kenedy out from under his mount. Other than the shoulder wound, he was in satisfactory condition. Kenedy asked the posse if he had killed Kelley. No, they replied, he had killed Dora Hand.[66] The posse brought Kenedy into Dodge the next day and put him in jail to await trial as he received medical attention.[67]

Poor Dora Hand was laid to rest in Dodge's cemetery. All the saloons and shops in town were closed. Over four hundred people attended the graveside service, including the poor, whom Dora had helped when not working.[68]

THE PLIGHT OF THE NORTHERN CHEYENNE

The Northern Cheyenne lived in the Tongue and Powder River basins of Wyoming and Montana Territories. After the battle of the Little Big Horn, they were harassed by the army until 1877, when most of the bands surrendered at Fort Robinson, Nebraska. They expected to settle on the Great Sioux Reservation in Dakota Territory as stipulated in the 1868 Fort Laramie Treaty, but a little known provision in the treaty stated they could also be settled on the Southern Cheyenne Reservation in Indian Territory.[69]

The federal government wanted to send them to Indian Territory. The Cheyenne leaders met with General George Crook about the move. It was their understanding Crook told them to go to Indian Territory, take a look, and return if they didn't like it. Nine hundred seventy-two Cheyenne men, women, and children left Fort Robinson heading south cross-country to Indian Territory. They arrived at the Cheyenne-Arapaho Reservation on August 5, 1877.[70]

They found deplorable conditions: no game to hunt, scanty and inferior rations, bad water, and oppressive heat. They were swarmed by mosquitos and came down with malaria. The leaders, Little Wolf and Dull Knife, wanted to take their people home, but their agent told them he could not let them leave. Only the Washington leadership could do that, and their response was no, the Cheyenne had to stay.[71]

By September 1878, the Cheyenne had had enough starvation, disease, and death. They told the agent they were returning north. They just wanted to be left alone and didn't plan to cause any trouble, but if they were attacked they would fight. The agent didn't believe they would leave on a long journey where the army could easily intercept and capture them, but on September 9, 1878, Little Wolf and Dull Knife led 297 men, women, and children on their exodus home.[72]

On September 13, they crossed the Cimarron River and were soon attacked by the army, but the warriors trapped the troops allowing the women and children to escape. Continuing to head north through Kansas and Nebraska, they were constantly harassed by troops and civilians. By mid-October, they split into two groups. Little Wolf, leading 134 people, continued north to the Tongue River, and Dull Knife led 150 people toward Red Cloud's agency in Nebraska.[73]

Little Wolf was able to reach Fort Keogh, Montana Territory, where they surrendered and awaited their fate. Dull Knife and his people surrendered and were taken to Fort Robinson. They were told they must return immediately to Indian Territory in the heart of the winter, but they refused. To force them into submission, the army locked them in a barracks building with no heat, food, or sanitation. The night of January 9, 1879, they broke out, attempting to escape. Most were either captured or killed; a few made it to the Lakota at Pine Ridge, Dakota Territory, only to be made prisoners there. [74] The federal government finally relented on sending the Northern Cheyenne south, and, in 1884, the government created a reservation for them. As of 2018, the Northern Cheyenne Indian Reservation in southeastern Montana was 444,000 acres in size with 11,266 enrolled tribal members, of which 5,012 lived on the reservation. [75]

CHAPTER 7

ENDINGS IN DODGE AND BEGINNINGS IN TOMBSTONE

With the advent of autumn, the cattle-shipping season was ending, but law enforcement's work never ended. The October 12, 1878, edition of the *Dodge City Times* listed six prisoners in the county jail including Spike Kenedy, another man accused of murder, and one accused of attempted murder.[1]

Kenedy was still in bad shape from his gunshot wound. Instead of holding the preliminary examination of Kenedy's guilt in the courtroom, Justice of the Peace R. G. Cook held it in the sheriff's office with no room for spectators. The law enforcement officers were the only ones willing to testify. No actual witnesses saw Kenedy murder Dora, and Kenedy recanted his confession to the posse that he had tried to kill Mayor Kelley. Cook acquitted Kenedy; he was a free man.[2] On October 29, 1878, the *Ford County Globe* reported, "We do not know what the evidence was, or upon what grounds he was acquitted. But he is free to go on his way rejoicing whenever he gets ready."[3] Rumors flew. Mifflin Kenedy paid for his son's release. Speculated amounts ranged from ten thousand to fifty thousand dollars.[4]

News reached Dodge that on Friday, October 25, 1878, Mike Rourke was planning a robbery when he was captured near Ellsworth, Kansas.[5] This was the same Mike Rourke whom Bat had chased into the Staked Plains and Wyatt had pursued across Texas.

Bat maintained a good record capturing horse thieves; on November 22, he arrested another one.[6] However, with Texas cowboys few and far between, there was not much action for Dodge City's three policemen. On December 3, 1878, the city council reduced Jim Masterson and Wyatt's salaries from one hundred to fifty dollars a month but kept Marshal Charlie Bassett's salary at a hundred dollars.[7]

The sheriff's office was embarrassed when four prisoners escaped from jail on December 6. The jailor was making improvements to the cell and had partially sawed through one of the bars. While he was gone picking up an item from the blacksmith shop, the inmates broke the bar at the cut, bent it back, and four of them made their escape. Jim Masterson caught one escapee a mile outside Dodge. Two more were caught in the town of Kinsley. The fourth was never captured.[8]

On December 9, Mifflin Kenedy, Spike's father, arrived in Dodge. The December 17 issue of the *Globe* reported Spike Kenedy was taken to the Fort Dodge hospital where three army doctors, including one from Fort Leavenworth, operated on Kenedy's shoulder.[9] The operation was a success, and Mifflin Kenedy took his son home to Texas.

Bat assisted the army on a pursuit of stolen animals. On the night of December 10, a small army detachment of two wagons on its way to Camp Supply, Indian Territory, was camped thirty-seven miles south of Dodge. During the night, eight mules were stolen. The army requested Bat's assistance, and on the evening of December 11, he accompanied Second Lieutenant Alexander Guard and eight enlisted men in pursuit of the thieves. The next day, a blizzard caught them out in the open, forcing them to stop and hunker down until it blew over on the morning of December 14. Traveling was difficult. Lieutenant Guard wrote in his report, "We found the country covered with snowdrifts which made it almost impossible to search ravines along the way." Rations and forage began to run low, so they headed to Camp Supply to recuperate and then returned to Dodge on December 21, traveling 232 miles without finding the mules or thieves.[10]

A few days later, Bat learned that one of the most notorious horse thieves, "Dutch Henry" Born, was enjoying himself in Trinidad, Colorado. Bat had known Dutch Henry from buffalo hunting days, but Dutch Henry had turned bad. Two years earlier, Dutch Henry had been arrested for stealing two mules in Ford County, but he had broken out of jail and continued his crime spree. Within the past year, he had escaped jail and law enforcement three times. Bat sent a telegraph message to Las Animas County Sheriff Dick Wootton to arrest Dutch Henry, which he did.[11]

On New Year's Day 1879, Bat boarded the westbound train for Trinidad to bring Dutch Henry back to Dodge, but it wasn't going to be easy. When Bat arrived in Trinidad, he found Dutch Henry was a wanted man elsewhere. If he intended to take Dutch Henry back to Dodge, he was going to have to pay five hundred dollars, which was what they were willing to pay for him in Nevada. On January 4, Bat went to court to extradite Dutch Henry to Kansas. After much back and forth between lawyers and Bat, the judge stated that Dutch Henry had to be detained in the Trinidad jail until district court was to be held in March. Somehow, Bat managed to get Dutch Henry on the train, instead of jail, without paying the five hundred dollars, and without an extradition request from the governor of Kansas. Bat had him back in Dodge in time to stand trial in the Ford County District Court on January 7— where Dutch Henry was acquitted of stealing the mules. Months later he was arrested by a deputy US marshal and sent to Arkansas to complete a prison sentence.[12]

If there was any consolation for Dutch Henry getting off, it was that the other eight prisoners Bat had in the county jail all received prison sentences. Among them was Limping Tom Roach, who received twelve years and three months for killing deputy US Marshal Mack McCarty.[13]

McCarty's position had been open since July, and Bat was appointed deputy US marshal on January 18, 1879.[14] The winter was busy for Bat, apprehending more horse thieves and rustlers, along with another jail break and capture of the escapees. Bat was at odds with the Ford County commissioners. He wanted money to improve the jail to cut down on escapes, but the commissioners refused to spend any more money.[15]

After the capture of most of the Northern Cheyenne who had fled Indian Territory, the governor of Kansas petitioned the federal government in November 1878 to have the leaders tried in Kansas civil court "as participants in the crimes of murder and woman ravishing." In December, the federal government agreed to the governor's request. The army transferred seven Cheyenne leaders from Nebraska to Fort Leavenworth, Kansas. Since Ford County was the principal Kansas county that the Northern Cheyenne passed through, they were to be tried in Dodge.[16]

Bat was responsible for the transfer of the Cheyenne leaders from Fort Leavenworth to the Ford County jail. He traveled by train to Leavenworth, taking with him Charlie Bassett, brother Jim, and two additional deputy sheriffs. The army transferred the seven Cheyenne leaders all wearing handcuffs and leg irons. At every stop on their return, crowds mobbed them wanting to gawk at the Indians. Bat and his men had to get rough pushing people out of the way, so they could force their way through the crowds. In Lawrence, Kansas, the mob was almost overpowering. Bat started using his fists to fight through. The first man he punched just happened to be the marshal of Lawrence, who arrested him, until they came to an understanding. At their stop in Topeka, Kansas, the crowd was estimated at one thousand people. They arrived in Dodge on February 17 and placed the Cheyenne leaders in the county jail.[17]

Bat and his men cared for the prisoners for over four months. A change of venue was requested and granted. In June, the governor directed Bat to take the prisoners by train to Lawrence. In

October 1879, the Cheyenne leaders' cases were dismissed due to a lack of evidence.[18]

High in the Rocky Mountains eighty miles southwest of Denver, a silver-lead ore bonanza was discovered at Leadville, Colorado. By 1879, Leadville mines' annual production was over eleven million dollars, making Leadville the nation's new mining boss camp. Producing ten thousand dollars a day of ore, the Little Pittsburg mine was Leadville's boss mine and was claimed to be "the richest silver depository the world could show."[19]

One thing Leadville lacked was a railroad. The only feasible and economic way to build a railroad through the mountains was to follow the Arkansas River one hundred miles and through its canyon called Royal Gorge from Canon City, Colorado, to Leadville. The Arkansas River grade of roughly one percent was excellent for railroads, but in places Royal Gorge's walls rose to over a thousand feet and the canyon narrowed to less than fifty feet. There was room for only one railroad. An additional benefit for any railroad making it to Leadville would be to extend the line from there all the way to Salt Lake City, Utah.[20]

In 1871, the Denver and Rio Grande Railroad staked a preliminary line from Canon City through the gorge to Leadville, inspected the route in 1872 and 1873, but failed to file with the federal General Land Office the plat required by the 1875 Right-of-Way Act.[21] In the meantime, the Rio Grande had built a line to Canon City.

The Santa Fe Railroad ran through Pueblo, Colorado, only forty-four miles from Canon City. It had its eye on the Leadville riches and a route from Leadville to Salt Lake City, Utah. On June 22, 1877, the Santa Fe filed the proper plat documents for the Arkansas River route with the General Land Office.[22]

In 1878, both the Rio Grande and the Santa Fe sent their workers to the route working over top of each other surveying and grading. Angry words were said, fights broke out, men armed themselves. The Rio Grande workers built a breastwork of logs and dirt to prevent Santa Fe men from passing through the gorge.[23] Lawyers from both sides got to work and a legal battle raged in state and federal courts. The two railroads attempted an agreement but in the end did not trust each other. The Rio Grande breastworks continued to be manned. By March 1879, the Santa Fe believed it needed not only to defend itself in court but to defend its workers and right-of-way through the gorge.[24] The test of wills became known as the Royal Gorge War.

The Santa Fe Railroad made Dodge City what it was, and the citizens of Dodge were extremely loyal to the Santa Fe. Bat received a telegram on March 25, 1879, from Santa Fe Railroad officers in Canon City requesting he bring a posse to defend their workers from Rio Grande Railroad thugs who were attacking them in an attempt to capture the Royal Gorge. Bat and Deputy Sheriff Duffy opened a recruiting office and signed up thirty-three men "armed to the teeth."[25] Entertainer Eddie Foy said Ben Thompson and Doc Holliday were heading to the Royal Gorge War with Bat. Holliday tried to recruit Eddie, but he declined, saying, "I wouldn't be able to hit a man if I shot at him."[26]

Bat Masterson, sheriff of Ford County, Kansas, had no authority in Canon City, Colorado, but he did have authority as a deputy US marshal. He and his posse left Dodge for Canon City aboard a westbound Santa Fe train on Friday morning, March 26. The Santa Fe was paying each posse member three dollars a day plus board.[27]

When the posse arrived in Canon City, they found the Rio Grande had fortifications in place along the route manned by fifty well-armed gunmen. Some of the posse were all for attacking and driving off the Rio Grande men, but Bat told them no. He was a peace officer, and his job was to maintain the peace, and that was exactly what he did as the standoff progressed from days to weeks as the railroads continued to battle in court.[28]

It was an easy assignment for the men as they kept watch over the Santa Fe workers laboring on the railroad. As time progressed, the Santa Fe hired one hundred gunmen to protect its workers, and through April all was quiet.[29] At some point, Bat and most of the Dodge City posse left Royal Gorge and returned to Dodge.

The cattle-shipping season was beginning again, and the business of keeping cowboys in line was picking up for Dodge's police force: Charlie, Jim, and Wyatt. The April 15, 1879, edition of the *Ford County Globe* reported the city council saw fit to restore Jim and Wyatt's salaries back to a hundred dollars per month and were allotted a two-dollar fee for every arrest.[30] Nothing noteworthy made the newspapers until the evening of May 5, 1879.

Three armed Missourians from Clay County were on their way to Leadville and stopped in Dodge to enjoy themselves. After consuming their fair share of whiskey, they started to "take the town." As they emerged from a saloon onto Front Street, Wyatt was going to put an end to it. He grabbed the worst offender by the ear. The man was squirming around, preventing Wyatt from disarming him. One of the other Missourians shouted to his friend to "Throw lead!" and they both drew their guns. Wyatt drew his six-shooter while still holding on to the Missourian's ear. The man grabbed Wyatt's gun arm, preventing him from shooting.[31]

Seeing the ruckus from across the street, Bat drew his six-gun and ran to assist Wyatt. The man was still struggling in Wyatt's grasp as Bat buffaloed him on top of the head. The man collapsed to the ground as Wyatt and Bat leveled their six-shooters on the other two Missourians, who promptly surrendered. They were marched off to spend the night in jail.[32]

The next day, the three men were released, but they were furious with Bat and were now determined to assassinate him. That night, they gathered in an alley behind a store. Stopping a young black boy, they told him to give Sheriff Masterson a message that

a man wished to see him behind the building. The boy found Bat, gave him the message, but told him to be careful, he smelled a mouse. Bat and his deputies captured the three would-be bushwhackers and hauled them off to jail. The Missouri hard cases found they were no match for the local lawmen.[33]

On May 21, Jim Masterson and Wyatt left town to track down a horse drover who failed to pay a black man for services rendered. They found the drover and six of his companions on Duck Creek. Backed by his friends, the drover refused to pay, but Wyatt and Jim refused to back down. The *Dodge City Times* reported that "the drover promptly [paid] the debt when resistance was no longer available."[34]

The evening of June 9 saw some lively action between cowboys who insisted on wearing their guns and the Dodge City police. Wyatt usually worked the night beat, so he was most likely involved. The police attempted to disarm "a squad of cow boys" who refused to obey "and war was declared," the June 10 issue of the *Ford County Globe* reported. "Several shots were fired, and one of the cow boys was wounded in the leg. The balance of the cow boys made their escape."[35]

Earlier that day, Bat learned the Royal Gorge War was heating up again. The Santa Fe believed a Colorado court was going to rule in favor of the Rio Grande, giving it control of the railroad. The Santa Fe management was confident this ruling would be overturned by a higher court. In the meantime, Santa Fe was going to hold onto all property until the case could be heard by a higher court. So again, they sent out messages to Dodge and other sympathetic cities requesting men to help defend Santa Fe interests.[36]

Within a half hour of receiving the telegram, Bat assembled sixty men, who headed west on a special Santa Fe train.[37] At Pueblo, Colorado, the Santa Fe management gave Bat and his men the responsibility to hold the opposition Rio Grande's depot and roundhouse. They began fortifying the buildings and commandeered the cannon from the state armory in Pueblo.[38]

On June 10, just as expected, the Colorado court ruled in favor of the Rio Grande. Believing the court ruling would be overturned on appeal, Santa Fe management told their men not to yield to the Rio Grande. But by the morning of June 11, Rio Grande men had seized all Santa Fe positions except for the Pueblo buildings held by Bat and his men.[39]

At 3:00 p.m., a force of fifty Rio Grande men armed with rifles and fixed bayonets fired upon the depot. As the Santa Fe defenders retreated to the roundhouse, one Dodge City man was fatally shot in the back.[40]

Bat and his men were surrounded and unable to communicate with Santa Fe management as to their legal status. The Rio Grande leaders requested a parley with Bat. They showed him the court order stating the Santa Fe must surrender its positions. He saw he had no legal standing and agreed to give up the roundhouse.[41] The Dodge City men left Pueblo arriving back home the next day.

The Royal Gorge War would continue in the courts and railroad boardrooms. With back and forth payments and deals between the two rival railroads, a final agreement, called the Treaty of Boston, was negotiated in Boston, Massachusetts, and signed on March 27, 1880, whereby the Rio Grande finally had control of the railroad to Leadville.[42]

Bat saw lots of action the summer of 1879. He escorted a prisoner to the state prison in Leavenworth and a troubled person to the insane asylum in Topeka. He tracked down and apprehended five horse thieves on three separate occasions. The county commissioners still had not provided funds to make the jail more secure. Prisoners were escaping by digging under the door and removing ceiling boards, requiring Bat and his men to recapture the escapees.[43]

Wyatt's summer was not as busy as Bat's. Ogallala, Nebraska, siphoned off some of the cattle-shipping business reducing the number of cowboys arriving in town. Wyatt made only nine arrests between April 13 and July 24.[44] On his off hours, he dealt monte and faro in the Long Branch Saloon for professional gambler Luke Short.[45]

Brother Jim Earp and wife Bessie had arrived in Dodge. The two brothers were contemplating developing a cattle ranch in the Texas Panhandle when they started receiving a series of letters from brother Virgil, who was living in Prescott, Arizona Territory. Virgil wrote about a silver strike at a new Arizona town called Tombstone. He believed if they all worked together they could make a profit in the new town. Wyatt and Jim decided to give it a go and head for Tombstone, since in Wyatt's words, "Dodge's edge was getting dull."[46]

Wyatt resigned from the Dodge City police force on Thursday, September 4, 1879. The next day, he engaged in what the *Globe* titled "A Day of Carnival." A large number of Dodge citizens began drinking early in the day. A young man started the carnival by dousing his friends with a bucket of water. They retaliated, and it bloomed into a massive water fight. It further evolved as combatants tossed the contents of slop buckets and threw cucumbers, potatoes, and rotten eggs at each other. As the town-wide, celebratory fight continued into the evening, it grew into a massive fistfight brawl. Several "gun plays" occurred, but nothing came of them. As to fistfighting, the newspaper reported, "The 'finest work' and neatest polishes were said to have been executed by Mr. Wyatt Earp, who has been our efficient assistant marshal for the past year."[47]

Wyatt had been proficient with his fists in Dodge. In later years, Bat told Wyatt's wife, Sadie, about Wyatt's Dodge City fistfights with Texas cowboys. The cowboys would put up their best champions against him, but each time, he won. Sadie wrote, "Bat always declared that there was not a man in the west that could whip Wyatt in rough and tumble fighting."[48]

Wyatt also served as a deacon in Reverend O. W. Wright's church. Two lawyers gave Wyatt a Bible and inscribed it with:

To Wyatt S. Earp as a slight recognition of his many Christian Virtues and steady following in the footsteps of the meek and lowly Jesus.

SUTTON AND COLBORN[49]

On Saturday, September 6, 1879, Wyatt and Mattie along with Jim and Bessie left Dodge City.[50] The September 9, 1879, edition of the *Globe* reported, "Mr. Wyatt Earp, who has been on our police force for several months, resigned his position last week and took his departure for Las Vegas, New Mexico."[51]

The Ford County sheriff's position was up for election in November 1879. Bat announced he would be running again and was nominated by the Independent party on October 18 in Dodge City. The *Times* editorialized, "Bat is acknowledged to be the best Sheriff in Kansas. He is the most successful officer in the State. . . . Horse thieves have a terror for the name of Masterson." His opponent was bartender George Hinkle, who had briefly been in the 1877 sheriff's race but dropped out. Hinkle worked for George Hoover, who had been Dodge City mayor before Dog Kelley. False rumors and unsubstantiated stories printed in the *Globe* and eastern Ford County newspapers tarnished Bat's public image. Bat was really no politician. He consulted a newspaper editor friend and an attorney friend asking if he should rebut the allegations. They both advised him not to do so. They said he did not need to worry, people knew his character and the good job he had done. He should not have listened to their advice. He lost the election 404 to 268.[52]

When the Earp party left Dodge their plan was to join Virgil in Prescott, Arizona. From there, they would travel together to

Tombstone. The Earps rode the Santa Fe Railroad westward. The railroad had been constructed as far as Las Vegas, New Mexico, which was now a boomtown. Earlier that summer, Doc Holliday and Kate Elder had left Dodge for Las Vegas, where Doc ran a gambling house. He found trouble again, killing a gambler named Mike Gordon, but he was never convicted.[53] The Earps remained in Las Vegas for most of September.[54] More than likely, Wyatt tried his hand at a few games of chance. There is a strong possibility at this time that James Hume, Wells, Fargo Chief of Detectives, hired Wyatt as a detective or special messenger to guard Wells, Fargo shipments.[55]

Wyatt had brought thirteen horses and two wagons loaded with supplies to Las Vegas. His plan was to use the horses and wagons to establish a stage line between Tombstone and Tucson, Arizona.[56] The Earps, now with Kate and Doc joining their party, traveled by wagon cross country over four hundred miles to Prescott, arriving November 1, 1879.[57]

Virgil and his wife, Allie, had been living in Prescott, Arizona's territorial capital, since 1877. In November 1878, he was elected to one of two constable positions for Prescott. Virgil was well known to US Marshal Crawley Dake and when he resigned his constable position to leave for Tombstone, Dake commissioned him a deputy US marshal for Pima County.[58]

Virgil and Allie joined the rest of the Earps as they traveled 250 miles from Prescott to Tucson.[59] Doc and Kate remained behind; they were experiencing a string of gambling luck and would head to Tombstone when it ran out.[60] Morgan Earp was leaving Montana and planned to link up with the rest of the Earps in Tombstone.[61] From Tucson, the Earp party traveled southeast through desert terrain for seventy-five miles, reaching Tombstone on December 1, 1879.[62]

Back in Kansas, Bat escorted two prisoners to prison in Leavenworth as his last official act as Ford County sheriff. January 12, 1880, was his last day as sheriff. That same day, he resigned as deputy US marshal.[63]

CHAPTER 8
TOMBSTONE

Tombstone, Arizona Territory, which would become known as "the town too tough to die" was being born when the Earps drove their wagons into town on December 1, 1879. Streets had been laid out that summer, as adobe and frame buildings replaced the initial tent city. Lumber had to be hauled in from Dragoon and Huachuca Mountains costing as much as sixty-five dollars per thousand feet. Water was just sufficient enough for the current population of one thousand people, who had voted to incorporate and elected a mayor.[1]

Back in the summer of 1877, Ed Schieffelin had prospected east of the San Pedro River. It was dangerous out there, Apaches still roamed the countryside. Friends told him the only rock he would find was his own tombstone. He found silver ore, naming the mining district Tombstone. When word of his discovery got out, people flocked to the area. The nearby booming tent camp took the same name, Tombstone.[2]

It was a rich silver strike. There were three major silver bonanzas: the Lucky Cuss, the Tough Nut, and the Contention. Investors rapidly constructed two mills and started processing ore in June 1879. The Tombstone mines would become the Southwest's largest silver bonanza, producing over twenty-five million dollars.[3] The Earps wanted a piece of the action.

By the time they arrived in Tombstone in December 1879, Wyatt learned two stage lines were already servicing town. Competition between the two was so brisk they were reducing fares to attract passengers. Wyatt would only lose money if he entered the stage business, so he sold his teams and wagons.[4]

The Earp brothers went to work staking mining claims, hoping for a bonanza and filing for water rights to tie up scarce water. They gambled not for pleasure but to make money. Virgil pursued his deputy US marshal duties in Pima County, while Jim worked as a saloonkeeper, and Wyatt took jobs as a shotgun messenger with Wells, Fargo and other outfits guarding their shipments. Following a brief visit to his mother and father in California and leaving his wife Louisa with them for the summer, Morgan Earp arrived in Tombstone in late July 1880.[5] The Earp brothers and their wives were settling in, becoming part of the fabric of Tombstone.

Voted out of office, twenty-five-year-old Bat Masterson spent most of January and February 1880 in Dodge, gambling and socializing. He had developed his card-playing skills and made a decent living at games of chance. Leadville, Colorado, was a gambling mecca. With all the profits rolling in from its silver mines, people were ready to stake their hard-earned cash gambling, and there were plenty of other people ready to win it from them. Leaving Dodge on February 25, Bat took a trip to Leadville to see the action for himself. He was back in Dodge two weeks later, impressed with booming Leadville and the richness of its mines.[6]

After attending the Ford County Republican convention on March 20 and the Kansas state convention in Topeka on March 31, Bat returned to Leadville and the surrounding countryside looking for money-making opportunities. The May 4, 1880, edition of the *Ford County Globe* reported a rumor, "Ex-Sheriff W.B. Masterson had made a big commotion up about Buna Vista [sic] [Colorado] by a dexterous use of his revolver." Bat soon realized that reports of new mineral wealth and booming business opportunities were "the worst fraud he ever saw." He was back in Dodge by June 5, living with nineteen-year-old Annie Ladue. The census taker called Annie a concubine. Nothing more is known about their relationship.[7]

In early July, Ben Thompson contacted Bat. Brother Billy Thompson was in trouble once again. This time it was in Ogallala, Nebraska. On June 26, 1880, Billy had quarreled with Texan Jim Tucker. Billy had received five bullet wounds but was expected to live. Rumor had it that as soon as he was healthy enough, the townsmen planned to hang him. Ben asked Bat to intervene.[8] Bat agreed to go and see what he could do, and the July 6 edition of the *Globe* reported he was on his way to Ogallala.[9]

Upon his arrival, Bat visited Billy, who was laid up in a hotel guarded by a deputy sheriff. Bat went to see Tucker, who was at home in bed recuperating from his wound. Billy had shot off his left thumb. Apparently, Billy had started the whole affair, and the town backed Tucker. He was willing to drop the matter if Billy paid an astronomical amount of money, quickly ending the conversation.[10]

Bat was determined to rescue Billy, but Billy was under constant guard. He was unable to ride a horse, and if they left by wagon, they would be quickly caught. The eastbound train stopped briefly at night in Ogallala to take on water. Bat decided that would be the way to get Billy out of town. If they could get to North Platte, Nebraska, Bat's friend, Buffalo Bill Cody, who had a ranch north of town, would help them.[11]

That Sunday night, the town held a dance at the schoolhouse, and most everyone was there as the sheriff led the festivities playing the fiddle. Bat was good friends with the hotel's bartender and let him in on the escape plan. Bat convinced the guarding deputy sheriff to have a few drinks with him. The bartender must have added a little something extra to the deputy's drinks as he was soon passed out. Bat dressed Billy, got him on his back, carried him down the stairs, then outside, and onto the train platform. The train arrived at midnight, and they quickly boarded, leaving town before the sheriff learned of their escape.[12]

Two hours later, they were in North Platte. Bat located Buffalo Bill and twelve friends enjoying themselves in a saloon. Bill found Bat and Billy a comfortable place to hide for the night. The next day, Bill was taking a group of foreign dignitaries to a ranch, twenty-five miles south of North Platte to view a small herd of tame buffalo and put on an exhibition for them. Bill had Bat and Billy accompany them on their excursion south, He insisted Bat and Billy take his wife's phaeton and "a fine, big Texas horse" for their 250-mile trip to Dodge City.[13]

Booze flowed like water for that first twenty-five-mile leg of the trip. Bat drove Buffalo Bill's mess wagon while Bill relaxed in the back. Bat had a little too much to drink and overturned the wagon. Fortunately, Buffalo Bill was not hurt, and Bat only received a split lip. Once Bat and Billy left Buffalo Bill's party, it began to rain and continued to rain the entire trip until they reached Dodge. Upon their arrival, Billy sent a telegram to the sheriff at Ogallala inviting him to come get him, which never happened.[14]

By 1880, Pima County, Arizona Territory, was relatively safe from major Apache attacks. Most were confined to their reservations although a few bands held out in Mexico. It was good grazing land, and ranchers began running cattle. Along with Tombstone, the major markets for beef were army forts and Indian reservations. Many ranchers were honest, but there were those who were not. These men would steal anything they could get away with: cattle, horses, and mules. They raided into Mexico and then sold the livestock in Tombstone or elsewhere. They were known to rob stagecoaches, travelers, and Mexican trading caravans. Although they were mostly independent, from time to time some would rise to temporary leadership such as John Ringo and Curly Bill Brocius. These outlaws became known as "cowboys."[15]

Many Tombstone residents thought well of the cowboys. They considered them jovial modern-day Robin Hoods. The cowboys might not have given to the poor in Tombstone, but they did sell their rustled horses, mules, and beef at discount prices and they did freely spend their money on sprees in Tombstone's saloons, gaming halls, and brothels.[16] Two prominent cowboy families were the Clantons and the McLaurys.

Newman "Old Man" Clanton was originally from Missouri. With four of his five sons—Phin, Ike, Peter, and Billy—Old Man Clanton settled on a ranch in the San Pedro Valley, twelve miles southwest of the future site of Tombstone in 1877. John Clum, agent at the San Carlos Apache Indian Reservation at the time, later editor of the *Tombstone Epitaph*, and eventually Tombstone's mayor, would write about the Clantons and their ranch: They "made it headquarters for outlaws in that section, a clearinghouse for cattle stolen in Mexico by rustlers and smuggled across the line."[17]

Brothers Frank and Tom McLaury, originally from New York, worked in Texas and moved to Arizona to invest in cattle about the same time the Clantons arrived. They lived on the Babacomari River near the Clantons. Frank and Tom were good-hearted, hardworking men; who also acted as go-betweens for rustlers bringing stolen cattle from Mexico and Tombstone merchants.[18]

Lieutenant J. H. Hurst and three enlisted men rode into Tombstone late July 1880. They were in search of six mules stolen from Camp Rucker, seventy-five miles to the east. Hurst requested deputy US Marshal Virgil Earp's assistance. Virgil formed a posse of Wells, Fargo agent Marshall Williams, Morgan, and Wyatt, who rode out of town with the four soldiers on July 25, 1880. They learned from a cowboy informant that a cowboy named Pony Deal, Billy Clanton, and Tom and Frank McLaury had stolen the mules. They rode to the McLaury ranch, where they found the six mules. A rancher named Frank Patterson was overseeing a group of cowboys changing the mules' brands from "U.S." to "D.8."[19]

Patterson was belligerent telling Lieutenant Hurst if he tried to arrest them and take the mules, there would be bloodshed. Patterson said if Hurst dropped all charges, he would bring the mules to the nearby town of Charleston the next day. Hurst weighed the situation and agreed.[20] The posse returned to Tombstone, and Hurst and his men rode to Charleston.

Hurst waited in Charleston for two days. On the second day, Patterson, Billy Clanton, and the McLaurys rode into town without the mules. They laughed at Hurst, and Patterson told him he only said he would bring in the mules because he did not want to confront Virgil's posse. Hurst was angry. He posted notices describing the stolen mules and naming Pony Deal and others as thieves and identified Frank Patterson and Frank McLaury as culprits for hiding the mules.[21]

Frank McLaury responded by placing an announcement in the *Tombstone Nugget* stating he was not a thief and that Hurst was a liar and coward. Toward the end he wrote, "Perhaps when the matter is ventilated it will be found that the Hon. Lieut. Hurst has stolen these mules and sold them, for a coward will steal."[22]

Frank and Tom stopped in Virgil's office; they wanted to know if he had any part in Hurst's notice. Virgil said he did not. They threatened him that if he ever came after them there would be a fight. Virgil responded that if he ever had a warrant for their arrest he would be coming for them.[23]

Pima County Sheriff Charlie Shibell, headquartered out of Tucson, had one deputy sheriff, Newton Babcock, located in Tombstone. He needed a second deputy sheriff there, and on July 27, 1880, he appointed Wyatt Earp as deputy sheriff.[24] Wyatt was busy through the rest of the summer and into the fall chasing rustlers, arresting claim jumpers, hunting down petty criminals, and hauling prisoners to Tucson. During one court case, he had to intervene when a scuffle erupted between Harry Jones, a defense lawyer, and James Reilly, the judge. Arresting them both, Wyatt created an enemy in Judge Reilly.[25] Tombstone was a rough town. In addition to his county responsibilities, Wyatt was always ready to help Tombstone's popular marshal, Fred White.

In September 1880, Doc Holliday and Kate Elder arrived in Tombstone. Kate did not like Tombstone and left for Globe,

Arizona, but would come back and visit Holliday from time to time. Holliday was soon in trouble again. A well-known gambler, Johnny Tyler, and Holliday were in the midst of a game in the Oriental Saloon on the evening of October 10, 1880. A shouting match broke out between the two. Others had to intervene, and Tyler walked out of the saloon. Milt Joyce, who had the concession for the Oriental's bar and restaurant, blamed Holliday for creating the disturbance. Holliday argued back, and Joyce threw him out of the saloon. Holliday returned demanding his gun from the bartender, which had been placed behind the bar. The bartender refused, and Holliday left. He soon returned with another pistol. Swearing loudly, he walked within ten feet of Joyce and fired. Joyce was hit in the hand. Several others fired their guns. One person was nicked by a shot. Joyce jumped on Holliday knocking him to the floor and then buffaloed him. Marshal White and a deputy ran in and disarmed everyone. Holliday went before Judge Reilly, who fined him $20 for assault and battery and $11.30 for court costs.[26]

The *Tombstone Epitaph* October 20, 1880, edition stated, "The appointment of Wyatt Earp as Deputy Sheriff by Sheriff Shibell, is an eminently proper one, and we in common with the citizens generally congratulate the latter in his selection. Wyatt has filled various positions in which bravery and determination were requisites, and in every instance proved himself the right man in the right place."[27]

It was after midnight, October 28. Curly Bill Brocious and a few other cowboys were whooping it up in a saloon and then took their revelry out into the street, shooting their six-guns at the moon and stars. Marshal White broke up the fun and chased Curly Bill into an alley.[28]

Wyatt heard the shots and ran to where they had been fired. Fred Dodge and Morgan joined him. Borrowing Dodge's gun, Wyatt ran into the alley Curly Bill and White had entered. White said to Curly Bill, "I am an officer, give me your pistol." Curly Bill removed his gun from its holster. White grabbed its barrel. Wyatt threw his arms around Curly Bill. White yelled, "Now you God-damned son of a bitch, give me that pistol." As White jerked the gun from Curly Bill, it fired. White fell to the ground holding the gun. He was shot in the groin and his clothes were on fire. Wyatt buffaloed Curly Bill dropping him to the ground.[29]

As others took care of Marshal White, Wyatt ordered Curly Bill to get up, he was under arrest. "What have I done?" Curly Bill asked. "I have not done anything wrong to be arrested for." Wyatt, with assistance from Fred Dodge and Morgan, hustled Curly Bill off to jail and stood guard. Rumors floated that Tombstone citizens were outraged and itching for a lynching.[30]

The next day, Curly Bill went before a justice of the peace and waived his examination, and Wyatt hauled him to jail in Tucson to await trial. Marshal Fred White died two days later. November 1, the day of the funeral, one thousand people attended, and all businesses were closed. Marshal White's death caused the city council to change its gun ordinances prohibiting the carrying of guns in town except for peace officers.[31]

The Arizona Territorial Assembly determined that the eastern portion of Pima County would become Cochise County on February 1, 1881. Pima County elections were being held November 9, 1880. Those people who would be residents of the new Cochise County could still vote for Pima County officials.

Politics were complicated in Pima County. Most of the early white inhabitants, as well as most of the ranchers and cowboys, including the Clantons and Sheriff Charlie Shibell, were Democrats. The people in town, including the Earps, were mostly Republican.[32]

Bob Paul, Wells, Fargo employee, ran against Charlie Shibell. Shibell won by a close margin. There were lots of election irregularities on both sides. One glaring concern was the San Simon Cienega precinct. One vote was cast for Paul and 103 votes for Shibell. The only problem was there were only fifty eligible voters. Election officials for the precinct were cowboys John Ringo and

Ike Clanton. The votes were certified by James Johnson, who had been with Curly Bill the night Marshal White was shot.[33]

Paul contested the election. Wyatt was a supporter of Paul and believed it was not right to work for Shibell while he helped Paul in his bid for a recount, so on November 9, 1880, Wyatt resigned as deputy sheriff.[34] Shibell replaced Wyatt with Democrat Johnny Behan, who had held a variety of law enforcement and political positions including twice being elected to the territorial legislature.[35] Wyatt and Johnny were on good terms.

Shortly after arriving in Tombstone, one of Wyatt's horses had been stolen. One night late in December, Wyatt and Doc Holliday were driving a wagon back to Tombstone after checking on a water right. They ran into a cowboy informant who told Wyatt his missing horse was in Charleston. They hurried there and found his horse in one of the corrals. He wired to brother Jim in Tombstone to put together the paperwork to claim his horse. Youngest brother Warren, who was now in Tombstone, would bring the paperwork out to Wyatt. While Wyatt was waiting, Billy Clanton learned Wyatt was in town and tried to take the horse out of the corral, but Wyatt prevented him until the papers arrived. Billy had no choice but to give up the horse. Billy asked if Wyatt had any more horses to lose. Wyatt responded he would be keeping his horses in the stable giving Billy no chance to steal them.[36]

December 27, 1880, Wyatt testified at the trial of Curly Bill Brocious. He probably could have lied and said Curly Bill shot Marshal White on purpose, but he said White had Curly Bill's gun barrel in his hand and when White pulled the barrel back, it fired. Other witnesses and evidence pointed to the same conclusion, and with Marshal White's deathbed statement that he believed it was an accident, Curly Bill was set free.[37]

Saturday night, January 8, 1881, Curly Bill went on a drunken spree in Charleston. He and a friend entered a crowded Mexican dance hall, each with his back to an exit with their guns drawn. Curly Bill ordered everyone to strip naked, then ordered the band to play and everyone to dance. A Charleston peace officer passing by looked in a window and saw the whole situation. He organized a five-man posse to capture Curly Bill and his partner. When the two emerged from the dance hall and walked toward the corral to saddle their horses, one of the posse's guns went off alerting the cowboys. They opened fire on the posse, driving them off. From there, they rode to Contention, where they disrupted a church service, shot their pistols around the pastor, and made him dance. They rode to Tombstone Monday night where they continued their rampage "capturing" the Alhambra Saloon and hurrahing the town, then riding away to continue their depredations in other towns.[38]

January 14, 1881, Wyatt allowed Virgil to take his racehorse Dick Naylor for a ride. Virgil was three miles from town on the road to Charleston when he saw a wagon racing toward him. It was the Charleston Constable George McKelvey with a prisoner named Johnny-Behind-the-Deuce. Johnny claimed he had killed a man in self-defense, but a mob of the dead man's friends, led by John Ringo, were fast approaching, planning to string him up. Virgil had Johnny jump up behind him on Dick Naylor, and they raced back to Tombstone. Seeing them gallop into town, Wyatt grabbed a Wells, Fargo shotgun and took Johnny into a bowling alley on Allen Street where Sheriff Behan, Fred Dodge, Doc Holliday, Virgil, Morgan, and others prepared their weapons to withstand the mob. The cowboy crowd in the street grew with the addition of off-duty miners. Wyatt planned to take Johnny to Tucson, but to do so, they had to enter the mob and cross town to the livery stable. Wyatt faced down the mob with his shotgun as he and the posse, with guns drawn, marched out through the crowd. No one had the nerve to take them on. They reached the livery, hitched a team to a wagon, and Wyatt drove Johnny to Tucson.[39,][40] As a private citizen, Wyatt took charge of the situation when others could have but didn't.

The Earp brothers' investments were starting to pay dividends. Wyatt continued to work off and on for Wells, Fargo and when called upon, as a field-commissioned deputy US marshal. Things were looking up for Wyatt and Mattie. They had a little house to live in, and Mattie made money sewing for other people.[41]

Mid-January, Wyatt went into partnership with Lou Rickabaugh and a small group of San Francisco gamblers in the Oriental Saloon's gambling concession. Clara Brown, a correspondent for the *San Diego Union*, wrote, "The 'Oriental' is simply gorgeous and is pronounced the finest place of its kind this side of San Francisco."[42] It was furnished with a beautiful bar, the gaming room had carpeted floors, and the interior was well lit. There was plenty of reading and writing material. In the evenings, musicians played piano and violin music, and numerous dances were held, although Clara reported, "but so long as many members of the demi-monder [sic] who are numerous and very showy here patronize them, many honest women will hesitate to attend."[43, 44]

Even top-of-the-line saloons could have problems with rowdy clientele, and this was one of the reason's Rickabaugh took in Wyatt as a partner. Rival gambling concessions hired hooligans to make trouble at the Oriental and drive business away. Shortly after Wyatt joined the partnership, troublemaker Johnny Tyler, leading twelve men, entered the Oriental. Tyler's men bellied up to the bar while Tyler walked over to Rickabaugh's faro table. Tyler was obnoxious, making threatening remarks to Rickabaugh. Pulling his six-gun on Rickabaugh, Tyler threatened to shoot the stack of chips in front of Rickabaugh if he did not win the next round.[45]

Tyler screamed in pain as he was lifted by an earlobe from his chair. When he saw it was Wyatt, he put away his gun. Doc Holliday had Tyler's henchmen at the bar covered with his nickel-plated revolver. Wyatt tossed Tyler out the door, and Holliday marched the others outside. With Wyatt's presence at the Oriental, the opposition gamblers' intimidation subsided, and profits increased.[46]

Soon after the rescue of Billy Thompson, Bat traveled east visiting his parents in Sedgwick, Kansas, and then moving on to Kansas City, Missouri. Kansas City was a gambler's paradise with over forty gambling halls from which to choose. He remained in town for several months, returning to Dodge City in December. In January 1881, Bat received a message from Wyatt offering him a job as a house gambler in Tombstone's Oriental Saloon. Bat accepted and boarded a westbound train on February 8, 1881.[47]

FARO, OR BUCK THE TIGER

Wyatt Earp and Bat Masterson were proficient at faro, one of the most popular gambling games in nineteenth-century America. Faro is a banking game where players do not play against each other but play against the house. Faro is also called Buck the Tiger because old playing cards had a tiger image on the back of the cards and if the player won, he bucked the tiger, or beat the house.

The game is played with cards and chips. A suit from the deuce to the ace of spades is glued face-up to a green felt board called the layout. A deck of fifty-two cards is used, and players buy chips for their play in the game. The dealer may shuffle and hold the cards or use a special faro card box to keep the cards. There may be a house employee called the case keeper who tracks the cards played with a type of abacus that players can view. Another house employee, the lookout, watches the play to spot cheating or mistakes in the game.[48]

Before the dealer begins, the players place their chips on the layout cards they think the dealer will display. Suits do not matter, only the number or character on the card. The dealer will use all fifty-two cards in the deck. The first card dealt is the soda card, which is turned face up for everyone to see and is not played. The second card played is the losing card. If a player has his chip on the losing card displayed, he loses that chip to the dealer. The third card played is the winning card. If a player has his chip on the winning card displayed, the dealer pays him. If the player has his chip on a card that is neither winning nor losing, it is neutral. He can keep his chip there, move it to a different card on the layout, or not play at all. A player can "copper" a bet where he places a penny on top of his chip, indicating he is betting on losing. If the losing card comes up and he has coppered the bet, he wins. There are rules for multiple betting in a variety of ways. The play continues until there are three cards left. The players are given the option to "call the turn" and bet the sequence of the last three cards. If the player is correct, he is paid at four to one odds.[49]

Faro is a straightforward game that, if played fairly, gives almost even odds to players and the house. Unfortunately, it is an easy game to cheat at and can came down to who is the better cheat, the player or the dealer. You can't play faro at a casino today. Most states have outlawed it. The Ramada Casino in Reno, Nevada, was the last to offer faro, ending in 1985.[50]

CHAPTER 9

BATTLE OF THE PLAZA AND TOMBSTONE TROUBLES

On February 1, 1881, Pima County was split, the eastern portion becoming Cochise County with Tombstone as its county seat.[1] All of Cochise County's government positions were appointed by Arizona's Republican Territorial governor, John C. Fremont, with the approval of the predominantly Democratic legislative council. The appointed positions would last until the next general election to be held in November 1882.[2]

Democrat and Pima County Deputy Sheriff Johnny Behan wanted the appointed sheriff position for Cochise County. There were Republican Tombstone citizens who wanted Wyatt Earp appointed sheriff. Johnny met with Wyatt, proposing if Wyatt stepped aside and allowed him to be appointed sheriff, he would appoint Wyatt as his undersheriff and allow him to appoint the deputies. Wyatt agreed to Johnny's proposal.[3] On February 10, Johnny was appointed sheriff of Cochise County. Instead of Wyatt, Johnny appointed as undersheriff fellow Democrat and editor of Tombstone's *Nugget* Harry Woods. Johnny never explained to Wyatt why he reneged on their agreement.[4]

Bat Masterson had arrived in Tombstone in mid-February and went to work as a house gambler for Wyatt and his partners in the Oriental Saloon. Wyatt also hired Luke Short, a Dodge City gambler friend of his and Bat's.

On the morning of February 25, Short was dealing faro in the Oriental. Charlie Storms was at his table. Storms, a professional gambler and gunman, was a friend of Bat, but Short had never met him. Storms had been up all night gambling and quarreling with other players. An argument erupted between Storms and Short. As Bat rushed into the gaming room, Storms slapped Short. They both were going for their guns as Bat grabbed Storms and asked Short not to shoot.[5]

Bat hustled Storms out onto the street telling him to go to his room and sleep. Storms asked Bat to go with him, which Bat did. Leaving Storms in his room, Bat returned to the Oriental and started to tell Short that Charlie Storms was a decent fellow, when Storms appeared in front of them. Storms pulled his pistol, but Short was faster, jamming his pistol's muzzle against Storms's chest. Pulling the trigger, Short shot Storms in the heart and shot him again as he fell to the floor dead. Short was given a preliminary hearing and let go.[6]

Meanwhile, the Southern Pacific Railroad had been building eastward from Tucson and constructed a station in Benson, Arizona, northwest of Tombstone. By March 1881, stagecoaches were hauling passengers and silver from Tombstone to Benson.

On the evening of March 15, 1881, a stagecoach hauling a Wells, Fargo shipment to Benson was outside Contention. Bud Philpott was the driver and Bob Paul rode alongside as Wells, Fargo shotgun messenger. A man stepped into the road shouting "Hold!" as other men emerged from hiding. Paul leveled his shotgun shouting, "By God, I hold for nobody!" The bandits fired, killing Philpott, his body falling forward off the wagon and between the horses. Paul shot and grabbed the lines as the horses ran. The robbers fired several volleys, hitting passenger Peter Roerig, who later died. Getting control of the runaway team, Paul continued to Benson and sent a telegram to Tombstone about the attempted robbery. On the stagecoach's return trip, Paul stopped at the scene of the crime, recovered Philpott's body, and brought it back to Tombstone.[7]

Sheriff Johnny Behan formed a posse of the Earps, Wells, Fargo agents Marshall Williams and Bob Paul, and Bat Masterson.

The posse rode to the site of the attempted robbery; from there they followed the robbers' trail for three days to the ranch of Len and Hank Redfield, who were suspected of being friends of outlaw cowboys. There, Morgan captured a man who was attempting to hide. The man said his name was Luther King. Hank Redfield talked briefly with King and immediately left the ranch. The posse questioned King, who finally admitted he was part of the attempted robbery. His job was to hold the others' horses during the holdup. He identified the other men as Billy Leonard, Jimmy Crane, and Harry Head and said they had left Redfield's with fresh mounts.[8]

Behan took King back to Tombstone while the rest of the posse continued to follow the robbers' trail for another six days. Virgil telegraphed Behan to bring fresh mounts, but when he arrived on March 24 with more men, he failed to bring along horses for the original posse members. Paul's horse died, and Bat and Wyatt's horses were done. Paul was able to obtain a fresh horse, but Bat and Wyatt couldn't and had to walk eighteen miles back to Tombstone.[9]

On March 28, Wells, Fargo detective Jim Hume and Wyatt learned there were seventy-five cowboys in Tombstone who were ready to help King escape. They went to the sheriff's office to tell Undersheriff Harry Woods the news and recommended he place King in irons. He said he would, but fifteen minutes later, King walked out the back door of the sheriff's office, mounted a saddled and readied horse, and rode out of town.[10] King was never apprehended; Wyatt heard he had crossed the border into Mexico.[11]

The rest of the posse continued through rough, waterless country, trailing the three cowboys into New Mexico where they lost their trail. After hundreds of miles and more than two weeks on the trail, running out of food and water and with their horses played out, the posse returned to Tombstone empty-handed.[12]

In April, Bat received a telegram from an unidentified source that sent him speeding as fast as he could back to Dodge City. The message read: "Come at once. Updegraff and Peacock are going to kill Jim."[13]

Mayor Dog Kelley had appointed Jim Masterson chief city marshal on November 4, 1879. Jim did a good job maintaining the peace, but on April 4, 1881, Kelley lost his bid for reelection, and two days later, the new mayor, A. B. Webster, replaced Jim with Fred Singer.[14]

Several months earlier, Jim had gone into partnership with A. J. Peacock owning the Lady Gay Saloon and Dance Hall. Jim and Peacock disagreed over management almost from the start. Peacock hired his brother-in-law, Al Updegraff, as bartender. Updegraff, a heavy drinker, was a shady character who had been involved in crooked land deals. Jim wanted Updegraff fired, and Peacock refused to do so. Jim stewed as he watched Updegraff consume free alcohol, drinking into his profits. Updegraff and Jim argued openly as clientele began taking sides. At one point, shots were fired, but no one was injured. It was then that the anonymous message was sent to Bat.[15]

Riding the rails north to Dodge must have been agonizing for Bat. He had already lost brother Ed, and he sure didn't want to lose brother Jim.

It was noon, Saturday, April 16, 1881, as the train pulled into Dodge. Bat wasn't sure what kind of reception he was going to receive, so he disembarked from the train while it was still pulling up to the station. As the caboose passed him, he saw two men walking in the same direction alongside the train. Bat recognized them—Peacock and Updegraff. Bat opened his coat to reach his six-shooter, and shouted, "Hold up there a minute, you two. I want to talk to you."[16]

Peacock and Updegraff recognized Bat's voice, took a quick look back toward him, and ran to get behind the jail. No one would admit who started firing first, but it most likely was those

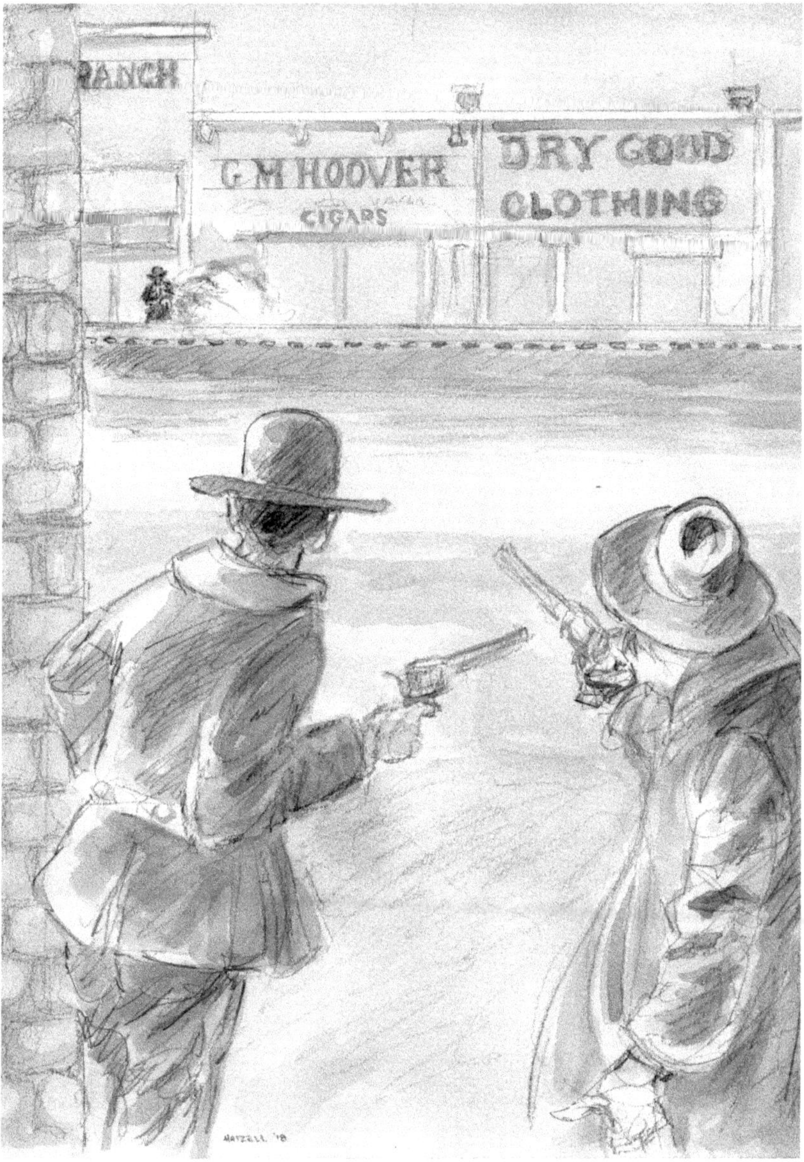
RANCH
G M HOOVER
CIGARS
DRY GOOD
CLOTHING

two. They were behind protection, and Bat stood out in the open. As shots rang out, Bat dove for cover behind the three-foot-high railroad embankment.[17]

As Peacock and Updegraff shot at Bat, their bullets were smashing into Front Street's north side businesses sending patrons in the Long Branch Saloon scrambling for cover. People supporting Bat started firing from the north side, while others supporting Peacock and Updegraff began shooting from the south side in a gunfight that would be named the Battle of the Plaza. Updegraff fell, a bullet slamming into his chest. The fighting soon came to an end when both Peacock and Bat ran out of bullets and their supporters stopped firing.[18]

With shotgun in hand, Mayor Webster ran up to Bat ordering him to surrender, which Bat did. He asked Webster if his brother Jim was all right, and Webster confirmed he was well. Up until that point, Bat had no idea if Jim was dead or alive.[19]

Later that day, Bat was charged with unlawfully discharging a pistol in town. He pled guilty and was fined eight dollars. Updegraff was shot through a lung but would live. He said Bat did not shoot him, but one of Bat's unknown supporters did.[20]

The people of Dodge turned against Bat and Jim. The Mastersons and two of their supporters were allowed to leave town. Jim and Peacock dissolved their partnership on mutually acceptable terms. The Mastersons were told if they ever returned to Dodge, they would be prosecuted.[21]

The Earps became wary of Sheriff Johnny Behan. He had reneged on his promise to appoint Wyatt as undersheriff; had failed to bring the posse fresh mounts for the search of the cowboy bandits; and his undersheriff, *Nugget* editor Woods, had allowed the cowboy bandit Luther King to escape. The clincher came when the Earps learned Sheriff Behan had paid all the posse members except them. He claimed he had never deputized them. When

Wells, Fargo learned Behan had stiffed the Earps, the company paid them for their time and effort.[22]

The Earps' relations with the cowboys worsened as they attempted to track down the cowboys' bandit friends: Lenard, Head, Crane, and King. Virgil claimed the cowboys, led by John Ringo, had sworn a blood oath to kill them.[23]

On June 6, 1881, Tombstone Marshal Ben Sippy left town for two weeks. Virgil was temporarily appointed to fill his position. Sippy never returned. He absconded with two hundred dollars of city money and left behind unpaid debts. Virgil stayed on as city marshal and remained deputy US marshal. Wyatt and Morgan served as deputy city marshals, and Wyatt helped Virgil as a field-commissioned deputy US marshal.[24]

Wyatt developed a plan to secretly work with cowboys to capture the stagecoach bandits. Wyatt met with Ike Clanton, Frank McLaury, and cowboy Joe Hill behind the Oriental Saloon. Wyatt was willing to give them the Wells, Fargo twelve hundred dollar reward money per each cowboy bandit if they brought them to a place where he could capture them. This sounded like a good deal to the cowboys, especially Ike Clanton, who had jumped Lenard's ranch and was running cattle on it until Lenard learned about it. They wanted to know if the reward was conditioned dead or alive because they knew the bandits would not be taken alive. Wyatt told them he would find out and let them know.[25]

Wyatt went to Wells, Fargo agent Marshall Williams and had him send a telegram to the San Francisco Wells, Fargo office asking if the reward was for dead or alive. The answer came back in the affirmative—the reward was for dead or alive. Clanton and Hill insisted on seeing the actual telegram that Earp got from Williams. After seeing the telegram, they agreed to bring in the bandits Lenard, Head, and Crane. Hill knew where to find them in New Mexico and would bring them to the McLaury ranch, where Ike and Frank would tell them there was a mine payroll shipment headed to Bisbee, Arizona, that they wanted them to take. Wyatt would take the bandits into custody at McLaury's ranch. Hill rode off to New Mexico to bring back Lenard, Head, and Crane.[26]

Hill was too late. On June 12, Lenard and Head were ambushed and killed by brothers Bill and Ike Haslett, who believed Lenard and Head were out to get them. The Haslett brothers in turn were murdered as they sat in a saloon celebrating when Crane and a band of cowboys entered and shot up the brothers and a third man.[27]

Wells, Fargo agent Marshall Williams must have figured out there was a deal between Wyatt and Ike based on the reward telegrams Wyatt asked him to send. Williams had too much to drink when he ran into Ike and mentioned he knew what was going on. Ike was upset; if news leaked out to his fellow cowboys that he was working with the law to turn in the cowboy bandits, he was a dead man. Ike found Wyatt and accused him of telling Williams of their plan. Wyatt denied it, saying Williams must have figured it out on his own. What little trust Ike had in Wyatt evaporated.[28]

Kate Elder had returned to Tombstone. She and Doc Holliday soon got into one of their fights. In a drunken rage, she swore out a warrant claiming Holliday was in on the stagecoach robbery outside Contention and he was the one who killed Philpott. Sheriff Behan arrested Holliday on July 5, and Wyatt and others posted his bond. The next day, Kate was arrested and fined for drunk and disorderly conduct, and then the day after that for making threats against life, but there was no reference who the threats were made against. Holliday was brought before Judge Wells Spicer, who after listening to witnesses, released him stating there was no evidence to even show the suspicion of guilt. But rumors had a way of continuing to float that Holliday had been in on the stagecoach robbery and was the one who shot and killed Bud Philpott. The rumors expanded to include one that the Earps had been in on the plot to rob the stagecoach.[29]

The Earps continued to keep law and order in Tombstone during the summer of 1881. On June 22, a major fire tore through town consuming four city blocks of businesses including the Oriental. The Earps, along with most able-bodied citizens, tried to contain and put out the fire. Lot jumpers tried to take over the burned-out lots, but the Earps and others forced them out. Rebuilding began almost immediately.[30]

News reached Tombstone that on August 13, Old Man Clanton leading a band of cowboys drove a cattle herd from Mexico across the border into Guadalupe Canyon, Arizona. Mexicans followed them across the border and attacked at night, killing five cowboys including Old Man Clanton and Jim Crane, the stagecoach robber. Besides mourning the loss of his father, Ike realized with Crane's death and King long gone to Mexico, there was no deal left to turn in cowboys for reward money. He began worrying Wyatt would tell people about the deal, placing his life in jeopardy.[31]

At 10:00 on the night of September 8, 1881, the stagecoach from Tucson to Bisbee, Arizona, was stopped when two masked and armed men stood in the road as one shouted, "Hold on!" The bandits stole the mail sack, the Wells, Fargo strongbox containing twenty-five hundred dollars, and plundered the passengers and driver. One of the robbers referred to money as "sugar."[32]

News of the stagecoach robbery reached Tombstone the next morning. A posse made up of Morgan and Wyatt Earp, their friend Fred Dodge, Wells, Fargo employee Marshall Williams, and two deputy sheriffs set off to find the culprits. When the posse interviewed the robbed passengers and driver, they mentioned one robber was jovial and used the expression "sugar" for money. That sounded a lot like the mannerisms and language used by Frank Stilwell—Cochise County Deputy Sheriff Frank Stilwell.[33]

The posse found the robbers' trail at the scene of the crime and began following it. One of the horses was unshod, which was unusual in that country. The robbers split up. Wyatt, Morgan, and Dodge followed one trail, and the others took the other trail. The Earp party found where the rider had dismounted on occasion and noticed from tracks that somewhere along the way, he had lost a boot heal, which they found. Following the trails into Bisbee, the trackers deduced that their quarry were Frank Stilwell and Pete Spencer, known as Spence. Finding that the two culprits were together in Bisbee, Dodge and Morgan kept an eye on the pair while Wyatt went to the shoemaker who said he had repaired Stilwell's boot.[34]

Wyatt, Morgan, and Dodge arrested them and hauled them back to Tombstone. Dodge wrote: "Stilwell and Spence both swore they would get Wyatt, Morg and myself for the arrest."[35]

Stilwell and Spence had a preliminary hearing before Judge Wells Spicer. They were released on two thousand dollars bail each. Ike Clanton was one of those who helped bail them out. Later, Spicer dropped the case due to insufficient evidence as well as witnesses providing alibis for the two.[36]

"Geronimo is coming!" shouted a breathless rider racing into Tombstone on the night of October 4, 1881. The town was thrown into a frenzy as men grabbed rifles, women and children took shelter, and mine whistles blew signaling danger. Geronimo and his band had broken out of the San Carlos Apache Reservation north of Tombstone. They were killing and looting as they went. The Apache hit the McLaury ranch stealing fourteen head of horses.[37]

Tombstone Mayor John Clum had been an agent at the reservation and had run-ins with Geronimo in the past. He did not like Geronimo, and he had no faith the army would capture him and his band, so he called for a posse to track down the Apaches and show them no quarter. Thirty-five men joined the posse, including Sheriff Johnny Behan, Wyatt, Virgil, and Morgan. They rode out of town heading east passing deserted ranches. When a torrential downpour hit them, some of the posse deserted. The next day they followed the Apaches' trail that turned south and crossed into Mexico. The posse turned back to Tombstone without firing a shot or seeing a hostile Apache.[38]

While the posse was out chasing elusive Apaches, five bandits stopped and robbed another stagecoach near Charleston on October 8. Five days later, Virgil and Wyatt again arrested Stilwell and Spence as members of the robber gang. Ike Clanton and Frank McLaury, as well as John Ringo and other cowboys, surrounded Morgan confronting him in the street in front of the Alhambra Saloon. In anger they shouted at him about the arrests of their friends Stilwell and Spence. Frank threatened the Earps' lives as Morgan walked away from them.[39]

What about Bat? What was he doing during the summer and early fall of 1881? He was traveling from town to town in Colorado playing faro and other gambling games.[40] There is no record of Bat getting into any kind of trouble.

THE BUNTLINE SPECIAL

Ned Buntline, whose real name was Edward Zane Carroll Judson, was a prolific writer of dime novels making William F. Cody famous when he wrote *Buffalo Bill: The King of the Border Men*.[41] Stuart Lake wrote in *Wyatt Earp: Frontier Marshal* that Ned Buntline arrived in Dodge City in 1876. Wyatt, Bat, and others sat down with Buntline providing frontier tales he could use in his writing. Buntline was so appreciative that he special ordered from Colt's Manufacturing Company five, .45-caliber, single-action six-guns with barrels four inches longer than standard or a foot in length, the gun being all together eighteen inches long. Each gun's walnut butt had the name "Ned" carved in it, and they all came with a wooden detachable shoulder stock.[42]

Buntline gave these guns he called "Buntline Specials" to Wyatt Earp, Bat Masterson, Bill Tilghman, Charlie Bassett, and Neil Brown. Tilghman and Bat did not like the long barrels and cut them down to standard length. Lake has Wyatt quoted as saying about the Buntline Special, "Mine was my favorite over any other gun."[43]

This is all interesting, but no one can seem to find any of the Buntline Specials. Colt's factory records do not mention them. None of the men presented Buntline Specials spoke of them. There is no record Ned Buntline was in Dodge City in 1876. There is no record he met any of the five men, and he never wrote about them.[44]

But on the other hand, there are those who believe the Buntline Specials existed. Avid weapons expert and historian Lee A. Silva believed Lake did not invent the Buntline Specials story. He believed Buntline gave the guns to Wyatt, Bat, and the others not because they were famous lawmen, which they were not in 1876, but because they had all been buffalo hunters. They had provided him buffalo hunting material, building upon what he had already learned from Buffalo Bill. Silva pointed to the fact that Lake wrote a letter to Colt Manufacturing on March 17, 1929, detailing the features of the Buntline Special and requesting factory records. Wyatt told Lake he gave his Buntline Special to Charles Hoxie, who was his business partner in the Dexter Saloon in Nome, Alaska, from 1900 to 1901. Lake wrote to a variety of people and Alaskan newspapers trying to track down Wyatt's Buntline Special, all dead ends.[45] Who knows? Maybe Wyatt's Buntline Special lies in a trunk in the attic of a Hoxie descendent or gathers dust on a bottom shelf in an Alaskan gun shop.

CHAPTER 10

THE GUNFIGHT NEAR THE O.K. CORRAL

Monday, October 24, 1881, was a day like any other day in Sheriff Johnny Behan's Cochise County jail. The inmates serving time included Jim Sharp for killing a Mexican in Charleston, Yank Thompson for grand larceny, and Milt Hicks for rustling. At 5:00 p.m., jailer Billy Soule left on business leaving assistant Charles Mason by himself with the prisoners. A boy arrived with the inmates' dinners. As Mason unlocked the cell to let the boy in, the three prisoners overpowered Mason and made their escape.[1]

Sheriff Behan put together a posse that included Wyatt, Morgan, and Virgil. They scoured the immediate area around town but had to stop when it became dark. Behan formed a new posse that included his deputies and Virgil. They left town at 11:00 p.m. to check the closest ranches. Finding no trace of the escapees, Behan and Virgil returned to Tombstone the next day, Tuesday, October 25, while the deputies continued the search.[2]

That same day, Ike Clanton and Frank McLaury arrived in town to conduct business. Ike was still worried that Wyatt had told others, especially Doc Holliday, about the old plan to capture the cowboys who had tried to rob the stagecoach near Contention and killed Bud Philpott. If Ike was exposed, he believed the cowboys would kill him. After finishing business, Ike went on an all-night drinking spree, visiting a variety of saloons as he bad-mouthed the Earps and Holliday and made threats against them.

About 1:00 a.m., on October 26, Ike sat at a table waiting for a meal in the Alhambra Saloon. Wyatt and Morgan were at the counter as Doc Holliday entered. He walked up to Ike cursing him and calling him "a son of a bitch of a cowboy" who "had been using his name." Holliday told Ike to get out his gun and get to work. Ike replied he didn't have a gun on him. Holliday called him "a damned liar" and said he had threatened the Earps. Ike said he had not threatened the Earps and Holliday should bring whoever said so to him and he would convince him he had said no such thing. Holliday challenged Ike to pull out his gun and, if there was any grit in him, to go to fighting. Holliday had his hand in his upper coat pocket, and Ike thought on his pistol. Morgan appeared ready to draw a pistol from his coat too.[3]

Morgan led the hothead Holliday outside. Ike got up from the table and walked out onto the sidewalk. Holliday said, "You son of a bitch, if you ain't heeled, go heel yourself."[4] Morgan added, "Yes, you son-of-a-bitch, you can have all the fight you want now!" Ike thanked him and told him he wasn't heeled. Virgil and Wyatt stood in the street but didn't say anything. Morgan told Ike the next time he came back on the street to be heeled. Ike walked off asking them not to shoot him in the back.[5]

Later, Ike entered the Occidental Saloon joining an all-night poker game with Virgil Earp, Tom McLaury, and Sheriff Johnny Behan. After leaving the game and arming himself with his Winchester and pistol, Ike continued his saloon tour bad-mouthing the Earps. About noon, Virgil and Morgan came up behind Ike on the street. Virgil buffaloed him on the side of the head with his six-shooter knocking him against a wall. Morgan cocked and pointed his pistol at Ike. Virgil took Ike's weapons and said, "You damned son of a bitch, we'll take you up here to Judge Wallace's."[6]

They dragged Ike to the recorder's office, Virgil searched for Judge Wallace while Morgan guarded Ike. Wyatt arrived and said to Ike, "You damn dirty cow thief, you have been threatening our lives, and I know it. I think I would be justified to shooting you down any place I would meet you, but if you are anxious to make a fight, I will go anywhere on earth to make a fight with you, even over to San Simon, among your crowd."[7]

"Fight is my racket and all I want is four feet of ground," Ike responded.[8] Morgan offered to pay Ike's fine if Ike would fight. "I'll fight you anywhere or any way," Ike replied. Morgan offered a weapon, but Ike declined saying he did not like the odds. After the exchange of threats, Judge Wallace arrived, fined Ike for carrying firearms in town, and released him.[9]

Wyatt ran into Tom McLaury on the street and said to him, "Are you heeled?" McLaury replied he had never done anything against the Earps and he was Wyatt's friend. But he went on to say, "If you want to make a fight, I'll make a fight with you anywhere."[10]

"All right, make a fight," Wyatt said, slapping McLaury's face with his left hand then buffaloing McLaury alongside his head bloodying his face.[11] After hitting McLaury several times with his pistol, Wyatt said, "I could kill the son-of-a-bitch," and walked away leaving him lying in the street.[12]

Billy Clanton and Frank McLaury rode into town stopping at the Grand Hotel. "How are you?" Doc Holliday greeted them and shook hands in passing. As they ordered drinks, Billy Allen, a Tombstone resident, walked in and told Frank that Wyatt had pistol-whipped Tom. "What did he hit Tom for?" Frank asked. Allen said he didn't know and Frank responded by saying, "I will get the boys out of town. We won't drink." He and Billy left without touching their drinks and rode west on Allen Street toward the O. K. Corral.[13]

On their way, they ran into cowboy friend Billy Claiborne, who had taken Ike to the doctor. He told them what had happened to Ike. Billy Clanton said, "I want to get him to go out home." Clanton continued saying he didn't come to town to fight anyone.[14] They met Tom and Ike at Spangenberg's Gun Shop. Billy Clanton and Frank bought ammunition. Ike wanted to buy a pistol, but owner George Spangenberg would not sell him one.

They left heading west on Allen Street to Dexter's Livery and Feed Stables, then crossed Allen Street to the O. K. Corral. The two Billys walked through the corral to a vacant lot on Fremont Street where Ike was having his team harnessed.[15] Ike joined them while the McLaurys went through the corral's rear entrance to Bauer's Union Meat Market on Fremont Street.

About 1:30 p.m., Sheriff Johnny Behan was getting a shave at Barron's Barbershop when someone said there was liable to be trouble between the Earps and Clantons. This was the first Behan had heard there were problems. He found Virgil at Hafford's Corner Saloon and asked what was going on. Virgil responded that there were "a lot of sons of bitches in town looking for a fight." Behan replied, "You had better disarm the crowd." Virgil said he would not. He would give them a chance to fight. Behan said, "It is your duty as a peace officer instead of encouraging a fight to disarm the parties."[16] Behan left to find the cowboys.

Learning the cowboys were on Fremont Street, Virgil decided to go disarm them, taking along Wyatt, Morgan, and a temporarily deputized Doc Holliday. Virgil gave Holliday his shotgun, which he concealed under his long coat.

Behan found Frank McLaury outside Bauer's Union Meat Market and told him to give up his weapons. Frank replied he did not intend to cause trouble, but he would only give up his guns after Behan disarmed the Earps.[17]

Behan walked with Frank leading his horse westward to the vacant lot where Billy Claiborne, the Clantons, and Tom McLaury stood. Behan searched Ike, finding no weapons. Tom opened his coat saying he carried no guns. Seeing the Earps and Holliday approaching, Behan told the cowboys, "Wait here. I see them coming down. I will go up and stop them."[18] As Behan walked toward the Earps, one of the Clantons said, "You need not be afraid Johnny, we are not going to have any trouble."[19]

Martha King was in Bauer's Union Meat Market when someone at the door said, "There they come." She stepped to the door and saw Holliday and the Earps pass on the sidewalk. She later said, "What frightened me and made me run back, I heard this man [one of the Earps] on the outside, looked at Holliday, and I heard him say 'Let them have it.' and Doc Holliday said, 'All right.'"[20]

Behan intercepted the Earps and Holliday, telling them not to go any farther. He was there to disarm the Clantons and McLaurys. They ignored him, but he continued talking, "Gentlemen, I am sheriff of this county, and I am not going to allow any trouble if I can help it." They brushed past, but he followed, calling for them to stop.[21] Virgil said, "Johnny, I am going to disarm them."[22]

With their horses saddled and their backs to the Harwood house, the cowboys stood in the vacant lot talking. The Earps and Holliday stopped about six feet from them.[23] Behan and Billy Claiborne both edged toward the front door of Fly's boarding house.

HOTZELL '16

Holliday and all the Earps, except for Virgil, had drawn their pistols. Virgil lifted a walking stick in this right hand. Holliday pointed his nickel-plated pistol at Billy Clanton. An Earp said, "You sons of bitches, you have been looking for a fight, and now you can have it!" Virgil yelled, "Boys, throw up your hands, I want your guns." Billy Clanton raised his hands saying, "Don't shoot me. I don't want to fight!" Tom McLaury threw open his coat saying, "I'm not armed." Frank held his horse's reins with no weapons in his hands, and Ike was unarmed.[24]

Holliday fired a shot followed by Morgan firing a shot. The action commenced fast and furious. Virgil switched the walking stick to his left hand and drew his gun. The Earps and Holliday got off six to seven shots before Billy Clanton and Frank McLaury could draw their pistols.[25]

Holliday's first shot hit Tom McLaury. Morgan's shots hit Billy Clanton in the chest and right wrist. As he slid to the ground his back against the wall of the Harwood house, Billy drew his six-shooter, and started shooting left-handed.[26] Wyatt shot Frank McLaury hitting him in the stomach. Frank staggered firing a shot back at Wyatt.[27]

Grabbing Billy Claiborne, Behan jerked him into Fly's boarding house.[28]

Unarmed, Ike stood in front of Wyatt, who pointed his pistol at him. "Go to fighting or get away," Wyatt told Ike. Ike's left hand darted out grasping Wyatt's right hand and pistol. At the same time, he grabbed Wyatt's shoulder with his right hand as Wyatt shot his gun. Pushing Wyatt away, Ike ran through Fly's front door and out the back.[29]

Wounded, Frank held the reins to his horse trying to use it as cover as he moved into Fremont Street, but the horse bolted in fear.[30] A bullet hit Virgil in the ankle, and he went down.[31]

Tom got behind his frightened horse, trying to control the animal long enough to retrieve his Winchester. Holliday must have shoved his pistol in a coat pocket. Pulling out the shotgun from under his coat and walking around Tom's horse, Holliday pointed the shotgun at Tom and blasted him under the right armpit. Tom staggered into the street and collapsed.[32]

Holliday saw Frank squatting in the street. Dropping the shotgun, he drew his pistol. Frank stood, lifted his pistol, and aimed at Holliday saying, "I've got you now."[33]

"Blaze away. You're a daisy if you have," Holliday said as he and Morgan fired simultaneously at Frank as Frank fired at Holliday. Hit by both bullets, Frank collapsed, but his shot nicked Holliday's hip.[34]

A bullet passed through Morgan's shoulder, chipped a vertebra, and passed out the other shoulder.[35] A third shot had hit Billy in the stomach, but he was not done fighting. He tried to reload his pistol, but it was taken from him.[36]

Thirty shots in thirty seconds, and the fight was over. Frank was dead. Still alive, Billy and Tom were carried into a house. As Doctor William Millar gave Billy morphine, Billy said, "They have murdered me. I have been murdered. Chase the crowd away from the door and give me air." Then he died. Tom did not say a word, later dying as well. When coroner Henry Matthews arrived, he found no gun or cartridges on Tom's body.[37]

CHAPTER 11

VENDETTA

After the shooting of Billy Clanton and Tom and Frank McLaury, only Wyatt stood without injury. The wounded Earps were taken to their homes to be cared for. Sheriff Johnny Behan tried to arrest Wyatt, but he wouldn't stand for it. Others who saw the attempt sided with Wyatt stating there was no need to arrest him, he would not be leaving town. Ike was arrested, and when Fin Clanton came to town, he asked to be placed under guard, so they both stayed in the county jail for the night with ten extra deputies to protect them.[1]

Feelings in town were mixed. Many believed the cowboys had it coming. Others thought the Earps were heavy-handed with their law enforcement. The Earps believed Behan had told them he had disarmed the cowboys, but Behan claimed he only told them he was there to disarm the cowboys.

Clara Brown, correspondent for the *San Diego Union*, wrote, "Opinion is pretty fairly divided as to the justification of the killing. You may meet one man who will support the Earps, and declare that no other course was possible to save their own lives, and the next man is just as likely to assert that there was no occasion whatever for bloodshed, and that this will be a 'warm place' for the Earps hereafter."[2]

Tombstone's *Epitaph* editorialized, "The feeling among the best class of our citizens is that the Marshal was entirely justified in his efforts to disarm these men, and that being fired upon they had to defend themselves, which they did most bravely."[3]

But a different point of view was emerging. The undertaker displayed the three bodies in their coffins in his business window

with a large sign, "MURDERED IN THE STREETS OF TOMBSTONE."
Tombstone's *Nugget*'s funeral heading read, "An Imposing Funeral."
Billy Clanton and Tom and Frank McLaury's funeral was the
largest held in Tombstone. A brass band led the two-block-long
procession with three hundred people on foot, over twenty-two
carriages, buggies, and wagons, and a line of horsemen.[4]

Coroner Henry Matthews picked an eight-man jury and held
an inquest on October 28 and 29, hearing eight witnesses. After
deliberating for two hours, the jury concluded "William Clanton,
Frank and Thomas McLaury came to their deaths in the town of
Tombstone on October 26, 1881, from the effects of pistol and
gunshot wounds inflicted by Virgil Earp, Morgan Earp, Wyatt
Earp and one—Holliday, commonly called 'Doc' Holliday."[5] The
conclusion did not determine if the marshal and his deputies had
acted in the line of duty. The next day, the city council suspended
Virgil from the police force pending investigation.[6]

Ike filed murder charges against the Earps and Doc Holliday. Wyatt and Doc were arrested on October 31 and placed in
jail. Since Virgil and Morgan were wounded, they were allowed to
remain at home. Friends came to Wyatt and Doc's assistance helping them raise the funds to post bail of $10,000 each.[7]

On October 31, Judge Wells Spicer began an inquest that
would last until November 29. Spicer's inquest was to determine
if there was enough evidence to try the Earps and Holliday for
murder in district court.[8]

On November 1, Virgil, as deputy US marshal, telegraphed
General Orlando Willcox at Fort Huachuca requesting a company of cavalry to protect Tombstone from the cowboys. Willcox
asked Arizona's acting governor if troops were needed and he said
no. Tombstone's *Nugget* had fun criticizing Virgil's request.[9]

Tom and Frank's brother, Will McLaury, arrived in Tombstone. He was a lawyer and, on November 4, joined the prosecu-
tion. Thirty witnesses were examined and cross-examined as their
testimony and other evidence was recorded.[10]

During the trial, Sheriff Johnny Behan may have been experiencing stress and sought consolation. Josephine Sarah Marcus had been living with Behan as his wife since at least December 1880. She had traveled to California visiting her parents and returned to Tombstone mid-November 1881 to find Behan in bed with a married woman he had been running around with. That was it, Josephine was done with him.[11]

After hearing a month's worth of testimony, Judge Spicer concluded there was not sufficient evidence that the Earps and Holliday were guilty of any offense, and he ordered them released. Spicer said if the Cochise County grand jury believed otherwise, it could review the case.[12] On December 1, the Earps and Holliday were once again free men; but they were concerned about cowboy retaliation. Virgil, Allie, and Morgan relocated to the Cosmopolitan Hotel where they believed they would be safer from cowboy retribution while Virgil and Morgan recovered from their gunshot wounds.[13] As anti-Earp anger increased, the rest of the Earps moved there too. Kate Elder left Tombstone for Globe, Arizona, having been warned by John Ringo that the Clantons planned to ambush Holliday at his room in Fly's boarding house.[14]

The cowboys rented their own room in the Grand Hotel right across Allen Street from the Earp's room in the Cosmopolitan. John Ringo, Pony Deal, Curly Bill, and Ike Clanton spent time in the room. The shutters were always closed, but one slat was removed giving a good view of the Earp room. The rumor floated that one of them aimed a rifle out the window of the room and was about to shoot Wyatt's gambling partner Lou Rickabaugh when the others stopped him.[15]

Tombstone Mayor John Clum, an Earp supporter, heard rumors of a cowboy "Death List" that included the Earps, Doc Holliday, and others including himself.[16] On the evening of December 14, Clum left on a stagecoach hauling nothing of value other than four other passengers bound for Benson. Four miles out of Tombstone, someone out along the road shouted "Hold!"

followed by a volley of sixteen shots. As the team of horses took off flying, two passengers heard someone shout, "Be sure to get the old bald-headed son of a bitch!" One person in a following wagon was shot in the leg, but no one else was hurt. Clum, who was bald, made it to Benson.[17]

The day after the attempt at stopping the stagecoach, the Earps walked up to the Oriental Saloon's bar for a drink. Virgil's wound had healed well enough that he could now walk. Democrat county supervisor Milt Joyce, who ran the Oriental's bar and restaurant, remarked, "See who's here. I expect there will be another stage robbed by morning." Virgil slapped Joyce's face as the Earps drew their guns. Joyce backed toward the door saying, "Your favorite method is to shoot a man in the back, but if you murder me you will be compelled to shoot me in the front." The next day, Joyce, carrying two six-shooters, walked into the Oriental and found the Earps and Holliday. He called them bastards and told them he was ready to fight. Sheriff Johnny Behan came up behind Joyce, grabbed him from behind, pulled him out of the Oriental, and arrested him for carrying guns. They had been good friends, but from then on Joyce had no time for Behan.[18]

Josephine Marcus and Wyatt began spending time together. Wyatt always called her Sadie.[19] Johnny Behan had introduced them in December 1880 when she first arrived in Tombstone.[20] "When Wyatt heard of my falling out with Johnny, he sought to court me for the first time," Sadie wrote. "I knew he was married, but it was no secret that his marriage was on the rocks."[21] Wyatt spent less and less time with Mattie, who suffered from severe gum disease and headaches. To relieve the pain, she took laudanum, an opioid. Her addiction to laudanum may have started in Tombstone.[22]

On December 16, the grand jury decided not to reverse the Spicer decision.[23] Ike would make two further attempts to get the Earps and Holliday charged with murder, but the attempts went nowhere.[24] From that time on, people have debated if the Earps and Holliday were doing their duty to enforce Tombstone's no-firearm carry ordinance or if it was just plain murder while hiding behind a badge as the rumors of Holliday's stagecoach holdup and possible Earp involvement just would not die.

Bat Masterson had been busy throughout the fall and into the winter traveling from town to town making a living at gambling. He became a nationally known character when in early November 1881, the *New York Sun* printed a story about him titled "A Mild-Eyed Man, Who Has Killed Twenty-six Persons," which was later picked up by various newspapers across the country including the *Ford County Globe* on November 22, 1881. The story was told by Dr. W. S. Cockrell to a *New York Sun* correspondent in Gunnison, Colorado. Cockrell pointed out Bat, who was standing in the doorway to the Tabor House billiards room, and said, "There is a man who has killed twenty-six men, and he is only twenty-seven years of age. He is W. B. Masterson of Dodge City, Kan. He has killed his men in the interest of law and order. Once he shot seven men dead within a few minutes." Cockrell went on to spin tales of Bat's alleged killings including the time he killed a father-and-son criminal team and brought back their heads for a reward.[25]

The *Kansas City Journal* learned Bat was visiting Kansas City, Missouri, and sent a reporter to interview him as he was emerging from a Main Street restaurant at 8:00 p.m. on November 14, 1881. The next day, the *Journal* printed a story entitled "Bat's Bullets. A Talk With The Frontiersman Who is 'On His Third Dozen,' Or At Least Is Said To Be." Bat must have had great fun with the reporter. When the reporter asked Bat if it was true he had killed twenty-six men, "Masterson said he had not killed as many men as was popularly supposed." When asked about killing the father-and-son criminals, Bat answered, "Oh, that story is straight, except that I did not cut off their heads." The *Journal* went on to embellish events of Bat's life. The story ended with, "Whether he has killed twenty-six men as is popularly asserted, cannot be positively ascertained without careful and extensive research, for he himself is quite reticent on the subject. But that many men have fallen by his deadly revolver and rifle is an established fact, and he furnishes a rare illustration of the fact that the thrilling stories of life on the frontier are not always overdrawn."[26]

Two days later, the *Atchison Champion* came out with an amusing editorial entitled "Too Much Blood" regarding the twenty-six men killed attributed to Bat. "We do not stickle about a few tubs of gore, more or less, nor have we any disposition to haggle about a corpse or two, but when it comes to a miscount or overlap of a dozen, no conscientious journalist, who values truth as well as the honor of our state, should keep silent." The editorial continued with exaggerated stories of Bat's exploits. It insisted that the numbers tallied by Bat's accountant and the undertaker should be verified because they would only discourage "some humble beginner in the field of slaughter." In the end, the editorial called for a recount.[27]

What were Bat's thoughts on all these exaggerated tales? In later years, he wrote to a friend, "The newspapers both East and West have devoted a great deal of space to me, and it seems that when they run out of a subject upon whom they can appropriately devote a column or two, their minds revert to me. They do it with such a recklessness and with such utter disregard of the truth that I make no kick—just let them go ahead. I have concluded that they can't do me any harm."[28] Bat was known to have killed, maybe at the most, two men: Corporal Melvin King at Sweetwater and Jack Wagner, who shot his brother Ed in Dodge City.

Back in Tombstone, Arizona, on December 28, 1881, at 11:30 p.m., Virgil Earp stepped out of the Oriental Saloon to walk back to the Cosmopolitan Hotel where he and the rest of the Earps were living. From out of the darkness about sixty yards away, three assailants fired double-barreled shotguns at him. As he fell to the street, three men ran out of a burned-out building and down Fifth Street toward Toughnut Street. No one chased them.[29]

The buckshot hit Virgil on his left side. Fortunately, the worst of the blasts hit his left arm and missed all vital organs, or he probably would have been killed. He was hauled to his room at the Cosmopolitan where the doctors debated about removing his arm. He insisted they try to keep it. They operated on him, removing buckshot and five and a half inches of splintered bone from his upper arm.[30]

Wyatt started to do some investigating. Looking around the burnt-out building where the assailants had fired at Virgil, he found a sombrero with Ike Clanton's name inside it. A watchman at the icehouse on Toughnut Street told Wyatt he saw Ike Clanton, Frank Stilwell, and Hank Swilling each with a shotgun run past him. A miner told Wyatt he saw the same three men mount horses in Tombstone Gulch and race off toward Charleston. John Ringo and an unidentified man were seen running down Allen Street.[31]

No one from the city or the county went after the culprits. The day after Virgil was shot, Wyatt wired US Marshal Crawley Dake in Phoenix, Arizona, telling him what had happened to Virgil and requesting appointment as a deputy US marshal. Dake responded by appointing Wyatt deputy US marshal with full power including appointing deputies.[32]

Wyatt did not pursue any suspects right away; he was preoccupied with Virgil, who wasn't doing well; but after ten days, Virgil was on the road to recovery. The Tombstone city election took place during Virgil's convalescence. The Earps' shooting of the McLaurys and Billy Clanton became an issue as well as their perceived heavy-handed law enforcement. The anti-Earp faction won big at the polls sweeping the mayor, marshal, and three of the four city council positions.[33] It was quite certain neither Wyatt nor Morgan would again be appointed as Tombstone deputy marshals.

On January 5, 1882, Wyatt received another blow to his finances. Milt Joyce took over complete control of Oriental Saloon forcing Wyatt and his partners out of the gaming concession and replacing them with Sheriff Johnny Behan.[34] Now Wyatt's main job was his deputy US marshal position.

Crime continued in Cochise County. At 3:00 a.m. on January 6, 1882, a stagecoach was robbed outside Bisbee, and the following night, the stagecoach from Benson to Tombstone was robbed. Rumors floated that John Ringo was one of the Bisbee stagecoach robbers.[35] Sheriff Behan sent out no posses to search for bandits.

On January 17, Ringo and Holliday almost had a showdown in the streets but were prevented by city Deputy Marshal Jim Flynn and Wyatt interceding.[36] Deputy Sheriff Billy Breakenridge was heading home on a dark and rainy night when he ran across Frank Stilwell with a gun ready to ambush and kill "a certain party" who had boasted he was going to kill him. Stilwell said he planned to shoot the other party first. Breakenridge told him he was in enough trouble and to go home, which he did. Breakenridge continued on his way and a half block later passed Doc Holliday walking in the opposite direction toward his rooming house. Breakenridge figured he had just saved Doc Holliday's life.[37]

The Earps and their friends began using Campbell and Hatch's Billiard Parlor as their headquarters located across Allen Street from the cowboy's Grand Hotel headquarters. Ringo stopped Wyatt in the street and proposed ending the feud by he and Holliday shooting it out in the street. Wyatt told him no and continued into Hatch's. Ringo remained in the middle of the street making a scene, wanting to fight with Holliday until Deputy Sheriff Breakenridge took him to the sheriff's office then let him leave town.[38]

Wyatt obtained warrants for the arrest of Pony Deal and Ike and Fin Clanton for the attempted murder of Virgil Earp. Monday morning, January 23, Wyatt rode out of town leading a heavily armed posse of seven men that included Doc Holliday and Morgan.[39]

John Ringo had been accused of two separate counts of robbery. Judge William Stilwell reviewed his bail bonds, determined they were insufficient, and ordered Ringo's arrest. Learning of his imminent arrest, Ringo quietly left Tombstone. Instead of going through Sheriff Behan's office, Judge Stilwell appointed John Henry Jackson to lead a posse after Ringo. Jackson had no law enforcement credentials, but that didn't stop him as he led a twenty-one-man posse out of town before sunrise on Wednesday, January 25. Jackson's posse arrived in Charleston later that morning and stopped at the Occidental Hotel for breakfast. Jackson ran into Ike Clanton and a group of cowboys. As the two talked about Ringo, Ike told Jackson that Ringo was in town and he would talk with him to see if he wanted to surrender to Jackson's posse. Ike's well-armed cowboy companions said the posse would not take Ringo unless he wanted to leave with them. Ringo decided not to go with the posse and raced back to Tombstone ahead of the posse turning himself in to Sheriff Behan.[40]

A third posse now was riding through Cochise County. This one was led by Charley Bartholomew, who was the shotgun messenger on the stage that had been robbed near Bisbee. His posse was looking for those robbers.[41]

On the evening of January 25, Wyatt's posse entered Charleston and went door to door looking for the Clantons and Pony Deal, without success. The next day, they roamed the countryside around Charleston looking for the fugitive cowboys. Charley Bartholomew brought his posse to Charleston and stayed there for the day and into the evening until someone built and lit a bonfire on Main Street and others started taking potshots at the posse until they left.[42]

Friday through Sunday, the Earp posse continued to search Cochise County for the Clantons and Deal. Judge Stilwell again sent out Jackson's posse this time to track down the Clantons. Jackson's posse joined Bartholomew's posse with cowboy Pete Spence acting as a guide. They found Ike and Fin Clanton on Monday,

January 30, at 2:30 a.m. Ike and Fin surrendered after the posse assured them they would protect them from the Earps.[43]

Ike and Fin were brought before Judge Stilwell later that day. They thought they were being arrested on robbery charges but found out they were being charged with attempted murder of Virgil Earp. Stilwell set bail for each at fifteen hundred dollars, which they met, and they were released.[44]

The next day, the attempted murder charges against Deal and Fin were dropped as there was no evidence against them. On February 2, Ike's case came before Judge Stilwell. Ike's hat found at the scene of the crime was produced as evidence as well as a witness overhearing Ike talking about Virgil's shooting saying he "would have to go back and do the job over." Ike said he had lost his hat before the shooting and had no idea how it wound up at the scene of the crime while seven witnesses testified Ike was in Charleston at the time of the attempt on Virgil's life. Stilwell ruled the evidence against Ike was inconclusive, and he was acquitted of the charges against him.[45]

Ike then went after the Earps in court. On February 9, he brought charges of murder against the Earps and Holliday before the justice of the peace in Contention. Sheriff Behan escorted the Earps, Holliday, and a large body of their supporters to Contention on February 14. The justice of the peace ruled the hearing to be held the next day back in Tombstone. After much legal wrangling back and forth, Cochise County probate judge John Lucas ruled that since the Spicer hearing found there was not enough evidence to proceed to a trial and the grand jury refused to indict, the Clantons needed to present new evidence for a trial to be considered. The Earps and Holliday were again free.[46]

Tombstone was still divided over the cowboys. There were constant rumors and veiled threats against the Earps. Morgan's wife, Louisa, left to stay with his parents in Colton, California.[47] The rest of the Earps continued to live at the Cosmopolitan Hotel. Problems continued with cowboy raids into Mexico. US Marshal Crawley

Dake authorized Wyatt to patrol Cochise County to apprehend criminals. Wyatt spent the rest of February and into March on the trail with Morgan and Warren in the hunt for desperados.[48]

Bat Masterson was a sports enthusiast and enjoyed a good boxing match. In February 1882, he traveled to New Orleans to witness, along with a thousand other boxing enthusiasts, a prizefight between Paddy Ryan, considered America's heavyweight champion, and an up-and-coming fighter, John L. Sullivan, "the Boston Strong Boy." There is no record on who Bat bet or how much, but it must have been exciting for him to be there. The fight was held on February 7 with the late odds favoring Sullivan five to four. By the end of the ninth round, Sullivan had pummeled Ryan to the ground, and Ryan's handlers had to throw in the sponge.[49]

After the fight, Bat headed back west, winding up in Trinidad, Colorado, on February 14, where brother Jim was on the city police force. Gambling establishments were big business in Trinidad, and Bat decided to stay.[50]

On Friday, March 17, 1882, the Earp brothers were back in Tombstone after patrolling the county to thwart criminal activities. Seen together in town that day were Frank Stilwell, Pete Spence, Hank Swilling, and Florentino Cruz, known as Indian Charlie. Saturday morning, Briggs Goodrich, who was an attorney for some of the cowboys, stopped Wyatt on Allen Street. Goodrich told Wyatt that those four cowboys and unnamed others were out to get him that night. He also told Wyatt that John Ringo wanted him to know that he was not a part of any of it. Wyatt thanked Goodrich and then searched the town with Morgan looking for the four cowboys but couldn't find them.[51]

After attending a play that night, Wyatt and Morgan went to Campbell and Hatch's Billiard Parlor. Wyatt sat with his back to the wall as he watched Bob Hatch and Morgan play a game of billiards. The billiard table was near the back door leading into the alley. The upper half of the door was glass allowing anyone in the alley to see who was inside without being seen themselves. Hatch was making a shot as Morgan watched standing near the door with his back to it. Two rapid shots rang out. The glass in the door shattered. A bullet hit the wall above Wyatt's head. A .45 slug entered the small of Morgan's back on the left side, shattering his spine, exiting the right side, and hitting George Berry in the thigh. Wyatt fired three shots through the door as they heard men running down the alley. By the time Wyatt and the others could get out the alley door, the assassins were gone.[52]

Morgan was moved to a couch in Bob Hatch's office. After examining Morgan's bullet wound, the doctor said he would not live. The Earp family gathered by Morgan's side, and shortly after midnight he died.[53]

That Sunday, the coroner impaneled a jury and held an inquest into Morgan's death. After hearing testimony from several people including Pete Spence's wife, Marietta, and her mother, the coroner's jury concluded Morgan was killed by gunshot wounds fired by Pete Spence, Frank Stilwell, John Doe Freeze, an Indian called Charlie, and another Indian, name unknown.[54]

Later that day, James Earp escorted the coffin holding Morgan's body to the Benson train station and then back to Colton, California, for burial. Wyatt convinced Virgil it was not safe for Allie and him in Tombstone and that they needed to go to California. Monday morning, March 20, Wyatt received a telegram from Tucson that Frank Stilwell, Pete Spence, Hank Swilling, and Ike Clanton were there.[55] Virgil and Allie would be taking the westbound train, which always stopped in Tucson. The cowboys must have known Virgil and Allie would be heading west. The Earps heard reports the cowboys were searching every westbound train looking for Virgil to kill him.[56]

Using his authority as a deputy US marshal, Wyatt led a posse of five trusted men to escort Virgil and Allie as far as Tucson. The posse was made up of Warren Earp, Doc Holliday, Turkey Creek Jack Johnson, Texas Jack Vermillion, and Sherman McMasters.[57] Virgil was still weak and had to be carried on and off the train. They reached the Tucson train station at dusk and had an hour stop for supper.[58] As posse members helped Virgil off the train, Virgil saw Frank Stilwell and his friends "armed to the teeth." When the cowboys saw Virgil's escort, they disappeared into the crowd.[59] The posse guarded Virgil and Allie as they ate and then saw them safely on the westbound train.

While they were waiting for the train to pull out of the station, Wyatt saw Frank Stilwell and Ike Clanton with shotguns lying prone on a flatbed car waiting for the moment they could shoot into the lighted passenger car where Virgil and Allie sat. Wyatt ran toward the cowboys with posse members following. Clanton and Stilwell saw him coming and ran. Wyatt said, "I ran straight for Stilwell. It was he who killed my brother. What a coward he was. He couldn't shoot when I came near him. He stood there helpless and trembling for his life. As I rushed upon him, he put out his hands and clutched at my shotgun. I let go both barrels, and he tumbled down dead and mangled at my feet. I started for Clanton then, but he escaped behind a moving train of cars."[60]

As the westbound train pulled out of the station, Wyatt ran alongside the passenger car with Virgil looking out the window. Wyatt held up a finger shouting, "It's all right, Virg! It's all right! One for Morg!"[61]

Wyatt and his posse searched through Tucson for two hours looking for the other cowboys without success. They boarded an eastbound train later that night and by Tuesday morning, March 21, they were back in Tombstone.[62]

Some of the other posse members must have shot into Stilwell's body as there were three bullets found in it besides the pellets from the shotgun blasts. A coroner's inquest was held, and arrest warrants for the murder of Frank Stilwell were issued for Wyatt Earp, Warren Earp, Doc Holliday, Sherman McMasters, and Jack Johnson.[63]

The Earp posse returned to Tombstone's Cosmopolitan Hotel to rest and then head out to find the other culprits who had killed Morgan. Pima County justice of the peace Charles Meyer sent a telegram to Sheriff Johnny Behan stating Wyatt Earp and his posse were wanted for the murder of Frank Stilwell and he should arrest them.[64] The telegraph office manager was a friend of the Earps and showed Wyatt the telegram first. Wyatt asked that he not show Sheriff Behan until the posse was prepared to leave.[65]

At 8:00 p.m., the posse was readying their horses in front of the Cosmopolitan when the telegraph office manager gave Sheriff Behan the telegram. Behan ordered his deputies to grab their shotguns and follow him as he raced unarmed to stop the posse.[66] A crowd gathered as the posse mounted their horses and Behan ran up to Wyatt.

"Wyatt, I want to see you," Behan said.

"You can't see me; you have seen me once too often," Wyatt answered and added, "I will see [Pima County Sheriff Bob] Paul."[67]

Sheriff Behan's supporters said that as he tried to arrest Wyatt the posse members drew their guns on him. Earp supporters claimed Behan never tried to arrest the posse and they never raised their guns but only carried them in normal riding position as they rode out of town.[68]

Wyatt was a deputy US marshal, carried warrants for the arrests of the men named in his brother's murder, and had the authority to appoint a posse. The Arizona newspapers had a heyday with the murders, confrontations, and search for the murderers. The stories quickly spread to the California newspapers where the posse's search took on the names "Arizona Vendetta" and "*the* Vendetta."[69]

Wyatt and his posse—made up of Warren Earp, Doc Holliday, Turkey Creek Jack Johnson, Texas Jack Vermillion, and Sherman

HATZELL '16

McMasters—rode to Pete Spence's wood camp in the Dragoon Mountains.[70] Arriving at the camp Wednesday morning, March 22, Wyatt hoped to find Spence and Morgan's other accused murderers there, but unknown to Wyatt, Spence, Swilling, and John Doe Freeze (who turned out to be Frederick Bode, a German who hauled wood out of Spence's wood camp), were now all sitting in jail.[71]

The posse questioned the Mexican wood camp workers, who told them Indian Charlie, whose real name was Florentino Cruz and who was identified as one of the suspected killers in Morgan's murder, was alone up on the slopes. The posse rode up the hillside toward him. Indian Charlie started running as the posse chased him. Shots were fired, and the workers saw Indian Charlie fall. Later the posse rode back down the slope at a leisurely pace then headed east.[72]

Wyatt said that as Indian Charlie was running, McMasters shot and hit him, causing a minor flesh wound. The posse ran him down and interrogated him. He confessed he was part of the group that killed Morgan. He said Ike Clanton, Curly Bill, John Ringo, and Frank Stilwell had plotted to kill Morgan and Wyatt. The night of the murder, John Ringo, Curly Bill, Hank Swilling, Frank Stilwell, Pete Spence, and he met behind the courthouse to make last-minute plans. Ringo held the horses at one end of the alley. Spence and Indian Charlie stood guard at Allen Street. Curly Bill, Swilling, and Stilwell walked into the alley and did the shooting. Later Stilwell boasted he was the one who killed Morgan and the one who had hit Virgil with the buckshot. Curly Bill paid Indian Charlie twenty-five dollars for his efforts and he was supposed to shoot anyone who tried to interfere with killing the Earps. Wyatt said this last statement made him angry. Indian Charlie wore two holstered six-guns. Wyatt said he gave him the chance to draw. As Indian Charlie drew his guns, Wyatt drew his guns faster and put three bullets in him.[73]

Meanwhile back in Tombstone, Cochise County Sheriff Johnny Behan organized a twelve-man posse to ride out and arrest deputy US Marshal Wyatt Earp's posse. Behan's posse, made up of mostly cowboys, included John Ringo and Ike and Fin Clanton. Behan took cowboys with him because he believed the Earp posse would resist arrest and the cowboys would fight them because of their ongoing feud.[74] Pima County Sheriff Bob Paul had arrived in Tombstone with the purpose of riding with Behan's posse, but after listening to and observing Behan's cowboy posse he saw they were so hostile to the Earps that there would be no possibility of arrest, only bloodshed. He wanted no part of that and returned to Tucson.[75] A second posse formed in Charleston to search for the Earp posse. This one numbered twenty cowboys and was led by Curly Bill, who said Sheriff Behan had deputized him.[76]

Friday, March 24, 1882, was a busy day in Cochise County. Wyatt's wife, Mattie, and James's wife, Bessie, left Tombstone bound for Colton, California, and the safety of their husbands' parents' home.[77] Sheriff Johnny Behan led his cowboy posse out of Tombstone in search of the Earp posse, and Curly Bill led his twenty-man posse into Contention, learning the Earp posse was a couple miles to the north.[78]

The Earp posse was supposed to meet a contact from Tombstone at Iron Springs with payroll for the posse members. Wyatt left Warren back along the road to wait for the contact in case he came in from that direction and proceeded onward to Iron Springs.[79]

As Wyatt led his posse approaching Iron Springs, the springs were hidden from view by a fifteen-foot high bank. Wyatt dismounted while the others remained mounted, strung out behind him. He advanced forward on foot holding his horse's reins in his left hand and his double-barreled shotgun in his right hand. Rounding the bank, Iron Springs came into view as two men jumped up not more than ten feet away. One raised a double-barreled, sawed-off shotgun.[80]

"Curly Bill!" yelled posse member Sherman McMasters, turning his horse and racing back the way they had come. Wyatt's other posse members panicked and turned their horses to run.[81]

Curly Bill Brocious fired a double blast at Wyatt, tearing through his coat but missing him altogether. Wyatt pulled both triggers of his double-barreled shotgun nearly cutting Curly Bill in half.[82]

The other man with Curly Bill was Pony Deal, who raced to join the rest of the cowboys at the springs. The cowboys reached for their firearms and began shooting at Wyatt and his posse. Texas Jack Vermillion's horse was hit and collapsed on top of his leg. Wyatt's other posse members retreated out of gunfire range. Wyatt's horse danced around, spooked by the gunfire. As bullets whizzed all around him, Wyatt had to first readjust his gun belt before he could mount his skittish horse. He made it safely to Texas Jack, who by now had extracted himself from under the horse and insisted on removing the saddle, tack, weapons, and gear and carrying it away while Wyatt provided him cover. Holliday and the other posse members must have felt embarrassed about turning tail and running. They wanted to return and attack the cowboys, but Wyatt said no there were too many of them and by now they would put up an organized resistance.[83]

Through the first part of April, Wyatt and his posse continued their search for other suspects in Morgan's assassination, but the posse needed provisions and fresh mounts. Behan and his posse never found the Earps, or maybe they really didn't want to find them. It seemed they rode all over the county except in the direction the Earp posse was located. Wyatt decided it was fruitless to stay any longer in Arizona, and on April 15, 1882, the Earp posse arrived in Silver City, New Mexico, then traveled to Albuquerque where they would eventually take a train to Colorado.[84]

GUN COLLECTORS BEWARE

When the *New York Sun* printed the story "A Mild-Eyed Man, Who Has Killed Twenty-Six Persons" and it was picked up by various newspapers across the country including the *Ford County Globe* on November 22, 1881, Bat Masterson became a national celebrity. People wanted to meet him and hear his tales of gun battles. Some wanted to collect memorabilia from him.

Wyatt Earp told his biographer, Stuart Lake, one tale of a persistent collector pestering Bat. While Bat was working in New York City, an old acquaintance made frequent stops by Bat's office pestering him for one of his six-guns he had used on the frontier. Bat finally decided to give the man a gun to get rid of him, but he didn't want to give him one of his good guns. So, he went to a pawn shop and bought an old Colt's .45. He took it back to his office where he had a bright idea. Using his penknife, he cut twenty-two notches on the grips. When the collector arrived, Bat handed him the gun. The collector studied the grips and asked Bat if he had killed twenty-two men with it. Bat didn't tell him yes, and he didn't tell him no. The happy collector left with his souvenir.[85]

The gun collector was Fred Sutton, who had been a buffalo skinner for Bat back in 1876. Sutton wrote in his book *Hands Up!*, "Bat had killed aplenty. I have his best six-shooter in my collection and it is pretty well covered with notches; but I am sure he never shed a tear over any of them."[86] Bat may have shed tears—tears of laughter.

CHAPTER 12
TRINIDAD

Bat Masterson had been living in Trinidad, Colorado, since February 14, 1882. His brother Jim worked for the city police force, while Bat was making a living in Trinidad's gambling halls. City elections were held the first week of April, and John Conkie was elected the new mayor along with a new city council. At the city council's April 17 meeting, Mayor Conkie asked the members to appoint Bat as city marshal, which they did on a vote of four to two. Lou Kreeger, the old city marshal, and Feliciano Vijil were appointed city policemen under Bat. Brother Jim was not reappointed and took a job bartending at the Grand Central Bar.[1]

Trinidad was peaceful enough during April and May. The *Trinidad Daily News* reported on May 3 that Bat evicted "a gang of harlots. . . . Their quarters had for some nights been the scene of disgraceful orgies that aroused the attention of the neighborhood and made it a public disgrace."[2]

Wyatt Earp and his posse had left Arizona for New Mexico staying a few days in Albuquerque where Wyatt and Doc Holliday had a falling out—cooling but not ending their relationship. The posse left on the train to Trinidad, Colorado, where they made camp outside town, during the first week of May. They were in a contradictory predicament being lawmen but also fugitives from the law.[3]

Voiced by competing newspapers, Arizona public opinion was divided on the Earp posse. It was a classic debate—law versus order. Many believed the cowboys were out of control. These citizens held a vigilante mentality that the Arizona legal system was broken. Criminals were caught and released to continue their depravations. If government-sanctioned posses eliminated a few desperados, good riddance. The other side of the debate believed in the rule of law. As government peace officers, the Earp posse had sworn to uphold the laws and was obligated to capture an offender if possible and bring him before the duly sanctioned legal system, not take the law into their own hands. The opposite is chaos with every man being his own judge and executioner.[4]

There is evidence the Earp posse had protection and financial support from business and government interests that wanted to see the cowboy threat to stability eliminated. These interests were on the side of order. This support included large Cochise County ranchers, Tombstone's vigilante Citizen Safety Committee, Wells, Fargo, the Santa Fe Railroad, and the governors of Arizona, New Mexico, and Colorado. Even though Pima County had an arrest warrant for Wyatt and Doc for the killing of Frank Stilwell and Cochise County had an arrest warrant for the entire posse for the killing of Indian Charlie, there was never a serious effort to arrest the posse members except for Doc Holliday and that effort would be thwarted.[5]

After arriving at Trinidad, Texas Jack Vermillion, Turkey Creek Jack Johnson, and Sherman McMasters drifted separately into the Texas Panhandle and New Mexico. Doc Holliday left with gambler friends for Pueblo, Colorado, and then on to Denver. Wyatt and brother Warren remained in Trinidad for a few days before traveling on to Gunnison, Colorado.[6] There they hired lawyers in Arizona to clear their cases. In the meantime, Wyatt ran a faro game in one of Gunnison's saloons.[7]

While Doc Holliday was in Pueblo, a man introduced himself as Perry Mallen, claiming Doc had saved his life years ago, and wanted to do the same for him, warning that people were out to murder him. The night of May 15, Doc and his friends attended the horse races in Denver. Mallen stepped in front of Doc pointing two six-guns in his face. With him were two Arapahoe County deputy sheriffs. They arrested Doc and hauled him to jail. Mallen claimed he was a deputy sheriff, showing telegrams ordering Holliday's arrest for the deaths of Frank Stilwell, Billy Clanton, Curly Bill Brocious, and an unnamed railroad conductor. Mallen added that Holliday had killed his partner, Harry White, seven years earlier in Park City, Utah.[8]

The Denver newspapers made a big deal over Holliday's arrest. Wyatt Earp could do nothing to help his friend, but Bat Masterson was in Denver and might be able to do something.

"Holliday had a mean disposition and an ungovernable temper, and under the influence of liquor was a most dangerous man," Bat said. "While I assisted him substantially on several occasions, it was not because I liked him any too well, but on account of my friendship with Wyatt Earp, who did."[9]

Bat wired Pueblo City Marshal Henry Jameson about Holliday's situation. Jameson soon arrived at the Arapahoe County sheriff's office with a warrant for Holliday's arrest for running a bunko confidence card game swindling $150 from a victim. Arapaho County Sheriff Michael Spangler refused to honor the warrant saying he was holding Holliday until Arizona officials with the proper paperwork arrived.[10]

In Arizona, a legal war raged between Pima County Sheriff Bob Paul and Cochise County Sheriff Johnny Behan over who had the right to deliver Holliday's extradition papers to Denver. Holliday told a *Denver Republican* reporter, "John Behan . . . would give any amount of money to have me killed. . . . Should he get me in his power, my life would not be worth much." The governor of Arizona finally decided in favor of Pima County Sheriff Paul.[11]

Bat was waging a campaign in the Denver papers stating Holliday was not as bad as his enemies made him out to be; then he attacked Mallen's credibility. He got Mallen to admit in public he might have been mistaken about Holliday killing his partner in Utah as Holliday had never been to Utah. Bat questioned Mallen's deputy sheriff credentials in the newspapers and reports circulated Mallen had been involved in a swindle. The *Republican* reported, "Masterson . . . claims that Mallen is a fraud and a friend of the cowboys, whose only object is to get Holladay [sic] back in order that he might be killed."[12]

Sheriff Paul arrived in Denver with the extradition paperwork, which did not have the proper Arizona seals, so he had to wait until Arizona's governor's office sent him new paperwork. Rumors circulated that the cowboys were lying in wait to ambush Sheriff Paul on his return to Arizona and kill Holliday.[13]

The extradition hearing was set for May 30. The night before the hearing, Bat met with Colorado Governor Fredrick Pitkin along with the *Denver Tribune* capitol reporter E. D. Cowen. Bat presented evidence there were plans to murder Holliday on his return to Arizona. The governor called Pima County Sheriff Paul into his office, who confirmed Bat's findings there was a plot to kill Holliday, but he assured the governor Holliday would be protected. Governor Pitkin denied extradition based on the faulty extradition papers and that the Pueblo warrant for Holliday's arrest took precedence.[14]

Pueblo City Marshal Jameson arrived the next day and took Holliday into custody. Bat went along to Pueblo and then continued on to Trinidad. This was the last he would see Holliday. Holliday put up a bond and was released. His case was put off indefinitely, and when he died of tuberculosis in 1887, he was still under bond in Pueblo. Bat later said, "The charge . . . was nothing more than subterfuge on my part to prevent him from being taken out of state by the Arizona authorities."[15]

Wyatt and Warren Earp remained in Gunnison. They believed the governor of Arizona would vindicate them and they would be able to return to Arizona. Wyatt told the *Gunnison News-Democrat*, "My lawyers will have a petition for a pardon drawn up. Everyone in Tombstone knows that we did nothing but our duty." He believed Arizona Governor Frederick Tritle knew the facts and would sign a pardon within a few weeks. He told the newspaper he had plans to run against Johnny Behan for Cochise County Sheriff.[16]

At the same time Doc Holliday was released on bond in Pueblo, it was learned Perry Mallen, the man who had arrested him, was not a lawman, but a fraud and swindler, cheating a Denver resident out of $310 before disappearing.[17]

Holliday joined the Earps in Gunnison for a couple of weeks. All three were well armed, and when Doc drank too much and got out of hand, the Earps quietly hustled him away.[18]

Throughout the summer of 1882, Wyatt and Warren continued to wait for their pardons, but the Earps were too much of a political issue in Arizona. If the governor pardoned them, he would be committing political suicide. Their only consolation would be no one ever made a serious attempt to extradite them to Arizona. Late that year, they left Gunnison traveling to California.[19]

The summer of 1882 was peaceful in Trinidad. Bat and his deputies did a good job tamping down violence and running undesirables out of town.

The most violent act that summer happened between peace officers while Bat was gone. On August 19, Las Animas County Undersheriff M. B. McGraw fought with George Goodell, one of Bat's policemen. Criminals had recently escaped from the jail managed by the sheriff's office. The *Trinidad News* printed editorials critical of the sheriff's office based on insider information.

Undersheriff McGraw became furious when he learned Officer Goodell was the informant. At 9:10 a.m., Goodell was standing in the street as McGraw walked up close to him, said something, put his right hand on his gun, and using his left hand slapped Goodell's face. Goodell pulled his gun and shot McGraw in the right arm. As McGraw dropped his gun, Goodell rapidly fired three more shots into McGraw. Deputy Sheriff H. E. Hardy jumped on Goodell's back trying to stop him as Goodell picked up McGraw's gun and fired two more shots at McGraw before being controlled. McGraw died two days later, but Goodell was not charged as the coroner's court found "that said shooting and killing was not done with felonious intent."[20]

In late October 1882, Las Animas County hired Jim Masterson as a deputy sheriff while Bat and his officers continued to keep the peace in town. Bat participated in his share of scuffles with troublemakers. While Bat was arresting a drunk, he gave Bat a severe whack to the head with a cane. In another arrest tussle, Bat lost a valuable diamond ring, offering a reward for its return. Bat displayed compassion for ne'er-do-wells. He ordered a drunken vagrant out of town, but later that cold night, he found the man shivering along the road and gave him a place to sleep for the night in the county jail.[21]

Through the winter of 1883, Bat continued to uphold the law in Trinidad while continuing with his avocation—gambling. He dealt faro and was always available for a high-stakes poker game.[22]

Trinidad's municipal elections were held April 3, 1883. Up until this election, the city marshal position had always been appointed, but the requirements changed. Now the city marshal's position was an elected position. Lou Kreeger, who had been city marshal before Bat, ran against him on the Democrat ticket. Bat's gambling became one of the issues. The Republican ticket went down in defeat losing almost all municipal positions including the mayor and marshal's office. Bat lost to Kreeger 637 to 248 votes. Brother Jim was soon on the police force once again working for Kreeger.[23]

Bat's last act as Trinidad's marshal was to interfere in a footrace between a New Mexican and a Denver runner. Betting was heavy. The odds were in favor of the Denver runner, who Bat knew threw races. Bat positioned himself near the finish line, so he could view the entire race. The two runners were at the starting line. Just before the starting pistol was fired, the Denver runner bent down to tie his shoe. The New Mexican runner sprinted ahead. The Denver runner straightened and ran fast but would never catch the New Mexican. Just before the New Mexican reached the finish line, Bat stuck out his foot tripping him. He fell to the ground short of the finish line forcing the Denverite to finish first. Chaos ensued. The race results were void based on Bat's interference. He obtained warrants for the arrest of the runners, their backers, and the race promoters, and all wagered money was returned to the rightful owners. On April 11, Bat said goodbye to Trinidad, relocating to Denver.[24]

When Wyatt and Warren Earp left Gunnison for California in late 1882, they did not go to their parents' home in Colton where Wyatt's wife, Mattie, was living, but they traveled to San Francisco where Virgil had gone to have the best surgeons examine his arm for further treatment and where Sadie Marcus lived. Turning his back on Mattie, Wyatt spent all his time with Sadie.[25]

Wyatt and Sadie left San Francisco together and in early 1883, settled in Gunnison, Colorado. Wyatt made a good living for them running faro games, investing, and occasionally working for Wells, Fargo. He tramped through the mountains prospecting, sometimes taking Sadie with him. They went on hunting and fishing trips, and Sadie said their life together in Gunnison was idyllic.[26]

CHAPTER 13

THE DODGE CITY WAR

Luke Short, Bat and Wyatt's gambler friend who had shot and killed Charlie Storms in Tombstone in 1881, had returned to Dodge City. Short became partners with Bill Harris owning half interest in the Long Branch Saloon as well as managing the saloon's gambling concession. Short, a Texan, was popular with the cowboys. Some of the Long Branch competitors including next-door neighbors George Hoover's liquor store and Mayor A. B. Webster's Alamo Saloon saw a drop in their businesses.[1]

City elections were to be held April 3, 1883. The anti–Dodge City Gang were pushing for more reform. Mayor Webster, who was part of the anti–Dodge City Gang, was not running again. Instead Larry Deger, who had once been city marshal, would run for mayor and protect Webster's interest. The Dodge City Gang ran Bill Harris, Short's partner, as their candidate for mayor. The mayoral campaign was bitter and fought in the two opposing newspapers. Deger won by a large majority.[2]

Three weeks after the election, the new city council passed two ordinances. Ordinance Number 70 dealt with prostitution, fining those who kept houses of ill fame between ten and one hundred dollars and fining prostitutes between ten and fifty dollars. Ordinance Number 71 had to do with vagrancy. The ordinance defined vagrants as more than just tramps. It included keepers of houses of ill fame and gambling houses. They could be fined from ten to one hundred dollars.[3] This was nothing new for prostitutes and gamblers. They saw it as a form of city tax. Usually the offender paid the fine and resumed business.

Saturday night, two days after the ordinances went into effect, City Marshal Jack Bridges and City Clerk L. C. Hartman, wearing a policeman badge, entered the Long Branch Saloon arresting three female singers on the grounds of prostitution. Short accepted the arrests until later that night he learned no other women had been arrested. All the other saloons still had women in them including two in Webster's Alamo Saloon next door.[4]

Short strapped on his guns and walked toward the jail with the purpose of freeing the Long Branch girls. Hartman stood outside the jail on the high wooden sidewalk. As he saw Short approaching, Hartman pulled his pistol and fired at Short, missing him. Short drew his pistol and shot at Hartman, who had already turned and started to run. Hartman tripped and fell headfirst off the sidewalk as Short's bullet flew past his head.[5]

Believing he had killed Hartman, Short returned to the Long Branch, barricaded the door, and waited with his shotgun. No one was willing to go in after him as the siege lasted through the night and into the next morning. The marshal sent a representative into the saloon, who told Short he had not killed Hartman; he had only scared him. If he surrendered, he would be taken to police court and fined a small amount for creating a disturbance.[6]

Short accepted the terms, laid down his shotgun and pistols, and stepped outside. Two police officers took him to jail where he was charged with assault. Short posted a two thousand dollar bond and was released. The next day, he was again arrested along with five other gamblers who were told they were undesirables. Short was denied access to his lawyers. One came in by train to see him, but he was met at the train station by Mayor Deger and armed men who prevented him from detraining in Dodge.[7]

Twenty-five armed men led by the mayor, city marshal, Alamo Saloon owner A. B. Webster, and City Clerk L. C. Hartman took Short and the other gamblers from jail, escorted them to the train station, and gave them the choice of taking the next eastbound or westbound train. Short took the train to Kansas City.[8]

Of course, Luke Short was angry about the way he was treated and run out of town, but he also was physically severed from his main investment, ownership in the Long Branch Saloon. No one offered him any compensation. He wired Bat Masterson in Denver for help.[9]

Bat took the next train east to Kansas City where he met with Luke and his old friend Charlie Bassett, former Ford County sheriff. Bat suggested Luke present his grievance to Kansas Governor George Washington Glick in Topeka to see if the governor would help reinstate him in his Dodge City business. In the meantime, Bat began organizing a band of gunfighters to protect Luke when he returned to Dodge.[10]

On May 10, Luke filed his petition with the governor. Governor Glick took it seriously, investigated the matter, and found what Luke had stated was correct. The governor wired Ford County Sheriff George Hinkle asking him to report on the matter. Hinkle responded, "Mr. L. E. Deger our mayor has compelled several persons to leave the city for refusing to comply with the ordinances. No mob exists nor is there any reason to fear any violence as I am amply able to preserve the peace. I showed your message to Mr. Deger who requests me to say that the act of compelling the parties to leave the city was simply to avoid difficulty and disorders. Everything is as quiet here as in the capital of the state and should I find myself unable to preserve the present quiet will unhesitatingly ask your assistance."[11]

While waiting for Sheriff Hinkle's response, Governor Glick contacted two companies of the Kansas National Guard to be ready to move on Dodge City. Their commanders responded stating they were ready. After receiving Sheriff Hinkle's response, a telegram arrived from two Dodge City businessmen, Robert Wright and Richard Hardesty, stating the town was peaceful.[12]

Instead of appeasing the governor, the Dodge City telegrams angered him. He responded with a lengthy letter to Sheriff Hinkle. In it he stated if Luke Short's petition was true then Mayor Deger was unfit for office, and "the man [Deger] whose duty it is to see that the ordinances are enforced by legal process in the courts, starts out to head a mob to drive people away from their homes and their business." The governor wrote it was wrong to enforce ordinances on only a few and not all equally. He told Hinkle it was his duty as sheriff to ensure "the life and property of every individual there is fully protected." He went on to say Hinkle needed to protect Short if he returned to his home and business. If Hinkle was incapable of doing this, the governor would send men who could do so. The governor ended the letter by stating he had assured Short that he and others could return to their homes and would be protected by Hinkle.[13]

Hinkle's telegram back to the governor read as if he still did not, or refused to, understand it was wrong to drive people out of town instead of trying them in court. He did not see it was his duty to protect Short if he returned to town. Hinkle said it was Short's own fault he was expelled from Dodge and the town's prominent citizens did not want him back.[14]

In the meantime, Bat sent a message to Wyatt in Gunnison telling him of Luke's predicament and asking for his assistance in reinstating Luke in the Long Branch Saloon. Wyatt headed east taking Sadie with him.[15]

The governor met with Luke and Bat telling them since the local authorities assured him there were no problems in Dodge City, he would not interfere. He said Luke could reestablish himself in the Long Branch and wished them good luck.[16]

Luke, Bat, and Wyatt began gathering gunfighter friends together in Caldwell, Kansas.[17] The Kansas newspapers were having a field day with all the back and forth between Dodge City, the governor, and the Luke Short supporters. They interviewed Bat, who said he was returning to Dodge to visit old friends. The papers told how Wyatt, who had killed many men, would be heading to Dodge with other gunmen.

Sheriff Hinkle began to worry. He sent a telegram to the governor on May 15, "Are parties coming with Short for the purpose of making trouble? Answer quick." There is no record of Governor Glick's response. However the governor responded, Hinkle began forming a forty-man posse to confront Short's gunmen. The governor stated he never gave Hinkle any order to do so. Hinkle and his posse began meeting trains to intercept Luke Short or any of his friends who might try to get off in Dodge.[18]

Short and his backers developed a plan that Wyatt and others would first enter Dodge City to negotiate Short's return. Wyatt was still respected by many in Dodge. Other gunmen would secretly enter town and take strategic positions in case there was trouble. Short and Bat would wait in Kinsley, Kansas, just outside of Dodge until it was safe to return.[19]

At 10:00 a.m., on June 4, 1883, the westbound train arrived in Dodge City with Wyatt and four friends: Texas Jack Vermillion, Dan Tipton, Johnny Millsap, and Johnny Green. Sheriff Hinkle must have given up meeting every train that arrived in town. The only person there to meet the train was Dodge City Special Policeman Prairie Dog Dave Morrow. Morrow greeted Wyatt and stated he believed Short had received a dirty deal from the city. Wyatt asked Morrow to appoint his friends and him city peace officers, so they could carry their guns. Morrow obliged him, walked over to the city marshal's office, and returned with five deputy marshal badges. Wyatt then placed his men at strategic positions around the plaza. Setting up his headquarters in the Long Branch Saloon, Wyatt sent word to A. B. Webster that he wanted to meet with the mayor and city council about Luke Short's situation.[20]

They agreed to meet with him. After much wrangling back and forth, Mayor Deger and the city council agreed Short could return to Dodge City to live and run his business and Bat was welcome in town.[21] However, that same day, Mayor Deger issued a proclamation closing all gambling places stating that some of

Short's friends, "several hard characters," had not left town quick enough.[22]

On June 5, Luke Short and Bat arrived in town and were met by a delegation of friends who escorted them to the Long Branch Saloon. Bat said, "I have conversed with a great many and they are unanimous in their expression of love for Short, both as a man and a good citizen."[23] That night, Major Harry Gryden, who was in town as an observer for Kansas Adjutant General Thomas Moonlight, sent him a telegram that arrived the morning of June 6: "Everything is settled. Parties have shook hands across the bloody chasm. A number of men with a record are here but all is lovely."[24]

A few minutes after the arrival of Gryden's telegram, Governor Glick received a telegram from Mayor Deger, Sheriff Hinkle, and four other officials: "Our city is overrun with desperate characters from Colorado, New Mexico, Arizona, and California. We cannot preserve the peace or enforce the laws. Will you send in two companies of militia at once to assist us in preserving the peace between all parties and enforcing the laws." Governor Glick responded saying he was sending Kansas Adjutant General Thomas Moonlight.[25]

Minutes after Moonlight left on the westbound train to Dodge, Sheriff Hinkle wired the governor: "The difficulty is settled, Shorts [sic] fighters have left town. I am satisfied we will not have any more trouble." Moonlight continued on to Dodge City anyway. Upon his arrival, everyone settled back down, and the city honored its agreement that Luke Short could continue running his business and live in Dodge City.[26] Moonlight organized a quasi-militia called the Glick Guards, a group made up of men from both factions.[27] Hopefully, they would be able to resolve any issues before they escalated into violence.

What would be called "the Dodge City War" was over. Right before Short's supporters started to drift away, photographer Charles Conkling took a photograph of those who did not mind having their picture taken. Some did not want a photograph record of their faces—maybe for good reasons. The photograph includes Wyatt Earp, Bat Masterson, Luke Short, Charlie Bassett, and others. It's one of the iconic pictures of the Old West and was dubbed "The Dodge City Peace Commission."[28] Bat and Wyatt, along with Sadie, left Dodge on June 10, 1883, heading back to Colorado on the westbound train.[29]

WYATT UNWELCOME IN JUNEAU, ALASKA

Wyatt Earp and Sadle had been in Alaska since 1897. After the first two years, they returned to the States and would travel by ship to Nome, Alaska, each summer season. Wyatt and his partner Charlie Hoxie ran the Dexter Saloon in that gold rush boomtown.[30]

In June 1901, Wyatt and Sadie were returning to Nome and planned a stopover in Juneau, Alaska, possibly looking to establish a business there. Learning "Wyatt Earp the notorious desperado" was about to disembark, the deputy US marshal based in Juneau formed a posse deputizing local citizens and met Wyatt at the docks. The marshal demanded Wyatt hand over his gun and said he was not welcome in Juneau.[31]

The marshal told Wyatt he could pick up his gun at the US marshal's office before his ship departed. Wyatt and Sadie left on the S.S. *Senator* that departed at 5:00 in the morning on June 29. This was well before the marshal's office was open, so Wyatt had to leave his weapon behind. He never returned to retrieve it.[32]

Wyatt's gun was a Smith & Wesson Model No. 3.[33] It's still in Juneau prominently displayed behind the bar in the Red Dog Saloon, a Juneau landmark since the gold rush days. Each year, thousands of visitors can gaze at Wyatt's Smith & Wesson as they enjoy good food and their favorite beverage.

CHAPTER 14

SEPARATE LIVES

After working together to help Luke Short in the Dodge City War, Wyatt and Bat went their separate ways. However, they did spend time together on occasion.

Bat's friend Pat Sughrue was running for Ford County sheriff in the fall of 1883, and Bat returned to Dodge to campaign for him. The anti–Dodge City Gang supported his opponent Fred Singer. The rival newspapers initiated a verbal war filled with barbs and banter with some of the anti-gang newspaper attacks aimed at Bat. He left for Colorado a few days before the election. As the voting polls opened, he returned to Dodge accompanied by Wyatt Earp. The *Globe* said both men's presence at the polls "had a moral effect on our would-be moral element, that was truly surprising. It is needless to say everything passed off quietly at the city precinct on election day." Sughrue won the election for Ford County sheriff.[1]

In January 1884, Bat was living in Trinidad, Colorado. Wyatt stopped to visit Bat after a Texas gambling tour.[2] During the late 1880s, Wyatt and Sadie were living in San Diego, California, when Bat visited them. He was on his way to Ensenada, California, to bring back an army deserter and asked Wyatt to help him. Sadie joined them, and they traveled by ship. It was a pleasant trip down and back with no problems from the prisoner.[3]

During the mid-1890s, Bat lived in Denver, Colorado, dealing cards and managing gambling houses. Wyatt and Sadie drifted into Denver for a short time, Wyatt dealing faro.[4] Bat and Wyatt must have spent time together—probably for the last time. Wyatt began spending most of his time on the West Coast, and Bat eventually moved to the East Coast. However, they remained friends supporting each other until their deaths.

Emma Walters was a singer and dancer from Philadelphia, Pennsylvania. She and Bat may have met in Trinidad or Denver sometime in the early 1880s. No record of their marriage has been found, but they lived together as husband and wife for the rest of their lives.[5]

Bat made Denver his headquarters off and on for twelve years, but he did spend time in Dodge and traveled around the West promoting prizefights, horse races, and other sporting events as well as his old standby profession dealing cards and gambling. People considered Bat a prizefight expert and he had plenty of engagements to act as referee in cities throughout the West. He helped organize Dodge City's baseball team and played football there. While in town, Bat and Bill Tilghman were judges for a three-hundred-yard foot race for a thousand-dollar prize between a white man named Sawyer and a black man named Hogan. The race was close with Hogan winning. The June 24, 1884, edition of the *Ford County Globe* stated, "'Bat' and 'Til' were the judges, therefore everything was on the square, and no grumbling was heard by the losers."[6]

Bat prided himself on being honest and running honest games. His pleasant nature attracted lots of people who became friends. Some of these people were not as honest as Bat such as the amoral Jeff Smith, better known as Soapy Smith, crime boss of Creed and Denver, Colorado.[7] Another bad man Bat met and corresponded with was Frank James, Jesse's older brother.[8]

In 1885, Bat's travels took him through Dakota Territory where he met the young Theodore Roosevelt. T. R., as Roosevelt liked to be called, and Bat hit it off and became lifelong friends.[9] At Dodge City's Fourth of July celebration that year, Bat was elected the most popular man in Dodge.[10] Things had changed since the days he was told to get out of Dodge after the Battle of the Plaza. Stories grew into legends over the years. One story was that in the late-1880s, Bat participated in a series of violent disputes over which Kansas towns would become county seats. The most famous of these disputes has been called "The Battle of the Cimarron." Bat was not involved in these disputes, but his brother Jim was.[11]

In late 1891, Creed, Colorado, was experiencing a silver boom, and Bat took a job managing the gambling at the Denver Exchange, a combination restaurant, saloon, and gambling hall, considered the most popular business in Creed. Bat was good at keeping order in the Exchange where other establishments had problems.[12] He resigned in the fall of 1892 and actively promoted and worked at major prizefights across the country. He was nationally recognized as a prizefight expert. He returned to Denver during the winter of 1894 where he continued in the gambling profession.[13]

In June 1895, Bat was hired as bodyguard for multi-millionaire George Gould, who had been receiving death threats. Bat and Emma moved to New York City and enjoyed living there until eight months later when the man threatening Gould was caught. Returning to Denver, Bat took up his old profession again.[14]

From time to time, Bat was appointed a special deputy sheriff for Arapaho County, Colorado. In one instance, he had to fire his pistol to stop an illegal vote count for city alderman when one candidate's supporters had excluded the opposition's supporters from the count.[15]

Bat became embroiled in Denver politics and disputes in Denver's sports and athletic scene. He finally became disgusted with it all, and in May 1902, Bat and Emma left Denver, never to return.[16]

The Mastersons moved to New York City, and in early 1903, William Lewis, managing editor for the New York newspaper *The Morning Telegraph*, hired Bat as a reporter and later as a staff writer concentrating on sports.[17] He worked for *The Morning Telegraph* for the next eighteen years.

In 1905, President Theodore Roosevelt personally requested US Marshal William Henkle appoint Bat Masterson as a deputy US marshal for the Southern District of New York. On February 5, 1905, Henkle made the announcement and Bat was sworn in on March 28, 1905. He didn't do much other than go to the White House when T. R. invited him. Roosevelt did not run for reelection in 1908, and his successor William Howard Taft's administration abolished Bat's position on August 1, 1909.[18]

In 1911, Bat became vice president of *The Morning Telegraph* and remained active in sports reporting. As in other towns, he remained a controversial character in New York City.[19]

Bat enjoyed western movies and especially the acting of William S. Hart. Bat wrote, "Mr. Hart [is] a true type of that reckless nomad who flourished on the border when the six-shooter was the final arbiter of all disputes between man and man." After meeting Bat in 1918, Hart and Bat became lifelong friends. Hart said, "I play the hero that 'Bat' Masterson inspired. . . . More than any other man I have ever met I admire and respect him."[20]

Bat was sixty-seven years old when on October 25, 1921, he died at his desk as he worked on a boxing match story.[21] At Bat's funeral, William Muldoon, New York Boxing Commissioner, who knew Bat for forty years, told the hundreds of people attending, "[I] had never known Bat Masterson to do a dishonorable deed, never to betray a friend, never to connive at dishonor and never to fear an enemy."[22]

In a December 3, 1896, *San Francisco Chronicle* interview, Wyatt Earp had said Bat Masterson was "the best friend I have on earth."[23]

After learning Wyatt was living with Sadie and would not be coming back to her, Wyatt's wife, Mattie, returned to Arizona. Alcohol and drugs further ruined her life, and she committed suicide by overdosing on laudanum in Pinal, Arizona, on July 3, 1888.[24]

At times Wyatt and Sadie's relationship was rocky, but they stayed together for the rest of their lives. There is no record of their marriage or what year it occurred, but Sadie claimed they were at sea with investor and racehorse enthusiast Lucky Baldwin on his yacht beyond the US territorial limit, where the captain of his yacht married them.[25]

In early 1884, Wyatt and Sadie followed the latest gold rush to the Coeur d'Alene area of Idaho where he and brother Jim opened the White Elephant Saloon in Eagle City.[26] The Earps partnered with others investing in property and claims. They had several disputes in court over claims; some they won, and some they lost. Kootenai County hired Wyatt as a deputy sheriff in Eagle City. The area was also claimed by Shoshone County that had a sheriff and deputy sheriff also in Eagle City.[27]

On March 29, two groups of men who had been disputing over the ownership of a downtown Eagle City lot started shooting at each other in town. Wyatt, Jim, and the Shoshone County sheriff stepped between the two warring groups, joked about their poor marksmanship, and ordered them to stop firing, which they did. Afterwards the opposing two leaders met, smoked, and complimented each other on their courage.[28]

The Coeur d'Alene mining boom soon ended, and the Earps left. They moved about the west the next couple of years arriving in the latest booming mining camp or town noted for gambling. While in Aspen, Colorado, Wyatt assisted a deputy US marshal from Arizona in the arrest of a stagecoach robber.[29]

In 1886, San Diego, California, was experiencing an economic boom with an influx of new people and rising property values. Wyatt and Sadie moved there and bought investment property. Wyatt gambled, judged horse races, and refereed prizefights. His notoriety continued to build in 1887 when the nationally circulated *Police Gazette* retold the story of Wyatt's exploits in Arizona stating, "Wyatt S. Earp is one of the most famous Western characters living . . . who created such a sensation a few years since at

Tombstone, Arizona, by completely exterminating a whole band of out-lawed cut-throats."[30]

After four years in San Diego, Wyatt and Sadie moved to her hometown, San Francisco. Wyatt was hired to manage a stable in Santa Rosa and continued working in the horse racing business—racing his own horses and betting on the races. Wyatt became friends with the rich and powerful such as investor Lucky Baldwin and newspaper publisher William Randolph Hearst.[31]

Wyatt was asked to referee the heavyweight championship of the world using for the first time the Marquess of Queensbury rules, one of which was no hitting below the belt. Wyatt did not want to do it but was finally convinced to referee. Bob Fitzsimmons would be defending his title of world champion against the contender Tom Sharkey. The fight was held on December 3, 1896, before a crowd of over ten thousand people. For the first time, women could be spectators.[32]

Before the fight began, police captain Charles Wittman noticed a bulge in Wyatt's pocket and asked him if he had a gun. Wyatt said he did, and Wittman told Wyatt to hand it over.[33]

Fitzsimmons got the better of Sharkey through seven rounds. During the eighth round, Fitzsimmons pummeled Sharkey without letup and it looked like Sharkey was done for when Fitzsimmons hit him with a blow below the belt that sent Sharkey to the floor writhing in pain. Wyatt ruled Fitzsimmons had fouled Sharkey and declared Sharkey the winner. The crowd broke into pandemonium. Fitzsimmons and his backers as well as all those who had bet on Fitzsimmons to win were furious.[34]

After the fight, Sharkey's people would not allow the official medical examiner and others into the room to see how bad Sharkey was. Rumors began to fly that he really wasn't injured and that Wyatt had fixed the fight. Fitzsimmons and his backers were constantly being interviewed about it by newspaper reporters, and it was the gossip of the saloons. Wyatt's reputation was damaged and there was no way to reclaim it. In the end only one of three things had to have happened: Fitzsimmons did hit Sharkey hard below the belt and Wyatt made the right call; Sharkey pretended to be fouled fooling Wyatt; or Wyatt took a bribe and fixed the fight.[35]

In Denver, Bat Masterson stepped up to defend Wyatt's honor. He had bet heavily on Fitzsimmons and lost, and so did Felix O'Neill, a Denver politician and sports gambler who was bad mouthing Wyatt around town. They ran into each other at a saloon. O'Neill called to Bat across the saloon that Wyatt was a scoundrel, thief, and bully. Bat tried to reason with O'Neill telling him Wyatt was his friend and no cheat, saying, "In all America there is not a fairer, squarer, straighter man than Wyatt Earp." O'Neill continued to run down Wyatt. Bat ended the argument with his fists.[36]

Alaska was the new gold mining frontier. Wyatt and Sadie headed to Nome, Alaska, in the fall of 1897. Wyatt and Charlie Hoxie opened the Dexter Saloon, making money and friends. The *Nome Gold Digger* wrote, "Wyatt Earp . . . is a celebrated personage in nearly all the mining camps of the country." The Earps stayed in Alaska the first two years through the winter, and then after that they would head to the States for the winter. In 1901, they sold their Alaskan assets and never returned.[37]

In 1902, the Earps moved to Tonopah, Nevada, where Wyatt partnered with Al Martin in a saloon, The Northern, and did some prospecting. US Marshal J. F. Emmitt hired Wyatt as a deputy US marshal, and John Hays Hammond hired him to supervise his mine site guards.[38]

Five years later, Wyatt and Sadie moved to Los Angeles where they lived the rest of their lives together. Wyatt continued to gamble, took a few special jobs for the Los Angeles police department, invested in mines and oil, and continued to prospect, never hitting it big.[39]

Wyatt had met the author Jack London while in Alaska. In 1915, London took Wyatt to a movie set outside Los Angeles.

Wyatt began visiting movie sets, especially Westerns, and started friendships with actors such as Tom Mix. The most notable actor he befriended was cowboy actor William S. Hart. Wyatt tried to teach Hart how to draw his pistol fast and laughed at Hart's fumbling. They began a correspondence that lasted for years.[40] Wyatt was concerned with what he thought was false information being spread in magazines and books about his time in Arizona, and Hart worked with him to find a writer and publisher who could help.[41]

Wyatt befriended a young man who was working as a prop man and extra whose name was Marion Morrison, who would later change his name to John Wayne. Wayne later told Hugh O'Brian, who portrayed Wyatt Earp in the television series, that he based his Western lawman character on his conversations with Wyatt Earp.[42]

In the 1920s, Wyatt and Sadie's funds were low, and they lived partly on charity from others. Wyatt continued to try to get someone to write and publish his story for him, but all efforts were flops.[43]

Stuart Lake, who had become friends with Bat Masterson in New York City, was fascinated with Wyatt's life. After hearing Bat tell stories of Wyatt's adventures in the West, Lake began writing to Wyatt on December 25, 1927. He got Wyatt's approval to write his story and moved to California to be able to interview Wyatt firsthand. They probably had at least six meetings together and extensive correspondence as Lake tried to fill in the gaps of the information he had to extract out of Wyatt. Unfortunately, the book would have to be finished without Wyatt's final review and approval. Wyatt had prostate complications and became weakened after a bout of the flu. On January 13, 1929, Wyatt Earp died.[44]

Bat Masterson wrote of Wyatt, "Wyatt Earp . . . has excited, by his display of great courage and nerve under trying conditions, the envy and hatred of those small minded creatures with which the world seems to be abundantly peopled, and whose sole delight in life seems to be in fly-specking the reputations of real men. I have known him since the early seventies and have always found him a quiet, unassuming man, not given to brag or bluster, but at all times and under all circumstances a loyal friend and an equally dangerous enemy."[45]

Bat Masterson and Wyatt Earp's legacies live on after their deaths in a variety of forms. Some of these are well known and others subtle.

In 1905, Alfred Henry Lewis published a fictionalized version of Bat's life on the frontier called *The Sunset Trail*. Lewis created fictional characters sprinkled in with "Mr. Masterson" and other real-life characters. He created dialogue and sentimental scenes such as the death of Mollie Brennan at Sweetwater, Texas:

> *Hard hit as he was, Mr. Masterson raised the Wild Rose [Mollie Brennan] in his arms. She opened her brown eyes, swimming with love.*
>
> *"He said you wanted me," whispered the Wild Rose.*
>
> *Mr. Masterson looked into the soft depths, saw that love and knew it for his own. Even as he gazed, the warm lights failed and faded; the rose flush deserted the cheek. In the arms of Mr. Masterson, the Wild Rose lay dead.*[46]

One of Bat's many friends was a young reporter, Damon Runyon, who enjoyed listening to Bat's tales of the West. Later, Runyon became famous writing humorous short stories. One was titled "The Idyll of Miss Sarah Brown." Runyon patterned the main male character after Bat naming him Sky Masterson. The story became the basis of a Broadway musical that later became a motion picture in 1955 starring Marlin Brando as Sky Masterson in *Guys and Dolls*.[47] Nine additional movies were made about Bat or had him involved as a character. A few of the films he was portrayed in were *Trail Street* (1947) starring Randolph Scott, *Masterson of Kansas* (1954) starring George Montgomery, and *The Gunfight at Dodge City* (1959) starring Joel McCrea. Gene Barry portrayed Bat in the television series *Bat Masterson* (1958–1961).[48]

Wyatt tried to get his life story written but experienced disappointment and shoddy writing until he met Stuart Lake. Unfortunately for Wyatt, Lake's biography *Wyatt Earp: Frontier Marshal* would not be published until after Wyatt's death. Lake had to rely on his notes taken during interviews with Wyatt and Wyatt's letters. Lake admitted to inventing dialogue, and he has been criticized at the worst making up stories and at the best embellishing them.[49]

As mentioned earlier, John Wayne modeled his Western lawman characters after Wyatt. Wyatt was portrayed in twelve movies. A few of the films were *Frontier Marshal* (1939) starring Randolph Scott, *My Darling Clementine* (1946) starring Henry Fonda, *Gunfight at the O.K. Corral* (1957) starring Burt Lancaster, *Tombstone* (1993) starring Kurt Russell, and *Wyatt Earp* (1994) starring Kevin Costner. Hugh O'Brian portrayed Wyatt in the television series *The Life and Legend of Wyatt Earp* (1955–1961).[50]

William Hart best summed up Wyatt and Bat's lives while they still lived in a tribute to them published in the October 9, 1921, edition of the *Morning Telegraph*:

> *Now I am just an actor—a mere player—seeking to reproduce the lives of those great gunmen who molded a new country for us to live in and enjoy peace and prosperity. And we have today in America two of these men with us in the flesh. It is not astounding that their deeds of heroism are not more known. The whole of our great continent separates them. One is on the Pacific, the other on the Atlantic Coast. One resides in Pasadena, Calif., the other in New York City. One is Wyatt Earp, the other William B. Masterson.*[51]

Hart went on to describe the dangerous characters of the West:

To enforce the law under such conditions and in such a country took the very highest order of manhood, coupled with a cool head and iron nerve.

Such men were Bat Masterson and Wyatt Earp. . . . They never sought trouble—they used every means at their command to avoid it, but once it came, the lawbreakers who opposed them suddenly found they were in the middle of hell with the lights out.

Let us not forget these living Americans who, when they pass on, will be remembered by hundreds of generations. For no history of the West can be written without their wonderful deeds being recorded.[52]

Amen.

CHAPTER 15
END OF THE TRAIL

Who was greatest lawman, Bat or Wyatt? It's not an easy question to answer. At times they failed to uphold the law or stretched their interpretation and use of the law. Being a lawman was only one of many jobs they performed during their lives.

I asked people who assisted me in the research and review of this book to give me their thoughts on Wyatt and Bat's law enforcement actions during their frontier days. Below are some of their comments.

Author of *Dodge City: Wyatt Earp, Bat Masterson, and the Wickedest Town in the American West*, Tom Clavin said, "To me, hands down, Bat was the better lawman. For one thing, he served as a sheriff and had postings elsewhere as a lawman and was a federal officer in New York. Wyatt didn't have as much experience and never served as a sheriff or marshal. However, he was the de facto marshal in Dodge City for a time and was hailed as a good peace officer. After Tombstone he was a (somewhat disputed) deputy US marshal."

Longtime friend Phil "Theta" Bowden, who critiqued this book, wrote, "Wyatt was a cold-blooded murderer and should have been arrested. When family was involved, he took a Godfather-like approach and killed several men in the name of vengeance. Bat, on the other hand, was a much more straightforward character. Straight up the line, he was a moral man, trying to do his best, time and again—a man truly to be admired."

B. Keith Williams, who edited the manuscript, wrote, "One of my strongest, long-standing pet peeves has been a person using his public office or position for personal or spiteful gains, personal agendas, prejudices, biases, political aspirations, or vengeful retaliations; and at the expense of the less powerful or less positioned. Wyatt Earp's propensity to 'hide behind the badge' causes me to choose Bat Masterson. While certainly not the only occurrence in history, but, in my opinion, it is certainly one of the more flagrant."

Lifelong cowboy, outdoorsman, and good friend Mike Pellerzi after reviewing this book said, "I would have done the same thing as Wyatt, but that's me."

Jim Hatzell, the book's illustrator, wrote, "After reading Bill's manuscript, I have to admit I'm a bit surprised to throw my lot with Mr. Masterson! What an amazing life and career he had! And when does he get his stand-alone movie?"

Mile Leidholt, Sheriff of Hughes County, South Dakota, said, "As someone who has spent over forty-three years enforcing the law and holding people accountable for their actions, I believe Bat Masterson was the better lawman. It appears that he had the best moral compass of the two and was a duly elected sheriff who was accountable to those who elected him."

For me, it was tough to decide who was the best lawman, Wyatt or Bat. As I researched and wrote, and went back and read and reread, to be honest, I just didn't know at first who was the best lawman. I flipped back and forth—one week it was clearly Bat, and the next it was definitely Wyatt.

In the end, it boils down to the rule of law for me. I believe for society to function, peace officers need to live by and enforce the laws and regulations created by the legislative branches of federal, state, and local governments. Peace officers are sworn to uphold the laws of the land—nothing more and nothing less. The judicial system is to determine if a person has broken the law and if so what the penalty is to be.

Bat upheld the law even when his own brother Ed was killed. He could have easily gone and killed both Wagner and Walker, but after shooting them to stop their actions, he did not proceed to kill them there on the spot. Wyatt, on the other hand, had had enough with the cowboys. He must have believed the legal system was broken. Every time one of the cowboys was taken before a judge they were released. After Virgil was severely wounded and Morgan murdered, Wyatt must have snapped when he saw Ike Clanton and Frank Stilwell waiting to ambush Virgil at the Tucson railroad station. Instead of arresting them, he executed Stilwell on the spot. The same can be said about Indian Charlie, whom Wyatt had surrounded with his posse. There was no way Indian Charlie could escape them, but again Wyatt became his own judge, jury, and executioner. If a law enforcement officer does this, the fabric of our system of government begins to break down. Wyatt not only failed to uphold the law during his vendetta, but he used the office of deputy US marshal to carry out his vengeance.

Therefore, I believe Bat Masterson was the best lawman.

But what about Wyatt as an individual? Finding your older brother lying in the street shotgunned and not knowing if he would live, and then recognizing those same men who shot him were out to kill him again, and seeing your little brother shot and killed before your eyes and knowing who those killers were and knowing most likely the judicial system would let them off, would drive most anyone to act. I cannot fault Wyatt for going after the cowboy murderers of his brother; but when people knowingly step outside the bounds of the law, they should expect whatever consequences might fall.

Remember, John Wayne said that when he played a Western lawman, he modeled his character after Wyatt Earp. So, it's fitting to end with a quote that personifies Wyatt Earp spoken by John Wayne in the 1953 movie *Hondo*, "A man ought'a do what he thinks is best."

NOTES

INTRODUCTION

1 W. B. (Bat) Masterson, *Famous Gunfighters of the Western Frontier: Wyatt Earp, Doc Holliday, Luke Short and Others* (Mineola, NY: Dover Publications Inc., 2009), 25–28.

2 Stuart N. Lake, *Wyatt Earp: Frontier Marshal* (New York, NY: Pocket Books, 1994), 36.

3 Stuart N. Lake, *Wyatt Earp: Frontier Marshal*, xvi.

CHAPTER 1: EARLY YEARS

1 Stuart N. Lake, *Wyatt Earp: Frontier Marshal*, 3.

2 Stuart N. Lake, *Wyatt Earp: Frontier Marshal*, 3–6.

3 Stuart N. Lake, *Wyatt Earp: Frontier Marshal*, 3.

4 Stuart N. Lake, *Wyatt Earp: Frontier Marshal*, 7.

5 Robert K. DeArment, *Bat Masterson: The Man and the Legend* (Norman: University of Oklahoma Press, 1979), 9–14.

6 Tom Clavin, *Dodge City: Wyatt Earp, Bat Masterson, and the Wickedest Town in the American West* (New York, NY: St. Martin's Press, 2017), 30.

7 Stuart N. Lake, *Wyatt Earp: Frontier Marshal*, 9–10.

8 Stuart N. Lake, *Wyatt Earp: Frontier Marshal*, 7–8.

9 Ibid.

10 Stuart N. Lake, *Wyatt Earp: Frontier Marshal*, 9.

11 Stuart N. Lake, *Wyatt Earp: Frontier Marshal*, 12–13.

12 Stuart N. Lake, *Wyatt Earp: Frontier Marshal*, 13.

13 Stuart N. Lake, *Wyatt Earp: Frontier Marshal*, 14–15.

14 Stuart N. Lake, *Wyatt Earp: Frontier Marshal*, 15.

15 Stuart N. Lake, *Wyatt Earp: Frontier Marshal*, 14–17.

16 Stuart N. Lake, *Wyatt Earp: Frontier Marshal*, 17.

17 City of San Bernardino, "Diary of the Earp Wagon Train to San Bernardino by Sarah Jane Rousseau." Accessed March 30, 2018. www.ci.san-bernardino.ca.us/about/history/pioneer_women/sarah_jane_rousseau.asp

18 City of San Bernardino, "Wyatt Earp in San Bernardino." Accessed March 4, 2018. www.ci.san-bernardino.ca.us/about/history/wyatt_earp.asp. Stuart N. Lake, *Wyatt Earp: Frontier Marshal*, 17–18.

19 Casey Tefertiller, *Wyatt Earp: The Life Behind the Legend* (New York, NY: John Wiley & Sons, Inc., 1997), 3.

20 Tom Clavin, *Dodge City: Wyatt Earp, Bat Masterson, and the Wickedest Town in the American West* 36–37.

21 Stuart N. Lake, *Wyatt Earp: Frontier Marshal*, 23–24.

22 Stuart N. Lake, *Wyatt Earp: Frontier Marshal*, 25–26.

23 Stuart N. Lake, *Wyatt Earp: Frontier Marshal*, 26.

24 Stuart N. Lake, *Wyatt Earp: Frontier Marshal*, 26–27.

25 Roger Jay, "Wyatt Earp's Lost Year," *Wild West Magazine*, June 12, 2006.

26 Sherry Monahan, *Mrs. Earp: The Lives and Lovers of the Earp Brothers* (Guilford, CT: Globe Pequot Press, 2013), 1.

27 Sherry Monahan, *Mrs. Earp: The Lives and Lovers of the Earp Brothers*, 4.

28 Casey Tefertiller, *Wyatt Earp: The Life Behind the Legend*, 4.

29 Sherry Monahan, *Mrs. Earp: The Lives and Lovers of the Earp Brothers*, 4.

30 Stuart N. Lake, *Wyatt Earp: Frontier Marshal*, 27.

31 Casey Tefertiller, *Wyatt Earp: The Life Behind the Legend*, 4.

32 Wyatt Earp History Page, accessed November 27, 2017, www.wyattearp.net.

33 Casey Tefertiller, *Wyatt Earp: The Life Behind the Legend*, 4–5.

34 Bartholomaeus Masterson in the 1870 US Census in St. Clair County, Illinois.

35 Stuart N. Lake, *Wyatt Earp: Frontier Marshal*, 28–31.

36 Casey Tefertiller, *Wyatt Earp: The Life Behind the Legend*, 5.

37 Stuart N. Lake, *Wyatt Earp: Frontier Marshal*, 31–32, 41–42.

38 Robert K. DeArment, *Bat Masterson: The Man and the Legend*, 14.

39 Ibid.

40 James A. Crutchfield, Candy Moulton, and Terry Del Bene (eds.), *The Settlement of America: Encyclopedia of Westward Expansion from Jamestown to the Closing of the Frontier*, Vol. 1 (Armonk, NY: M. E. Sharpe Inc., 2011), 83–84.

41 Wayne Gard, *The Great Buffalo Hunt* (New York, NY: Alfred A. Knopf, 1960), 90–91.

42 Henry Crawford, retired curator of history, Museum of Texas Tech University, and founder of History by Choice, personal e-mail communication, March 29, 2018. Wayne Gard, *The Great Buffalo Hunt*, 123–124.

43 Henry Crawford, personal e-mail communication, March 29, 2018.

44 James A. Crutchfield, Candy Moulton, and Terry Del Bene (eds.), *The Settlement of America: Encyclopedia of Westward Expansion from Jamestown to the Closing of the Frontier*, 84.

45 National Bison Association, accessed December 12, 2017, https://bisoncentral.com/general-info/bison-1-millionbison-1-million-2/bison-1-million/.

CHAPTER 2: HUNTING BUFFALO AND CROSSING PATHS

1 Robert K. DeArment, *Bat Masterson: The Man and the Legend*, 16.

2 Robert K. DeArment, *Bat Masterson: The Man and the Legend*, 16–17.

3 Wayne Gard, *The Great Buffalo Hunt*, 125–126.

4 Wayne Gard, *The Great Buffalo Hunt*, 127.

5 Stuart N. Lake, *Wyatt Earp: Frontier Marshal*, 42–45.

6 Stuart N. Lake, *Wyatt Earp: Frontier Marshal*, 53–54.

7 Stuart N. Lake, *Wyatt Earp: Frontier Marshal*, 51–52.

8 Personal communication with historian Henry B. Crawford, retired curator of history, Museum of Texas Tech University, and founder of History by Choice, who wrote "As for using a shotgun, it can be done if he is loading a solid round ball and shooting relatively close range. Hunters on the early frontier have taken down buffalo with smoothbore muzzleloaders of large caliber. It made me think about how fur trappers shot buffalo and other large western game with a Northwest Trade Gun, a smoothbore .62 caliber flintlock. A 12-gauge shotgun shooting a .69 round ball would have no problem."

9 Ibid.

10 Casey Tefertiller, *Wyatt Earp: The Life Behind the Legend*, 5.

11 Wayne Gard, *The Great Buffalo Hunt*, 92.

12 Sherry Monahan, *Mrs. Earp: The Wives and Lovers of the Earp Brothers*, 10.

13 Sherry Monahan, *Mrs. Earp: The Wives and Lovers of the Earp Brothers*, 10–11.

14 Stuart N. Lake, *Wyatt Earp: Frontier Marshal*, 66.

15 Robert K. DeArment, *Bat Masterson: The Man and the Legend*, 19–20.

16 Walter R. Borneman, *Rival Rails: The Race to Build America's Greatest Transcontinental Railroad* (New York, NY: Random House, 2010), 68–69.

17 Walter R. Borneman, *Rival Rails: The Race to Build America's Greatest Transcontinental Railroad*, 69.

18 Robert K. DeArment, *Bat Masterson: The Man and the Legend*, 19–20.

19 Robert K. DeArment, *Bat Masterson: The Man and the Legend*, 20.

20 Wayne Gard, *The Great Buffalo Hunt*, 101.

21 Robert K. DeArment, *Bat Masterson: The Man and the Legend*, 21.

22 Roger Jay, "Wyatt Earp's Lost Year," *Wild West Magazine*, June 12, 2006.

23 Robert K. DeArment, *Bat Masterson: The Man and the Legend*, 21.

24 Robert K. DeArment, *Bat Masterson: The Man and the Legend*, 23.

25 Olive K. Dixon, *Life of Billy Dixon: Plainsman, Scout and Pioneer* (Abilene, TX: State House Press, 1987), 115.

26 Miles Gilbert, *Getting a Stand* (Union City, TN: Pioneer Press, 1986), 35.

27 Miles Gilbert, *Getting a Stand*, 36.

28 Miles Gilbert, *Getting a Stand*, 37.

29 Ibid.

30 Robert K. DeArment, *Bat Masterson: The Man and the Legend*, 25.

31 Robert K. DeArment, *Bat Masterson: The Man and the Legend*, 29.

32 Robert K. DeArment, *Bat Masterson: The Man and the Legend*, 27.

33 Tom Clavin, *Dodge City: Wyatt Earp, Bat Masterson, and the Wickedest Town in the American West*, 27.

34 Miles Gilbert, *Getting a Stand*, 41.

35 Ford County Historical Society, accessed December 17, 2017. www.kansas history.us/fordco.

36 Stuart N. Lake, *Wyatt Earp: Frontier Marshal*, 66.

37 Robert K. DeArment, *Bat Masterson: The Man and the Legend*, 32.

38 Robert K. DeArment, *Bat Masterson: The Man and the Legend*, 32–33.

39 Robert K. DeArment, *Bat Masterson: The Man and the Legend*, 33.

40 James A. Crutchfield, Candy Moulton, and Terry Del Bene (eds.), *The Settlement of America: Encyclopedia of Westward Expansion from Jamestown to the Closing of the Frontier*, 118.

41 Stuart N. Lake, *Wyatt Earp: Frontier Marshal*, 66, 74–75.

42 Bill O'Neal, *Encyclopedia of Western Gunfighters* (Norman: University of Oklahoma Press, 1979), 315–318.

43 Bill O'Neal, *Encyclopedia of Western Gunfighters*, 321–322.

44 Stuart N. Lake, *Wyatt Earp: Frontier Marshal*, 79.

45 Casey Tefertiller, *Wyatt Earp: The Life Behind the Legend*, 6–7.

46 W. M. Walton, annotated by Lisa Lach, *Life and Adventures of Ben Thompson Famous Texan* (Austin, TX: The Steck Company Publishers, 2016), 178.

47 Casey Tefertiller, *Wyatt Earp: The Life Behind the Legend*, 7.

48 Lee A. Silva, *Wyatt Earp: A Biography of the Legend, Vol. 1: The Cowtown Years* (Santa Anna, CA: Graphic Publishers, 2002), 200.

49 Casey Tefertiller, *Wyatt Earp: The Life Behind the Legend*, 7.

50 Casey Tefertiller, *Wyatt Earp: The Life Behind the Legend*, 7–8.

51 Lee A. Silva, *Wyatt Earp: A Biography of the Legend, Vol. 1: The Cowtown Years*, 208–243.

52 Stuart N. Lake, *Wyatt Earp: Frontier Marshal*, 93.

CHAPTER 3: IN AND OUT OF TROUBLE

1 Robert K. DeArment, *Bat Masterson: The Man and the Legend*, 35.

2 Ibid.

3 Stuart N. Lake, *Wyatt Earp: Frontier Marshal*, 93.

4 "No Man's Land" was also called "Public Land" and "Public Land Strip." The area was not assigned to any state or territory until 1890 when Congress made it a part of Oklahoma Territory. Today it is called the Oklahoma Panhandle.

5 Miles Gilbert, *Getting a Stand*, 2, 6.

6 T. Lindsay Baker and Billy R. Harrison, *Adobe Walls: The History and Archeology of the 1874 Trading Post* (College Station: Texas A&M University Press, 1986), 10.

7 Wayne Gard, *The Great Buffalo Hunt*, 138–139.

8 T. Lindsay Baker and Billy R. Harrison, *Adobe Walls: The History and Archeology of the 1874 Trading Post*, 13–14.

9 T. Lindsay Baker and Billy R. Harrison, *Adobe Walls: The History and Archeology of the 1874 Trading Post*, 13–22.

10 Robert K. DeArment, *Bat Masterson: The Man and the Legend*, 38.

11 T. Lindsay Baker and Billy R. Harrison, *Adobe Walls: The History and Archeology of the 1874 Trading Post*, 24.

12 Ibid.

13 Walter R. Borneman, *Rival Rails: The Race to Build America's Greatest Transcontinental Railroad*, 68.

14 Sherry Monahan, *Mrs. Earp: The Wives and Lovers of the Earp Brothers*, 14.

15 Stuart N. Lake, *Wyatt Earp: Frontier Marshal*, 95–97.

16 Casey Tefertiller, *Wyatt Earp: The Life Behind the Legend*, 10–11.

17 Sherry Monahan, *Mrs. Earp: The Wives and Lovers of the Earp Brothers*, 14.

18 Lee A. Silva, *Wyatt Earp: A Biography of the Legend, Vol. 1: The Cowtown Years*, 280.

19 Wayne Gard, *The Great Buffalo Hunt*, 147, 152–153, and 166.

20 T. Lindsay Baker and Billy R. Harrison, *Adobe Walls: The History and Archeology of the 1874 Trading Post*, 55.

21 Olive K. Dixon, *Life of Billy Dixon: Plainsman, Scout and Pioneer*, 157–159.

22 T. Lindsay Baker and Billy R. Harrison, *Adobe Walls: The History and Archeology of the 1874 Trading Post*, 55.

23 T. Lindsay Baker and Billy R. Harrison, *Adobe Walls: The History and Archeology of the 1874 Trading Post*, 60–61.

24 Robert K. DeArment, *Bat Masterson: The Man and the Legend*, 42.

25 Robert K. DeArment, *Bat Masterson: The Man and the Legend*, 43–44.

26 Olive K. Dixon, *Life of Billy Dixon: Plainsman, Scout and Pioneer*, 178.

27 T. Lindsay Baker and Billy R. Harrison, *Adobe Walls: The History and Archeology of the 1874 Trading Post*, 64–65.

28 Wayne Gard, *The Great Buffalo Hunt*, 177–178.

29 Robert K. DeArment, *Bat Masterson: The Man and the Legend*, 45–46.

30 Olive K. Dixon, *Life of Billy Dixon: Plainsman, Scout and Pioneer*, 180–181.

31 Robert K. DeArment, *Bat Masterson: The Man and the Legend*, 46.

32 Olive K. Dixon, *Life of Billy Dixon: Plainsman, Scout and Pioneer*, 187–188.

33 Lee A. Silva, *Wyatt Earp: A Biography of the Legend, Vol. 1: The Cowtown Years*, 305–306.

34 Lee A. Silva, *Wyatt Earp: A Biography of the Legend, Vol. 1: The Cowtown Years*, 297–308.

35 Lee A. Silva, *Wyatt Earp: A Biography of the Legend, Vol. 1: The Cowtown Years*, 309–312.

36 Lee A. Silva, *Wyatt Earp: A Biography of the Legend, Vol. 1: The Cowtown Years*, 316–317.

37 Stuart N. Lake, *Wyatt Earp: Frontier Marshal*, 125–127.

38 Casey Tefertiller, *Wyatt Earp: The Life Behind the Legend*, 11–12.

39 Robert K. DeArment, *Bat Masterson: The Man and the Legend*, 50.

40 Robert K. DeArment, *Bat Masterson: The Man and the Legend*, 51.

41 Olive K. Dixon, *Life of Billy Dixon: Plainsman, Scout and Pioneer*, 192–193.

42 Olive K. Dixon, *Life of Billy Dixon: Plainsman, Scout and Pioneer*, 193–195.

43 Robert K. DeArment, *Bat Masterson: The Man and the Legend*, 52.

44 Ibid.

45 Robert K. DeArment, *Bat Masterson: The Man and the Legend*, 53–54.

46 T. Lindsay Baker and Billy R. Harrison, *Adobe Walls: The History and Archeology of the 1874 Trading Post*, 107–109.

47 Robert K. DeArment, *Bat Masterson: The Man and the Legend*, 54.

48 Ibid.

49 Robert K. DeArment, *Bat Masterson: The Man and the Legend*, 403, endnote 8.

50 Lee A. Silva, *Wyatt Earp: A Biography of the Legend, Vol. 1: The Cowtown Years*, 291–292.

51 Lee A. Silva, *Wyatt Earp: A Biography of the Legend, Vol. 1: The Cowtown Years*, 292.

52 Casey Tefertiller, *Wyatt Earp: The Life Behind the Legend*, 13.

53 Lee A. Silva, *Wyatt Earp: A Biography of the Legend, Vol. 1: The Cowtown Years*, 344.

54 Casey Tefertiller, *Wyatt Earp: The Life Behind the Legend*, 13.

55 Lee A. Silva, *Wyatt Earp: A Biography of the Legend, Vol. 1: The Cowtown Years*, 337–338.

56 Casey Tefertiller, *Wyatt Earp: The Life Behind the Legend*, 13.

57 Lee A. Silva, *Wyatt Earp: A Biography of the Legend, Vol. 1: The Cowtown Years*, 352.

58 Robert K. DeArment, *Bat Masterson: The Man and the Legend*, 55.

59 Robert K. DeArment, *Bat Masterson: The Man and the Legend*, 55–56.

60 Tom Clavin, *Dodge City: Wyatt Earp, Bat Masterson, and the Wickedest Town in the American West*, 120–121.

61 Robert K. DeArment, *Bat Masterson: The Man and the Legend*, 58.

62 Robert K. DeArment, *Bat Masterson: The Man and the Legend*, 63.

63 Robert K. DeArment, *Bat Masterson: The Man and the Legend*, 57 and 63.

64 Tom Clavin, *Dodge City: Wyatt Earp, Bat Masterson, and the Wickedest Town in the American West*, 124.

65 Ibid.

66 Ibid.

67 Casey Tefertiller, *Wyatt Earp: The Life Behind the Legend*, 14.

68 Lee A. Silva, *Wyatt Earp: A Biography of the Legend, Vol. 1: The Cowtown Years*, 359.

69 Casey Tefertiller, *Wyatt Earp: The Life Behind the Legend*, 15.

70 T. Lindsay Baker and Billy R. Harrison, *Adobe Walls: The History and Archeology of the 1874 Trading Post*, 39–42.

71 Dee Brown, *Bury My Heart at Wounded Knee: An Indian History of the American West* (New York, NY: Henry Holt and Company, 1970), 265.

72 Dee Brown, *Bury My Heart at Wounded Knee: An Indian History of the American West*, 266 and 268.

CHAPTER 4: IN AND OUT OF DODGE

1 Early Ford County, by Ida Ellen Rath, Ford County Historical Society. Available from www.kansashistory.us/fordco/rath2/05.html, accessed January 5, 2018.

2 Tom Clavin, *Dodge City: Wyatt Earp, Bat Masterson, and the Wickedest Town in the American West*, 117.

3 Lee A. Silva, *Wyatt Earp: A Biography of the Legend, Vol. 1: The Cowtown Years*, 392.

4 Lee A. Silva, *Wyatt Earp: A Biography of the Legend, Vol. 1: The Cowtown Years*, 248.

5 Lee A. Silva, *Wyatt Earp: A Biography of the Legend, Vol. 1: The Cowtown Years*, 264.

6 Ford County Historical Society, accessed January 7, 2018, www.kansashistory .us/fordco/dodgecity.html.

7 Robert K. DeArment, *Bat Masterson: The Man and the Legend*, 69–71.

8 Lee A. Silva, *Wyatt Earp: A Biography of the Legend, Vol. 1: The Cowtown Years*, 351.

9 Stuart N. Lake, *Wyatt Earp: Frontier Marshal*, 142.

10 Sherry Monahan, *Mrs. Earp: The Lives and Lovers of the Earp Brothers*, 14.

11 Sherry Monahan, *Mrs. Earp: The Lives and Lovers of the Earp Brothers*, 15.

12 Stuart N. Lake, *Wyatt Earp: Frontier Marshal*, 135–136.

13 Stuart N. Lake, *Wyatt Earp: Frontier Marshal*, 142.

14 Stuart N. Lake, *Wyatt Earp: Frontier Marshal*, 143, 151–153.

15 Stuart N. Lake, *Wyatt Earp: Frontier Marshal*, 143.

16 Ibid.

17 Stuart N. Lake, *Wyatt Earp: Frontier Marshal*, 154.

18 Robert K. DeArment, *Bat Masterson: The Man and the Legend*, 74–75.

19 Stuart N. Lake, *Wyatt Earp: Frontier Marshal*, 154.

20 Stuart N. Lake, *Wyatt Earp: Frontier Marshal*, 155.

21 Stuart N. Lake, *Wyatt Earp: Frontier Marshal*, 156.

22 Sherry Monahan, *Mrs. Earp: The Lives and Lovers of the Earp Brothers*, 90.

23 Stuart N. Lake, *Wyatt Earp: Frontier Marshal*, 157.

24 Robert K. DeArment, *Bat Masterson: The Man and the Legend*, 77–78.

25 Stuart N. Lake, *Wyatt Earp: Frontier Marshal*, 160–164.

26 Agnes Wright Spring, *The Cheyenne and Black Hills Stage and Express Routes* (Lincoln: University of Nebraska Press, 1948), 208.

27 Stuart N. Lake, *Wyatt Earp: Frontier Marshal*, 162–163.

28 Tom Clavin, *Dodge City: Wyatt Earp, Bat Masterson, and the Wickedest Town in the American West*, 153.

29 Stuart N. Lake, *Wyatt Earp: Frontier Marshal*, 164–166.

30 Robert K. DeArment, *Bat Masterson: The Man and the Legend*, 79.

31 Ibid.

32 Robert K. DeArment, *Bat Masterson: The Man and the Legend*, 80.

33 Robert K. DeArment, *Bat Masterson: The Man and the Legend*, 80–81.

34 Robert K. DeArment, *Bat Masterson: The Man and the Legend*, 81.

35 Charles Siringo, *Riata and Spurs: The Story of a Lifetime Spent in the Saddle as Cowboy and Detective* (New York, NY: Coslino Classico, 1927), 36–37,

CHAPTER 5: BAT GETS A LAWMAN'S JOB, AND WYATT WANDERS

1 Stuart N. Lake, *Wyatt Earp: Frontier Marshal*, 164–166.

2 Lee A. Silva, *Wyatt Earp: A Biography of the Legend, Vol. 1: The Cowtown Years*, 433–434.

3 Lee A. Silva, *Wyatt Earp: A Biography of the Legend, Vol. 1: The Cowtown Years*, 369.

4 Stuart N. Lake, *Wyatt Earp: Frontier Marshal*, 190–191.

5 Robert K. DeArment, *Bat Masterson: The Man and the Legend*, 81.

6 Lee A. Silva, *Wyatt Earp: A Biography of the Legend, Vol. 1: The Cowtown Years*, 381.

7 Robert K. DeArment, *Bat Masterson: The Man and the Legend*, 97–98.

8 Lee A. Silva, *Wyatt Earp: A Biography of the Legend, Vol. 1: The Cowtown Years*, 379.

9 Robert K. DeArment, *Bat Masterson: The Man and the Legend*, 82.

10 Ibid.

11 Ibid.

12 Robert K. DeArment, *Bat Masterson: The Man and the Legend*, 85.

13 Stuart N. Lake, *Wyatt Earp: Frontier Marshal*, 191–192.

14 Lee A. Silva, *Wyatt Earp: A Biography of the Legend, Vol. 1: The Cowtown Years*, 374.

15 Lee A. Silva, *Wyatt Earp: A Biography of the Legend, Vol. 1: The Cowtown Years*, 437.

16 Robert K. DeArment, *Bat Masterson: The Man and the Legend*, 86.

17 Ibid.

18 Robert K. DeArment, *Bat Masterson: The Man and the Legend*, 99.

19 Robert K. DeArment, *Bat Masterson: The Man and the Legend*, 86–87.

20 Robert K. DeArment, *Bat Masterson: The Man and the Legend*, 99–101.

21 Robert K. DeArment, *Bat Masterson: The Man and the Legend*, 87.

22 Stuart N. Lake, *Wyatt Earp: Frontier Marshal*, 192.

23 Legends of America, www.legendsofamerica.com/tx-fortgriffin/ accessed January 11, 2018.

24 Lee A. Silva, *Wyatt Earp: A Biography of the Legend, Vol. 1: The Cowtown Years*, 445.

25 Stuart N. Lake, *Wyatt Earp: Frontier Marshal*, 192, 195.

26 Lee A. Silva, *Wyatt Earp: A Biography of the Legend, Vol. 1: The Cowtown Years*, 458, 466.

27 Lee A. Silva, *Wyatt Earp: A Biography of the Legend, Vol. 1: The Cowtown Years*, 466–471.

28 Lee A. Silva, *Wyatt Earp: A Biography of the Legend, Vol. 1: The Cowtown Years*, 460, 473–475.

29 Lee A. Silva, *Wyatt Earp: A Biography of the Legend, Vol.1: The Cowtown Years*, 474–476.

30 Stuart N. Lake, *Wyatt Earp: Frontier Marshal*, 198.

31 Stuart N. Lake, *Wyatt Earp: Frontier Marshal*, 198–199.

32 Robert K. DeArment, *Bat Masterson: The Man and the Legend*, 101.

33 Robert K. DeArment, *Bat Masterson: The Man and the Legend*, 87.

34 Robert K. DeArment, *Bat Masterson: The Man and the Legend*, 89.

35 Ibid.

36 Robert K. DeArment, *Bat Masterson: The Man and the Legend*, 90.

37 Nyle H. Miller and Joseph W. Snell, *Why the West Was Wild: A Contemporary Look at the Antics of Some Highly Publicized Kansas Cowtown Personalities* (Norman: University of Oklahoma Press, 1963), 608–609.

38 Nyle H. Miller and Joseph W. Snell, *Why the West Was Wild: A Contemporary Look at the Antics of Some Highly Publicized Kansas Cowtown Personalities*, 334.

39 Nyle H. Miller and Joseph W. Snell, *Why the West Was Wild: A Contemporary Look at the Antics of Some Highly Publicized Kansas Cowtown Personalities*, 335.

40 Robert K. DeArment, *Bat Masterson: The Man and the Legend*, 93.

41 Nyle H. Miller and Joseph W. Snell, *Why the West Was Wild: A Contemporary Look at the Antics of Some Highly Publicized Kansas Cowtown Personalities*, 338.

42 Robert K. DeArment, *Bat Masterson: The Man and the Legend*, 94.

43 Stuart N. Lake, *Wyatt Earp: Frontier Marshal*, 199.

44 Nyle H. Miller and Joseph W. Snell, *Why the West Was Wild: A Contemporary Look at the Antics of Some Highly Publicized Kansas Cowtown Personalities*, 297–299.

45 Robert K. DeArment, *Bat Masterson: The Man and the Legend*, 103.

46 Ibid.

47 Robert K. DeArment, *Bat Masterson: The Man and the Legend*, 103–104.

48 Lee A. Silva, *Wyatt Earp: A Biography of the Legend, Vol 1: The Cowtown Years*, 518–531.

49 Robert K. DeArment, *Bat Masterson: The Man and the Legend*, 104–105.

50 Robert K. DeArment, *Bat Masterson: The Man and the Legend*, 107–109.

51 Nyle H. Miller and Joseph W. Snell, *Why the West Was Wild: A Contemporary Look at the Antics of Some Highly Publicized Kansas Cowtown Personalities*, 304.

52 Lee A. Silva and Susan Leiser Silva, *Wyatt Earp: A Biography of the Legend, Vol. 2: Part 1: Tombstone before the Earps* (Santa Ana, CA: Graphic Publishers, 2010), 261–262.

53 Bill O'Neal, *Encyclopedia of Western Gunfighters*, 98.

54 Bill O'Neal, *Encyclopedia of Western Gunfighters*, 96–97.

55 Bill O'Neal, *Encyclopedia of Western Gunfighters*, 99–100.

56 Bill O'Neal, *Encyclopedia of Western Gunfighters*, 215–216.

57 Bill O'Neal, *Encyclopedia of Western Gunfighters*, 217–219.

58 Robert K. DeArment, *Bat Masterson: The Man and the Legend*, 109.

CHAPTER 6: DODGE CITY ON EDGE

1 Lee A. Silva, *Wyatt Earp: A Biography of the Legend, Vol. 1: The Cowtown Years*, 379.

2 Robert K. DeArment, *Bat Masterson: The Man and the Legend*, 109.

3 Nyle H. Miller and Joseph W. Snell, *Why the West Was Wild: A Contemporary Look at the Antics of Some Highly Publicized Kansas Cowtown Personalities*, 344.

4 Stuart N. Lake, *Wyatt Earp: Frontier Marshal*, 199, 201.

5 Nyle H. Miller and Joseph W. Snell, *Why the West Was Wild: A Contemporary Look at the Antics of Some Highly Publicized Kansas Cowtown Personalities*, 151–152.

6 Nyle H. Miller and Joseph W. Snell, *Why the West Was Wild: A Contemporary Look at the Antics of Some Highly Publicized Kansas Cowtown Personalities*, 307.

7 Nyle H. Miller and Joseph W. Snell, *Why the West Was Wild: A Contemporary Look at the Antics of Some Highly Publicized Kansas Cowtown Personalities*, 221.

8 Lee A. Silva, *Wyatt Earp: A Biography of the Legend, Vol. 1: The Cowtown Years*, 453.

9 Nyle H. Miller and Joseph W. Snell, *Why the West Was Wild: A Contemporary Look at the Antics of Some Highly Publicized Kansas Cowtown Personalities*, 345.

10 Robert K. DeArment, *Bat Masterson: The Man and the Legend*, 111–112.

11 Eddie Foy and Alvin F. Harlow, *Clowning Through Life* (New York, NY: E.P. Dutton & Company, 1928), 98.

12 Eddie Foy and Alvin F. Harlow, *Clowning Through Life*, 109–110.

13 Nyle H. Miller and Joseph W. Snell, *Why the West Was Wild: A Contemporary Look at the Antics of Some Highly Publicized Kansas Cowtown Personalities*, 273–276.

14 Andy Adams, *The Log of a Cowboy: A Narrative of the Old Trail Days* (New York, NY: Houghton, Mifflin and Company, 1903), 191.

15 Robert K. DeArment, *Bat Masterson: The Man and the Legend*, 114.

16 Ibid.

17 Robert K. DeArment, *Bat Masterson: The Man and the Legend*, 115.

18 Robert K. DeArment, *Bat Masterson: The Man and the Legend*, 116.

19 Ibid.

20 Robert K. DeArment, *Bat Masterson: The Man and the Legend*, 117.

21 Casey Tefertiller, *Wyatt Earp: The Life Behind the Legend*, 27.

22 Nyle H. Miller and Joseph W. Snell, *Why the West Was Wild: A Contemporary Look at the Antics of Some Highly Publicized Kansas Cowtown Personalities*, 346–347.

23 Nyle H. Miller and Joseph W. Snell, *Why the West Was Wild: A Contemporary Look at the Antics of Some Highly Publicized Kansas Cowtown Personalities*, 25.

24 Bill O'Neal, *Encyclopedia of Western Gunfighters*, 19–20.

25 Lee A. Silva, *Wyatt Earp: A Biography of the Legend, Vol. 1: The Cowtown Years*, 550.

26 Nyle H. Miller and Joseph W. Snell, *Why the West Was Wild: A Contemporary Look at the Antics of Some Highly Publicized Kansas Cowtown Personalities*, 25–26.

27 Robert K. DeArment, *Bat Masterson: The Man and the Legend*, 165.

28 Nyle H. Miller and Joseph W. Snell, *Why the West Was Wild: A Contemporary Look at the Antics of Some Highly Publicized Kansas Cowtown Personalities*, 308.

29 Nyle H. Miller and Joseph W. Snell, *Why the West Was Wild: A Contemporary Look at the Antics of Some Highly Publicized Kansas Cowtown Personalities*, 143.

30 Robert K. DeArment, *Bat Masterson: The Man and the Legend*, 117–118.

31 Nyle H. Miller and Joseph W. Snell, *Why the West Was Wild: A Contemporary Look at the Antics of Some Highly Publicized Kansas Cowtown Personalities*, 155.

32 Robert K. DeArment, *Bat Masterson: The Man and the Legend*, 115.

33 Nyle H. Miller and Joseph W. Snell, *Why the West Was Wild: A Contemporary Look at the Antics of Some Highly Publicized Kansas Cowtown Personalities*, 155.

34 Nyle H. Miller and Joseph W. Snell, *Why the West Was Wild: A Contemporary Look at the Antics of Some Highly Publicized Kansas Cowtown Personalities*, 26.

35 Stuart N. Lake, *Wyatt Earp: Frontier Marshal*, 175–176.

36 Charles Siringo, *Riata and Spurs: The Story of a Lifetime Spent in the Saddle as Cowboy and Detective*, 59.

37 Lee A. Silva, *Wyatt Earp: A Biography of the Legend, Vol. 1: The Cowtown Years*, 574.

38 Nyle H. Miller and Joseph W. Snell, *Why the West Was Wild: A Contemporary Look at the Antics of Some Highly Publicized Kansas Cowtown Personalities*, 347–348.

39 Robert K. DeArment, *Bat Masterson: The Man and the Legend*, 166.

40 Robert K. DeArment, *Bat Masterson: The Man and the Legend*, 167.

41 Nyle H. Miller and Joseph W. Snell, *Why the West Was Wild: A Contemporary Look at the Antics of Some Highly Publicized Kansas Cowtown Personalities*, 350.

42 Robert K. DeArment, *Bat Masterson: The Man and the Legend*, 167.

43 Lee A. Silva, *Wyatt Earp: A Biography of the Legend, Vol. 1: The Cowtown Years*, 483, 863, and Chuck Hornung and Gary L. Roberts, "The Split: Did Doc & Wyatt Split Because of a Racial Slur?", *True West Magazine*, November 1, 2001.

44 Stuart N. Lake, *Wyatt Earp: Frontier Marshal*, 170–171.

45 Stuart N. Lake, *Wyatt Earp: Frontier Marshal*, 111–112.

46 Lee A. Silva, *Wyatt Earp: A Biography of the Legend, Vol. 1: The Cowtown Years*, 864.

47 Stuart N. Lake, *Wyatt Earp: Frontier Marshal*, 477–485.

48 Alford E. Turner (ed.), *The O.K. Corral Inquest* (College Station, TX: Creative Publishing Company, 1981), 158.

49 Howard Kazanjian and Chris Enss, *Thunder Over the Prairie: The True Story of a Murder and a Manhunt by the Greatest Posse of All Time* (Guilford, CT: Globe Pequot Press, 2009), 2, 3, 5. Tom Clavin, *Dodge City: Wyatt Earp, Bat Masterson, and the Wickedest Town in the American West*, 247.

50 Howard Kazanjian and Chris Enss, *Thunder Over the Prairie: The True Story of a Murder and a Manhunt by the Greatest Posse of All Time*, 12–13.

51 Nyle H. Miller and Joseph W. Snell, *Why the West Was Wild: A Contemporary Look at the Antics of Some Highly Publicized Kansas Cowtown Personalities*, 362.

52 Howard Kazanjian and Chris Enss, *Thunder Over the Prairie: The True Story of a Murder and a Manhunt by the Greatest Posse of All Time*, 13, 24.

53 Nyle H. Miller and Joseph W. Snell, *Why the West Was Wild: A Contemporary Look at the Antics of Some Highly Publicized Kansas Cowtown Personalities*, 352–363.

54 Nyle H. Miller and Joseph W. Snell, *Why the West Was Wild: A Contemporary Look at the Antics of Some Highly Publicized Kansas Cowtown Personalities*, 362.

55 Robert K. DeArment, *Bat Masterson: The Man and the Legend*, 120.

56 Nyle H. Miller and Joseph W. Snell, *Why the West Was Wild: A Contemporary Look at the Antics of Some Highly Publicized Kansas Cowtown Personalities*, 363.

57 Ibid.

58 Nyle H. Miller and Joseph W. Snell, *Why the West Was Wild: A Contemporary Look at the Antics of Some Highly Publicized Kansas Cowtown Personalities*, 352.

59 Nyle H. Miller and Joseph W. Snell, *Why the West Was Wild: A Contemporary Look at the Antics of Some Highly Publicized Kansas Cowtown Personalities*, 363.

60 Howard Kazanjian and Chris Enss, *Thunder Over the Prairie: The True Story of a Murder and a Manhunt by the Greatest Posse of All Time*, 39–40.

61 Howard Kazanjian and Chris Enss, *Thunder Over the Prairie: The True Story of a Murder and a Manhunt by the Greatest Posse of All Time*, 40–41.

62 Howard Kazanjian and Chris Enss, *Thunder Over the Prairie: The True Story of a Murder and a Manhunt by the Greatest Posse of All Time*, 50–51.

63 Howard Kazanjian and Chris Enss, *Thunder Over the Prairie: The True Story of a Murder and a Manhunt by the Greatest Posse of All Time*, 41–42.

64 Nyle H. Miller and Joseph W. Snell, *Why the West Was Wild: A Contemporary Look at the Antics of Some Highly Publicized Kansas Cowtown Personalities*, 363.

65 Nyle H. Miller and Joseph W. Snell, *Why the West Was Wild: A Contemporary Look at the Antics of Some Highly Publicized Kansas Cowtown Personalities*, 364.

66 Stuart N. Lake, *Wyatt Earp: Frontier Marshal*, 219–220.

67 Nyle H. Miller and Joseph W. Snell, *Why the West Was Wild: A Contemporary Look at the Antics of Some Highly Publicized Kansas Cowtown Personalities*, 364.

68 Tom Clavin, *Dodge City: Wyatt Earp, Bat Masterson, and the Wickedest Town in the American West*, 247.

69 Dee Brown, *Bury My Heart at Wounded Knee: An Indian History of the American West*, 332.

70 Dee Brown, *Bury My Heart at Wounded Knee: An Indian History of the American West*, 333 and 334.

71 Dee Brown, *Bury My Heart at Wounded Knee: An Indian History of the American West*, 334–338.

72 Dee Brown, *Bury My Heart at Wounded Knee: An Indian History of the American West*, 340.

73 Dee Brown, *Bury My Heart at Wounded Knee: An Indian History of the American West*, 343.

74 Dee Brown, *Bury My Heart at Wounded Knee: An Indian History of the American West*, 345–349.

75 Northern Cheyenne Tribe website www.cheyennenation.com/.

CHAPTER 7: ENDINGS IN DODGE AND BEGINNINGS IN TOMBSTONE

1 Nyle H. Miller and Joseph W. Snell, *Why the West Was Wild: A Contemporary Look at the Antics of Some Highly Publicized Kansas Cowtown Personalities*, 365.

2 Howard Kazanjian and Chris Enss, *Thunder Over the Prairie: The True Story of a Murder and a Manhunt by the Greatest Posse of All Time*, 109–111.

3 Nyle H. Miller and Joseph W. Snell, *Why the West Was Wild: A Contemporary Look at the Antics of Some Highly Publicized Kansas Cowtown Personalities*, 364.

4 Lee A. Silva, *Wyatt Earp: A Biography of the Legend, Vol. 1: The Cowtown Years*, 600.

5 Nyle H. Miller and Joseph W. Snell, *Why the West Was Wild: A Contemporary Look at the Antics of Some Highly Publicized Kansas Cowtown Personalities*, 609–610.

6 Nyle H. Miller and Joseph W. Snell, *Why the West Was Wild: A Contemporary Look at the Antics of Some Highly Publicized Kansas Cowtown Personalities*, 366.

7 Nyle H. Miller and Joseph W. Snell, *Why the West Was Wild: A Contemporary Look at the Antics of Some Highly Publicized Kansas Cowtown Personalities*, 308.

8 Nyle H. Miller and Joseph W. Snell, *Why the West Was Wild: A Contemporary Look at the Antics of Some Highly Publicized Kansas Cowtown Personalities*, 366–368.

9 Nyle H. Miller and Joseph W. Snell, *Why the West Was Wild: A Contemporary Look at the Antics of Some Highly Publicized Kansas Cowtown Personalities*, 364–365.

10 Nyle H. Miller and Joseph W. Snell, *Why the West Was Wild: A Contemporary Look at the Antics of Some Highly Publicized Kansas Cowtown Personalities*, 369–370.

11 Robert K. DeArment, *Bat Masterson: The Man and the Legend*, 134–135.

12 Robert K. DeArment, *Bat Masterson: The Man and the Legend*, 135–136.

13 Robert K. DeArment, *Bat Masterson: The Man and the Legend*, 137.

14 Lee A. Silva, *Wyatt Earp: A Biography of the Legend, Vol. 1: The Cowtown Years*, 380–381.

15 Robert K. DeArment, *Bat Masterson: The Man and the Legend*, 138–139.

16 Robert K. DeArment, *Bat Masterson: The Man and the Legend*, 169.

17 Robert K. DeArment, *Bat Masterson: The Man and the Legend*, 169–171.

18 Robert K. DeArment, *Bat Masterson: The Man and the Legend*, 173.

19 Richard E. Lingenfelter, Western Lands and Waters Series XXVI, *Bonanzas and Borrascas: Gold Lust & Silver Sharks, 1848–1889* (Norman: University of Oklahoma Press, 2012), 276, 278.

20 Walter R. Borneman, *Rival Rails: The Race to Build America's Greatest Transcontinental Railroad*, 141–142, 144.

21 Walter R. Borneman, *Rival Rails: The Race to Build America's Greatest Transcontinental Railroad*, 142.

22 Walter R. Borneman, *Rival Rails: The Race to Build America's Greatest Transcontinental Railroad*, 144.

23 Walter R. Borneman, *Rival Rails: The Race to Build America's Greatest Transcontinental Railroad*, 146–148.

24 Walter R. Borneman, *Rival Rails: The Race to Build America's Greatest Transcontinental Railroad*, 152–153.

25 Nyle H. Miller and Joseph W. Snell, *Why the West Was Wild: A Contemporary Look at the Antics of Some Highly Publicized Kansas Cowtown Personalities*, 391.

26 Eddie Foy and Alvin F. Harlow, *Clowning Through Life*, 102–104.

27 Robert K. DeArment, *Bat Masterson: The Man and the Legend*, 149–150.

28 Robert K. DeArment, *Bat Masterson: The Man and the Legend*, 150.

29 Nyle H. Miller and Joseph W. Snell, *Why the West Was Wild: A Contemporary Look at the Antics of Some Highly Publicized Kansas Cowtown Personalities*, 392.

30 Nyle H. Miller and Joseph W. Snell, *Why the West Was Wild: A Contemporary Look at the Antics of Some Highly Publicized Kansas Cowtown Personalities*, 156.

31 Nyle H. Miller and Joseph W. Snell, *Why the West Was Wild: A Contemporary Look at the Antics of Some Highly Publicized Kansas Cowtown Personalities*, 392. Robert K. DeArment, *Bat Masterson: The Man and the Legend*, 155.

32 Nyle H. Miller and Joseph W. Snell, *Why the West Was Wild: A Contemporary Look at the Antics of Some Highly Publicized Kansas Cowtown Personalities*, 392. Robert K. DeArment, *Bat Masterson: The Man and the Legend*, 155–156.

33 Ibid.

34 Nyle H. Miller and Joseph W. Snell, *Why the West Was Wild: A Contemporary Look at the Antics of Some Highly Publicized Kansas Cowtown Personalities*, 156.

35 Lee A. Silva, *Wyatt Earp: A Biography of the Legend, Vol. 1: The Cowtown Years*, 606–607.

36 Walter R. Borneman, *Rival Rails: The Race to Build America's Greatest Transcontinental Railroad*, 154.

37 Nyle H. Miller and Joseph W. Snell, *Why the West Was Wild: A Contemporary Look at the Antics of Some Highly Publicized Kansas Cowtown Personalities*, 392.

38 Walter R. Borneman, *Rival Rails: The Race to Build America's Greatest Transcontinental Railroad*, 154–155.

39 Walter R. Borneman, *Rival Rails: The Race to Build America's Greatest Transcontinental Railroad*, 154.

40 Walter R. Borneman, *Rival Rails: The Race to Build America's Greatest Transcontinental Railroad*, 155.

41 Ibid.

42 Walter R. Borneman, *Rival Rails: The Race to Build America's Greatest Transcontinental Railroad*, 158.

43 Nyle H. Miller and Joseph W. Snell, *Why the West Was Wild: A Contemporary Look at the Antics of Some Highly Publicized Kansas Cowtown Personalities*, 393–394.

44 Casey Tefertiller, *Wyatt Earp: The Life Behind the Legend*, 30.

45 Stuart N. Lake, *Wyatt Earp: Frontier Marshal*, 228.

46 Ibid.

47 Nyle H. Miller and Joseph W. Snell, *Why the West Was Wild: A Contemporary Look at the Antics of Some Highly Publicized Kansas Cowtown Personalities*, 157.
48 Lee A. Silva, *Wyatt Earp: A Biography of the Legend, Vol. 1: The Cowtown Years*, 632–633.
49 Casey Tefertiller, *Wyatt Earp: The Life Behind the Legend*, 31 and 32. Lee A. Silva, *Wyatt Earp: A Biography of the Legend, Vol. 1: The Cowtown Years*, 629.
50 Robert K. DeArment, *Bat Masterson: The Man and the Legend*, 176. Casey Tefertiller, *Wyatt Earp: The Life Behind the Legend*, 36.
51 Nyle H. Miller and Joseph W. Snell, *Why the West Was Wild: A Contemporary Look at the Antics of Some Highly Publicized Kansas Cowtown Personalities*, 157.
52 Robert K. DeArment, *Bat Masterson: The Man and the Legend*, 176. Casey Tefertiller, *Wyatt Earp: The Life Behind the Legend*, 177–179.
53 Casey Tefertiller, *Wyatt Earp: The Life Behind the Legend*, 36.
54 Nyle H. Miller and Joseph W. Snell, *Why the West Was Wild: A Contemporary Look at the Antics of Some Highly Publicized Kansas Cowtown Personalities*, 157–158.
55 Nyle H. Miller and Joseph W. Snell, *Why the West Was Wild: A Contemporary Look at the Antics of Some Highly Publicized Kansas Cowtown Personalities*, 158. Lee A. Silva, *Wyatt Earp: A Biography of the Legend, Vol. 1: The Cowtown Years*, 603, 902 and 903, footnote 50. Alford E. Turner (ed.), *The O. K. Corral Inquest*, 155.
56 Stuart N. Lake, *Wyatt Earp: Frontier Marshal*, 229.
57 Lee A. Silva, *Wyatt Earp: A Biography of the Legend, Vol. 1: The Cowtown Years*, 653.
58 Lee A. Silva and Susan Leiser Silva, *Wyatt Earp: A Biography of the Legend, Vol. 2: Part 1: Tombstone before the Earps*, 262.
59 Stuart N. Lake, *Wyatt Earp: Frontier Marshal*, 230. Lee A. Silva, *Wyatt Earp: A Biography of the Legend, Vol. 1: The Cowtown Years*, 653.
60 Casey Tefertiller, *Wyatt Earp: The Life Behind the Legend*, 36.
61 Stuart N. Lake, *Wyatt Earp: Frontier Marshal*, 230.
62 Alford E. Turner (ed.), *The O. K. Corral Inquest*, 155.
63 Robert K. DeArment, *Bat Masterson: The Man and the Legend*, 176. Casey Tefertiller, *Wyatt Earp: The Life Behind the Legend*, 182.

CHAPTER 8: TOMBSTONE

1 Sherry Monahan, *Tombstone's Treasure: Silver Mines and Golden Saloons* (Albuquerque: University of New Mexico Press, 2007), 9.
2 Bill Markley, "The Legendary West: 10 Destinations You Must Visit in a Lifetime," *True West Magazine*, July 2017.
3 Richard E. Lingenfelter, Western Lands and Waters Series XXVI, *Bonanzas and Borrascas: Gold Lust & Silver Sharks, 1848–1889* (Norman: University of Oklahoma Press, 2012), 305–307.
4 Casey Tefertiller, *Wyatt Earp: The Life Behind the Legend*, 36.

5 Casey Tefertiller, *Wyatt Earp: The Life Behind the Legend*, 37–39.
6 Nyle H. Miller and Joseph W. Snell, *Why the West Was Wild: A Contemporary Look at the Antics of Some Highly Publicized Kansas Cowtown Personalities*, 408.
7 Nyle H. Miller and Joseph W. Snell, *Why the West Was Wild: A Contemporary Look at the Antics of Some Highly Publicized Kansas Cowtown Personalities*, 408–409.
8 Bill O'Neal, *Encyclopedia of Western Gunfighters*, 323.
9 Nyle H. Miller and Joseph W. Snell, *Why the West Was Wild: A Contemporary Look at the Antics of Some Highly Publicized Kansas Cowtown Personalities*, 409.
10 The William F. Cody Archive: Documenting the life and times of Wild Bill, Col. Cody, Scout and Indian Fighter, W. B. (Bat) Masterson, "A Few Incidents in the Adventurous Career of the Famous Buffalo Bill that Have Passed Under My Personal Observation—His Early Days on the Frontier" (Human Life Publishing Co., 1908). Accessed January 25, 2018, http://codyarchive.org/texts/wfc.nsp02038.html.
11 Ibid.
12 Ibid.
13 Ibid.
14 Ibid.
15 Lee A. Silva and Susan Leiser Silva, *Wyatt Earp: A Biography of the Legend, Vol. 2: Part 1: Tombstone before the Earps*, 377–378.
16 Lee A. Silva and Susan Leiser Silva, *Wyatt Earp: A Biography of the Legend, Vol. 2: Part 1: Tombstone before the Earps*, 395.
17 Lee A. Silva and Susan Leiser Silva, *Wyatt Earp: A Biography of the Legend, Vol. 2: Part 1: Tombstone before the Earps*, 142.
18 Lee A. Silva and Susan Leiser Silva, *Wyatt Earp: A Biography of the Legend, Vol. 2: Part 1: Tombstone before the Earps*, 143. Casey Tefertiller, *Wyatt Earp: The Life Behind the Legend*, 43.
19 Casey Tefertiller, *Wyatt Earp: The Life Behind the Legend*, 43–44.
20 Casey Tefertiller, *Wyatt Earp: The Life Behind the Legend*, 44.
21 Ibid.
22 Ibid.
23 Ibid.
24 Lee A. Silva and Susan Leiser Silva, *Wyatt Earp: A Biography of the Legend, Vol. 2: Part 1: Tombstone before the Earps*, 244–245.
25 Casey Tefertiller, *Wyatt Earp: The Life Behind the Legend*, 47–48.
26 Casey Tefertiller, *Wyatt Earp: The Life Behind the Legend*, 49.
27 Casey Tefertiller, *Wyatt Earp: The Life Behind the Legend*, 45.
28 Casey Tefertiller, *Wyatt Earp: The Life Behind the Legend*, 51
29 Ibid.
30 Ibid.
31 Casey Tefertiller, *Wyatt Earp: The Life Behind the Legend*, 51–52.
32 Casey Tefertiller, *Wyatt Earp: The Life Behind the Legend*, 53.
33 Casey Tefertiller, *Wyatt Earp: The Life Behind the Legend*, 54.

34 Lee A. Silva and Susan Leiser Silva, *Wyatt Earp: A Biography of the Legend,* *Vol. 2: Part 1: Tombstone before the Earps,* 245.
35 Lee A. Silva and Susan Leiser Silva, *Wyatt Earp: A Biography of the Legend,* *Vol. 2: Part 1: Tombstone before the Earps,* 447.
36 Casey Tefertiller, *Wyatt Earp: The Life Behind the Legend,* 55–56.
37 Casey Tefertiller, *Wyatt Earp: The Life Behind the Legend,* 59–60.
38 Casey Tefertiller, *Wyatt Earp: The Life Behind the Legend,* 60–61.
39 Johnny-Behind-the-Deuce never stood trial. He escaped from the Tucson jail and was never captured.
40 Stuart N. Lake, *Wyatt Earp: Frontier Marshal,* 247–252. Casey Tefertiller, *Wyatt Earp: The Life Behind the Legend,* 56–59.
41 Sherry Monahan, *Mrs. Earp: The Wives and Lovers of the Earp Brothers,* 25.
42 Casey Tefertiller, *Wyatt Earp: The Life Behind the Legend,* 65.
43 Demimonde was a class of women on the fringes of respectable society.
44 Sherry Monahan, *Tombstone's Treasure: Silver Mines and Golden Saloons,* 78.
45 Stuart N. Lake, *Wyatt Earp: Frontier Marshal,* 254–255.
46 Stuart N. Lake, *Wyatt Earp: Frontier Marshal,* 255.
47 Robert K. DeArment, *Bat Masterson: The Man and the Legend,* 193.
48 Sherry Monahan, *The Wicked West: Boozers, Cruisers, Gamblers, and More* (Tucson, AZ: Rio Nuevo Publishers, 2005), 82–85. The Diagram Group, *The Way to Play: The Illustrated Encyclopedia of the Games of the World* (New York, NY: Paddington Press Ltd. 1975), 206–207.
49 Ibid.
50 G. R. Williamson, *Frontier Gambling: The Games, The Gamblers & The Great Gambling Halls of The Old West* (CreateSpace Independent Publishing Platform, 2011), 18–19.

CHAPTER 9: BATTLE OF THE PLAZA AND TOMBSTONE TROUBLES

1 Lee A. Silva and Susan Leiser Silva, *Wyatt Earp: A Biography of the Legend,* *Vol. 2: Part 1: Tombstone before the Earps,* 239.
2 Casey Tefertiller, *Wyatt Earp: The Life Behind the Legend,* 68.
3 Stuart N. Lake, *Wyatt Earp: Frontier Marshal,* 252–253.
4 Casey Tefertiller, *Wyatt Earp: The Life Behind the Legend,* 69.
5 W. B. (Bat) Masterson, *Famous Gunfighters of the Western Frontier,* 13–14.
6 Ibid.
7 Casey Tefertiller, *Wyatt Earp: The Life Behind the Legend,* 76.
8 Casey Tefertiller, *Wyatt Earp: The Life Behind the Legend,* 77.
9 Ibid.
10 Casey Tefertiller, *Wyatt Earp: The Life Behind the Legend,* 78.
11 Stuart N. Lake, *Wyatt Earp: Frontier Marshal,* 264.
12 Casey Tefertiller, *Wyatt Earp: The Life Behind the Legend,* 78–79.
13 Robert K. DeArment, *Bat Masterson: The Man and the Legend,* 203–204.

14 Robert K. DeArment, *Bat Masterson: The Man and the Legend*, 204–205, 208. Nyle H. Miller and Joseph W. Snell, *Why the West Was Wild: A Contemporary Look at the Antics of Some Highly Publicized Kansas Cowtown Personalities*, 310.
15 Robert K. DeArment, *Bat Masterson: The Man and the Legend*, 206.
16 Robert K. DeArment, *Bat Masterson: The Man and the Legend*, 206–207.
17 Robert K. DeArment, *Bat Masterson: The Man and the Legend*, 207.
18 Ibid.
19 Robert K. DeArment, *Bat Masterson: The Man and the Legend*, 208.
20 Robert K. DeArment, *Bat Masterson: The Man and the Legend*, 208–209.
21 Robert K. DeArment, *Bat Masterson: The Man and the Legend*, 209.
22 Casey Tefertiller, *Wyatt Earp: The Life Behind the Legend*, 80.
23 Ibid.
24 Casey Tefertiller, *Wyatt Earp: The Life Behind the Legend*, 86.
25 Stuart N. Lake, *Wyatt Earp: Frontier Marshal*, 272 and 273. Casey Tefertiller, *Wyatt Earp: The Life Behind the Legend*, 83.
26 Casey Tefertiller, *Wyatt Earp: The Life Behind the Legend*, 85.
27 Casey Tefertiller, *Wyatt Earp: The Life Behind the Legend*, 84–85.
28 Casey Tefertiller, *Wyatt Earp: The Life Behind the Legend*, 86.
29 Casey Tefertiller, *Wyatt Earp: The Life Behind the Legend*, 86–88.
30 Casey Tefertiller, *Wyatt Earp: The Life Behind the Legend*, 89.
31 Casey Tefertiller, *Wyatt Earp: The Life Behind the Legend*, 97–98.
32 Casey Tefertiller, *Wyatt Earp: The Life Behind the Legend*, 103.
33 Ibid.
34 Ibid.
35 Ibid.
36 Ibid.
37 Paul Andrew Hutton, *The Apache Wars: The Hunt for Geronimo, the Apache Kid, and the Captive Boy Who Started the Longest War in American History* (New York, NY: Broadway Books, 2016), 286.
38 Paul Andrew Hutton, *The Apache Wars*, 286–288.
39 Casey Tefertiller, *Wyatt Earp: The Life Behind the Legend*, 107.
40 Robert K. DeArment, *Bat Masterson: The Man and the Legend*, 213.
41 Steve Friesen, *Buffalo Bill: Scout, Showman, Visionary* (Golden, CO: Fulcrum Publishing Inc., 2010), 20.
42 Stuart N. Lake, *Wyatt Earp: Frontier Marshal*, 145–146.
43 Ibid.
44 William B. Shillingberg, "Wyatt Earp and the Buntline Special Myth," *Kansas Historical Quarterly Summer 1996 Vol. 42, No2* (Kansas Historical Society, 1976), 113–154. Accessed February 22, 2018, www.kshs.org/p/kansas-historical-quarterly%20 wyatt-earp-and-the-buntline-special-myth/13255.
45 Lee A. Silva, *Wyatt Earp: A Biography of the Legend, Vol 1: The Cowtown Years*, 744, 746.

CHAPTER 10: THE GUNFIGHT NEAR THE O.K. CORRAL

1 Casey Tefertiller, *Wyatt Earp: The Life Behind the Legend*, 113.
2 Casey Tefertiller, *Wyatt Earp: The Life Behind the Legend*, 114.
3 Alford Turner (ed.), *The O. K. Corral Inquest*, 97.
4 The term "heeled" refers to being armed.
5 Alford Turner (ed.), *The O. K. Corral Inquest*, 97.
6 Alford Turner (ed.), *The O. K. Corral Inquest*, 98.
7 Alford Turner (ed.), *The O. K. Corral Inquest*, 162.
8 Alford Turner (ed.), *The O. K. Corral Inquest*, 204–205.
9 Casey Tefertiller, *Wyatt Earp: The Life Behind the Legend*, 117–118.
10 Casey Tefertiller, *Wyatt Earp: The Life Behind the Legend*, 118.
11 Ibid.
12 Alford Turner (ed.), *The O. K. Corral Inquest*, 123.
13 Alford Turner (ed.), *The O. K. Corral Inquest*, 55–56.
14 Alford Turner (ed.), *The O. K. Corral Inquest*, 45.
15 Arizona Memory Project, Legal and Court History of Cochise County, Coroner's Inquest of the Gunfight at the OK Corral, Joseph Clanton Transcript.
16 Alford Turner (ed.), *The O. K. Corral Inquest*, 136–137.
17 Ibid.
18 Alford Turner (ed.), *The O. K. Corral Inquest*, 137–138.
19 Arizona Memory Project, Legal and Court History of Cochise County, Coroner's Inquest of the Gunfight at the OK Corral, Coleman Transcript.
20 Arizona Memory Project, Legal and Court History of Cochise County, Coroner's Inquest of the Gunfight at the OK Corral, King Transcript.
21 Alford Turner (ed.), *The O. K. Corral Inquest*, 138.
22 Alford Turner (ed.), *The O. K. Corral Inquest*, 193.
23 Alford Turner (ed.), *The O. K. Corral Inquest*, 146.
24 Alford Turner (ed.), *The O. K. Corral Inquest*, 56, 76–77, 138–139.
25 Alford Turner (ed.), *The O. K. Corral Inquest*, 56, 71–72, 93, 138–139. Casey Tefertiller, *Wyatt Earp: The Life Behind the Legend*, 122.
26 Alford Turner (ed.), *The O. K. Corral Inquest*, 76–77.
27 Alford Turner (ed.), *The O. K. Corral Inquest*, 165.
28 Alford Turner (ed.), *The O. K. Corral Inquest*, 46.
29 Alford Turner (ed.), *The O. K. Corral Inquest*, 93–95.
30 Casey Tefertiller, *Wyatt Earp: The Life Behind the Legend*, 123.
31 Casey Tefertiller, *Wyatt Earp: The Life Behind the Legend*, 122.
32 Ibid.
33 Casey Tefertiller, *Wyatt Earp: The Life Behind the Legend*, 123.
34 Ibid.
35 Ibid.
36 Casey Tefertiller, *Wyatt Earp: The Life Behind the Legend*, 122–123.
37 Casey Tefertiller, *Wyatt Earp: The Life Behind the Legend*, 124.

CHAPTER 11: VENDETTA

1 Casey Tefertiller, *Wyatt Earp: The Life Behind the Legend*, 125.
2 Casey Tefertiller, *Wyatt Earp: The Life Behind the Legend*, 127.
3 Casey Tefertiller, *Wyatt Earp: The Life Behind the Legend*, 125.
4 Casey Tefertiller, *Wyatt Earp: The Life Behind the Legend*, 126.
5 Alford Turner (ed.), *The O. K. Corral Inquest*, 22–23. Casey Tefertiller, *Wyatt Earp: The Life Behind the Legend*, 128–129.
6 Casey Tefertiller, *Wyatt Earp: The Life Behind the Legend*, 129.
7 Casey Tefertiller, *Wyatt Earp: The Life Behind the Legend*, 130.
8 Alford Turner (ed.), *The O. K. Corral Inquest*, 50.
9 Casey Tefertiller, *Wyatt Earp: The Life Behind the Legend*, 131.
10 Alford Turner (ed.), *The O. K. Corral Inquest*, 50–51.
11 Sherry Monahan, *Mrs. Earp: The Wives and Lovers of the Earp Brothers*, 51.
12 Alford Turner (ed.), *The O. K. Corral Inquest*, 226.
13 Casey Tefertiller, *Wyatt Earp: The Life Behind the Legend*, 161.
14 Casey Tefertiller, *Wyatt Earp: The Life Behind the Legend*, 162.
15 Casey Tefertiller, *Wyatt Earp: The Life Behind the Legend*, 163, 174.
16 Casey Tefertiller, *Wyatt Earp: The Life Behind the Legend*, 163.
17 Casey Tefertiller, *Wyatt Earp: The Life Behind the Legend*, 164–166.
18 William M. Breakenridge, *Helldorado: Bringing the Law to the Mesquite* (Lincoln: University of Nebraska Press, 1928), 259 and 260. Casey Tefertiller, *Wyatt Earp: The Life Behind the Legend*,167.
19 Glen G. Boyer, *I Married Wyatt Earp: The Recollections of Josephine Sarah Marcus Earp* (Stamford, CT: Longmeadow Press, 1976), 137, note 3.
20 Glen G. Boyer, *I Married Wyatt Earp: The Recollections of Josephine Sarah Marcus Earp*, 6. Sherry Monahan, *Mrs. Earp: The Wives and Lovers of the Earp Brothers*, 51.
21 Glen G. Boyer, *I Married Wyatt Earp: The Recollections of Josephine Sarah Marcus Earp*, 30.
22 Sherry Monahan, *Mrs. Earp: The Wives and Lovers of the Earp Brothers*, 23.
23 Casey Tefertiller, *Wyatt Earp: The Life Behind the Legend*, 161.
24 Alford Turner (ed.), *The O. K. Corral Inquest*, 51.
25 Nyle H. Miller and Joseph W. Snell, *Why the West Was Wild: A Contemporary Look at the Antics of Some Highly Publicized Kansas Cowtown Personalities*, 415–416.
26 Nyle H. Miller and Joseph W. Snell, *Why the West Was Wild: A Contemporary Look at the Antics of Some Highly Publicized Kansas Cowtown Personalities*, 417–419.
27 Nyle H. Miller and Joseph W. Snell, *Why the West Was Wild: A Contemporary Look at the Antics of Some Highly Publicized Kansas Cowtown Personalities*, 420–421.
28 Robert K. DeArment, *Bat Masterson: The Man and the Legend*, 216.
29 Casey Tefertiller, *Wyatt Earp: The Life Behind the Legend*, 174.

30 Casey Tefertiller, *Wyatt Earp: The Life Behind the Legend*, 175.
31 Stuart N. Lake, *Wyatt Earp: Frontier Marshal*, 312–313.
32 Stuart N. Lake, *Wyatt Earp: Frontier Marshal*, 175.
33 Stuart N. Lake, *Wyatt Earp: Frontier Marshal*, 178.
34 Stuart N. Lake, *Wyatt Earp: Frontier Marshal*, 312–316.
35 Casey Tefertiller, *Wyatt Earp: The Life Behind the Legend*, 179–181.
36 Casey Tefertiller, *Wyatt Earp: The Life Behind the Legend*, 183.
37 William M. Breakenridge, *Helldorado: Bringing the Law to the Mesquite*, 261–262.
38 William M. Breakenridge, *Helldorado: Bringing the Law to the Mesquite*, 265–266.
39 Casey Tefertiller, *Wyatt Earp: The Life Behind the Legend*, 184.
40 Casey Tefertiller, *Wyatt Earp: The Life Behind the Legend*, 184–185.
41 Casey Tefertiller, *Wyatt Earp: The Life Behind the Legend*, 185.
42 Casey Tefertiller, *Wyatt Earp: The Life Behind the Legend*, 187.
43 Casey Tefertiller, *Wyatt Earp: The Life Behind the Legend*, 187–188.
44 Casey Tefertiller, *Wyatt Earp: The Life Behind the Legend*, 188–189.
45 Casey Tefertiller, *Wyatt Earp: The Life Behind the Legend*, 193.
46 Alford Turner (ed.), *The O. K. Corral Inquest*, 230–246. Casey Tefertiller, *Wyatt Earp: The Life Behind the Legend*, 194–196.
47 Sherry Monahan, *Mrs. Earp: The Wives and Lovers of the Earp Brothers*, 115–117.
48 Casey Tefertiller, *Wyatt Earp: The Life Behind the Legend*, 198.
49 Michael T. Isenberg, *John L. Sullivan and His America* (Chicago: University of Illinois Press, 1988) 108–109. Robert K. DeArment, *Bat Masterson: The Man and the Legend*, 218–219.
50 Robert K. DeArment, *Bat Masterson: The Man and the Legend*, 219–220.
51 Stuart N. Lake, *Wyatt Earp: Frontier Marshal*, 322–323.
52 Stuart N. Lake, *Wyatt Earp: Frontier Marshal*, 324. Glen G. Boyer, *I Married Wyatt Earp: The Recollections of Josephine Sarah Marcus Earp*, 103.
53 Stuart N. Lake, *Wyatt Earp: Frontier Marshal*, 325.
54 The Tombstone Epitaph, March 27, 1882. Library of Congress, accessed March 30, 2018. https://chroniclingamerica.loc.gov/lccn/sn84021939/1882-03-27/ed-1/seq-1/#date1=1882&index=1&rows=20&words=Earp+Earps&searchType=basic&sequence=0&state=Arizona&date2=1882&proxtext=Earp&y=11&x=10&dateFilterType=yearRange&page=1.
55 Stuart N. Lake, *Wyatt Earp: Frontier Marshal*, 327.
56 Casey Tefertiller, *Wyatt Earp: The Life Behind the Legend*, 226.
57 Stuart N. Lake, *Wyatt Earp: Frontier Marshal*, 327.
58 Stuart N. Lake, *Wyatt Earp: Frontier Marshal*, 327–328.
59 Casey Tefertiller, *Wyatt Earp: The Life Behind the Legend*, 226.
60 Casey Tefertiller, *Wyatt Earp: The Life Behind the Legend*, 227.
61 Stuart N. Lake, *Wyatt Earp: Frontier Marshal*, 330.
62 Stuart N. Lake, *Wyatt Earp: Frontier Marshal*, 331.

63 Casey Tefertiller, *Wyatt Earp: The Life Behind the Legend*, 227–228.
64 Casey Tefertiller, *Wyatt Earp: The Life Behind the Legend*, 231.
65 William M. Breakenridge, *Helldorado: Bringing the Law to the Mesquite*, 287–288.
66 William M. Breakenridge, *Helldorado: Bringing the Law to the Mesquite*, 288.
67 Casey Tefertiller, *Wyatt Earp: The Life Behind the Legend*, 231.
68 Ibid.
69 Casey Tefertiller, *Wyatt Earp: The Life Behind the Legend*, 232.
70 Casey Tefertiller, *Wyatt Earp: The Life Behind the Legend*, 233.
71 Casey Tefertiller, *Wyatt Earp: The Life Behind the Legend*, 230–231.
72 Casey Tefertiller, *Wyatt Earp: The Life Behind the Legend*, 234–235.
73 Stuart N. Lake, *Wyatt Earp: Frontier Marshal*, 336–340.
74 William M. Breakenridge, *Helldorado: Bringing the Law to the Mesquite*, 297–298. Casey Tefertiller, *Wyatt Earp: The Life Behind the Legend*, 233.
75 Casey Tefertiller, *Wyatt Earp: The Life Behind the Legend*, 237.
76 Casey Tefertiller, *Wyatt Earp: The Life Behind the Legend*, 238.
77 Sherry Monahan, *Mrs. Earp: The Wives and Lovers of the Earp Brothers*, 27.
78 Casey Tefertiller, *Wyatt Earp: The Life Behind the Legend*, 238.
79 Ibid.
80 Stuart N. Lake, *Wyatt Earp: Frontier Marshal*, 342–343.
81 Stuart N. Lake, *Wyatt Earp: Frontier Marshal*, 343.
82 Ibid.
83 Stuart N. Lake, *Wyatt Earp: Frontier Marshal*, 344–346.
84 Casey Tefertiller, *Wyatt Earp: The Life Behind the Legend*, 247.
85 Robert K. DeArment, *Bat Masterson: The Man and the Legend*, 217.
86 Fred E. Sutton and A. B. MacDonald, *Hands Up! Stories of the Six-Gun Fighters of the Old Wild West* (Indianapolis, IN: The Bobbs-Merrill Company, 1926), 109.

CHAPTER 12: TRINIDAD

1 Robert K. DeArment, *Bat Masterson: The Man and the Legend*, 219–223, 239.
2 Robert K. DeArment, *Bat Masterson: The Man and the Legend*, 223.
3 Casey Tefertiller, *Wyatt Earp: The Life Behind the Legend*, 247, 255.
4 Casey Tefertiller, *Wyatt Earp: The Life Behind the Legend*, 248–255.
5 Chuck Hornung and Gary L. Roberts, "The Split: Did Doc & Wyatt Split Because of a Racial Slur?" *True West Magazine*, November 1, 2001. Robert K. DeArment, *Bat Masterson: The Man and the Legend*, 225–226.
6 Robert K. DeArment, *Bat Masterson: The Man and the Legend*, 225.
7 Casey Tefertiller, *Wyatt Earp: The Life Behind the Legend*, 255.
8 Casey Tefertiller, *Wyatt Earp: The Life Behind the Legend*, 255–257.
9 W. B. (Bat) Masterson, *Famous Gunfighters of the Western Frontier*, 35, 42.
10 Casey Tefertiller, *Wyatt Earp: The Life Behind the Legend*, 256–257.
11 Casey Tefertiller, *Wyatt Earp: The Life Behind the Legend*, 258.

12 Casey Tefertiller, *Wyatt Earp: The Life Behind the Legend*, 257.
13 Casey Tefertiller, *Wyatt Earp: The Life Behind the Legend*, 258–259.
14 Casey Tefertiller, *Wyatt Earp: The Life Behind the Legend*, 259–260.
15 W. B. (Bat) Masterson, *Famous Gunfighters of the Western Frontier*, 41. Robert K. DeArment, *Bat Masterson: The Man and the Legend*, 231.
16 Casey Tefertiller, *Wyatt Earp: The Life Behind the Legend*, 262.
17 Casey Tefertiller, *Wyatt Earp: The Life Behind the Legend*, 265–266.
18 Casey Tefertiller, *Wyatt Earp: The Life Behind the Legend*, 262.
19 Casey Tefertiller, *Wyatt Earp: The Life Behind the Legend*, 264–265.
20 Robert K. DeArment, *Bat Masterson: The Man and the Legend*, 235–237.
21 Robert K. DeArment, *Bat Masterson: The Man and the Legend*, 239–241.
22 Robert K. DeArment, *Bat Masterson: The Man and the Legend*, 246.
23 Robert K. DeArment, *Bat Masterson: The Man and the Legend*, 246–247, 249.
24 Robert K. DeArment, *Bat Masterson: The Man and the Legend*, 248–249, 251.
25 Casey Tefertiller, *Wyatt Earp: The Life Behind the Legend*, 265.
26 Glen G, Boyer, *I Married Wyatt Earp: The Recollections of Josephine Sarah Marcus Earp*, 112–114.

CHAPTER 13: THE DODGE CITY WAR

1 Robert K. DeArment, *Bat Masterson: The Man and the Legend*, 252.
2 Nyle H. Miller and Joseph W. Snell, *Why the West Was Wild: A Contemporary Look at the Antics of Some Highly Publicized Kansas Cowtown Personalities*, 520. Robert K. DeArment, *Bat Masterson: The Man and the Legend*, 252–253.
3 Nyle H. Miller and Joseph W. Snell, *Why the West Was Wild: A Contemporary Look at the Antics of Some Highly Publicized Kansas Cowtown Personalities*, 520–521.
4 Nyle H. Miller and Joseph W. Snell, *Why the West Was Wild: A Contemporary Look at the Antics of Some Highly Publicized Kansas Cowtown Personalities*, 522. Robert K. DeArment, *Bat Masterson: The Man and the Legend*, 254.
5 Robert K. DeArment, *Bat Masterson: The Man and the Legend*, 255.
6 Ibid.
7 Robert K. DeArment, *Bat Masterson: The Man and the Legend*, 256.
8 Robert K. DeArment, *Bat Masterson: The Man and the Legend*, 257.
9 Ibid.
10 Ibid.
11 Nyle H. Miller and Joseph W. Snell, *Why the West Was Wild: A Contemporary Look at the Antics of Some Highly Publicized Kansas Cowtown Personalities*, 530.
12 Nyle H. Miller and Joseph W. Snell, *Why the West Was Wild: A Contemporary Look at the Antics of Some Highly Publicized Kansas Cowtown Personalities*, 531.
13 Nyle H. Miller and Joseph W. Snell, *Why the West Was Wild: A Contemporary Look at the Antics of Some Highly Publicized Kansas Cowtown Personalities*, 531–534.

14 Nyle H. Miller and Joseph W. Snell, *Why the West Was Wild: A Contemporary Look at the Antics of Some Highly Publicized Kansas Cowtown Personalities*, 534.
15 Glen G. Boyer, *I Married Wyatt Earp: The Recollections of Josephine Sarah Marcus Earp*, 116–117.
16 W. B. (Bat) Masterson, *Famous Gunfighters of the Western Frontier*, 17.
17 Ibid.
18 Nyle H. Miller and Joseph W. Snell, *Why the West Was Wild: A Contemporary Look at the Antics of Some Highly Publicized Kansas Cowtown Personalities*, 538–540.
19 Robert K. DeArment, *Bat Masterson: The Man and the Legend*, 261.
20 Stuart N. Lake, *Wyatt Earp: Frontier Marshal*, 364–365.
21 Robert K. DeArment, *Bat Masterson: The Man and the Legend*, 263.
22 Nyle H. Miller and Joseph W. Snell, *Why the West Was Wild: A Contemporary Look at the Antics of Some Highly Publicized Kansas Cowtown Personalities*, 558.
23 Nyle H. Miller and Joseph W. Snell, *Why the West Was Wild: A Contemporary Look at the Antics of Some Highly Publicized Kansas Cowtown Personalities*, 560.
24 Nyle H. Miller and Joseph W. Snell, *Why the West Was Wild: A Contemporary Look at the Antics of Some Highly Publicized Kansas Cowtown Personalities*, 558.
25 Ibid.
26 Nyle H. Miller and Joseph W. Snell, *Why the West Was Wild: A Contemporary Look at the Antics of Some Highly Publicized Kansas Cowtown Personalities*, 558, 561.
27 Robert K. DeArment, *Bat Masterson: The Man and the Legend*, 264.
28 Jack Demattos and Chuck Parsons, "The Man Behind the Dodge City War: Luke Short's troubles brought about one of the American West's most famous photographs," *True West Magazine*, July 2015. Robert K. DeArment, *Bat Masterson: The Man and the Legend*, 264–265.
29 Nyle H. Miller and Joseph W. Snell, *Why the West Was Wild: A Contemporary Look at the Antics of Some Highly Publicized Kansas Cowtown Personalities*, 561. Glen G. Boyer, *I Married Wyatt Earp: The Recollections of Josephine Sarah Marcus Earp*, 118.
30 Casey Tefertiller, *Wyatt Earp: The Life Behind the Legend*, 306.
31 Laurel Downing Bill, "Tombstone temporarily transplanted in Alaska" *Senior Voice*, January 1, 2014, accessed February 27, 2018. www.seniorvoicealaska.com/story/2014/01/01/columns/tombstone-temporarily-transplanted-in-alaska/344.html.
32 Red Dog Saloon display information with Wyatt Earp's Smith & Wesson Model No. 3 pistol. Juneau, Alaska, August 2, 2017.
33 Eric Forst, Red Dog Saloon Owner, personal communication to Bill Markley, February 26, 2018.

CHAPTER 14: SEPARATE LIVES

1 Nyle H. Miller and Joseph W. Snell, *Why the West Was Wild: A Contemporary Look at the Antics of Some Highly Publicized Kansas Cowtown Personalities*, 422–423. Robert K. DeArment, *Bat Masterson: The Man and the Legend*, 267–268.

2 Robert K. DeArment, *Bat Masterson: The Man and the Legend*, 270.

3 Glen G. Boyer, *I Married Wyatt Earp: The Recollections of Josephine Sarah Marcus Earp*, 132–135.

4 Robert K. DeArment, *Bat Masterson: The Man and the Legend*, 344.

5 Robert K. DeArment, *Bat Masterson: The Man and the Legend*, 325–326.

6 Robert K. DeArment, *Bat Masterson: The Man and the Legend*, 271.

7 Robert K. DeArment, *Bat Masterson: The Man and the Legend*, 344.

8 Tom Clavin, *Dodge City: Wyatt Earp, Bat Masterson, and the Wickedest Town in the American West*, 257.

9 Jack DeMattos, *Masterson and Roosevelt* (College Station, TX: Creative Publishing Company, 1984), 16, 29.

10 Robert K. DeArment, *Bat Masterson: The Man and the Legend*, 285.

11 Robert K. DeArment, *Bat Masterson: The Man and the Legend*, 301–305.

12 Robert K. DeArment, *Bat Masterson: The Man and the Legend*, 330.

13 Robert K. DeArment, *Bat Masterson: The Man and the Legend*, 339–343.

14 Robert K. DeArment, *Bat Masterson: The Man and the Legend*, 345–346. Jack DeMattos, *Masterson and Roosevelt*, 26–27.

15 Robert K. DeArment, *Bat Masterson: The Man and the Legend*, 346.

16 Robert K. DeArment, *Bat Masterson: The Man and the Legend*, 367.

17 Robert K. DeArment, *Bat Masterson: The Man and the Legend*, 371–372.

18 Jack DeMattos, *Masterson and Roosevelt*, 20–24, 49, 59, 80.

19 Robert K. DeArment, *Bat Masterson: The Man and the Legend*, 385–386.

20 Robert K. DeArment, *Bat Masterson: The Man and the Legend*, 393.

21 Robert K. DeArment, *Bat Masterson: The Man and the Legend*, 396–397.

22 Robert K. DeArment, *Bat Masterson: The Man and the Legend*, 398.

23 Casey Tefertiller, *Wyatt Earp: The Life Behind the Legend*, 289.

24 Sherry Monahan, *Mrs. Earp: The Wives and Lovers of the Earp Brothers*, 27.

25 Glen G. Boyer, *I Married Wyatt Earp: The Recollections of Josephine Sarah Marcus Earp*, 119.

26 Casey Tefertiller, *Wyatt Earp: The Life Behind the Legend*, 275.

27 Casey Tefertiller, *Wyatt Earp: The Life Behind the Legend*, 275–276.

28 Casey Tefertiller, *Wyatt Earp: The Life Behind the Legend*, 276.

29 Casey Tefertiller, *Wyatt Earp: The Life Behind the Legend*, 278.

30 Casey Tefertiller, *Wyatt Earp: The Life Behind the Legend*, 279.

31 Casey Tefertiller, *Wyatt Earp: The Life Behind the Legend*, 279, 281.

32 Casey Tefertiller, *Wyatt Earp: The Life Behind the Legend*, 284, 286.

33 Casey Tefertiller, *Wyatt Earp: The Life Behind the Legend*, 286.

34 Casey Tefertiller, *Wyatt Earp: The Life Behind the Legend*, 287.

35 Casey Tefertiller, *Wyatt Earp: The Life Behind the Legend*, 285–303.

36 Casey Tefertiller, *Wyatt Earp: The Life Behind the Legend*, 303–304.
37 Casey Tefertiller, *Wyatt Earp: The Life Behind the Legend*, 306–310.
38 Casey Tefertiller, *Wyatt Earp: The Life Behind the Legend*, 310.
39 Casey Tefertiller, *Wyatt Earp: The Life Behind the Legend*, 314.
40 Casey Tefertiller, *Wyatt Earp: The Life Behind the Legend*, 317–318.
41 Ibid.
42 Casey Tefertiller, *Wyatt Earp: The Life Behind the Legend*, 318.
43 Casey Tefertiller, *Wyatt Earp: The Life Behind the Legend*, 320–324.
44 Casey Tefertiller, *Wyatt Earp: The Life Behind the Legend*, 326–327.
45 W. B. (Bat) Masterson, *Famous Gunfighters of the Western Frontier*, 65.
46 Alfred Henry Lewis, *The Sunset Trail* (New York, NY: A.L Burt Company, 1905) 99, accessed Internet archive March 2, 2018 archive.org/details/sunsettrail00lewigoog.
47 Robert K. DeArment, *Bat Masterson: The Man and the Legend*, 387.
48 "Bat Masterson," Wikipedia, accessed March 2, 2018, en.wikipedia.org/wiki/Bat_Masterson.
49 Casey Tefertiller, *Wyatt Earp: The Life Behind the Legend*, 333.
50 "Wyatt Earp," Wikipedia, accessed March 2, 2018, en.wikipedia.org/wiki/Wyatt_Earp.
51 Jack DeMattos, *Masterson and Roosevelt*, 113.
52 Jack DeMattos, *Masterson and Roosevelt*, 114.

BIBLIOGRAPHY

MANUSCRIPTS AND PRIMARY RESOURCES

Arizona Memory Project, Legal and Court History of Cochise County, Coroner's Inquest of the Gunfight at the OK Corral, Joseph Clanton Transcript.

Arizona Memory Project, Legal and Court History of Cochise County, Coroner's Inquest of the Gunfight at the OK Corral, Coleman Transcript.

Arizona Memory Project, Legal and Court History of Cochise County, Coroner's Inquest of the Gunfight at the OK Corral, King Transcript.

Crawford, Henry, personal e-mail communication to Bill Markley, March 29, 2018.

Forst, Eric, Red Dog Saloon Owner, personal communication to Bill Markley, February 26, 2018.

Red Dog Saloon display information with Wyatt Earp's Smith & Wesson Model No. 3 pistol. Juneau, Alaska, August 2, 2017.

BOOKS

Adams, Andy, *The Log of a Cowboy: A Narrative of the Old Trail Days*, New York, NY: Houghton, Mifflin and Company, 1903.

Baker, T. Lindsay, and Harrison, Billy R., *Adobe Walls: The History and Archeology of the 1874 Trading Post*, College Station: Texas A&M University Press, 1986.

Borneman, Walter R., *Rival Rails: The Race to Build America's Greatest Transcontinental Railroad*, New York, NY: Random House, 2010.

Boyer, Glen G., *I Married Wyatt Earp: The Recollections of Josephine Sarah Marcus Earp*, Stamford, CT: Longmeadow Press, 1976.

Breakenridge, William M., *Helldorado: Bringing the Law to the Mesquite*, Lincoln: University of Nebraska Press, 1928.

Brown, Dee, *Bury My Heart at Wounded Knee: An Indian History of the American West*, New York, NY: Henry Holt and Company, 1970.

Clavin, Tom, *Dodge City: Wyatt Earp, Bat Masterson, and the Wickedest Town in the American West*, New York, NY: St. Martin's Press, 2017.

Crutchfield, James A., Moulton, Candy, and Del Bene, Terry (eds.), *The Settlement of America: Encyclopedia of Westward Expansion from Jamestown to the Closing of the Frontier*, Vol. 1, Armonk, NY: M. E. Sharpe Inc., 2011.

DeArment, Robert K., *Bat Masterson: The Man and the Legend*, Norman: University of Oklahoma Press, 1979.

DeMattos, Jack, *Masterson and Roosevelt*, College Station, TX: Creative Publishing Company, 1984.

Dixon, Olive K., *Life of Billy Dixon: Plainsman, Scout and Pioneer*, Abilene, TX: State House Press, 1987.

Foy, Eddie, and Harlow, Alvin F., *Clowning Through Life*, New York, NY: E.P. Dutton & Company, 1928.

Friesen, Steve, *Buffalo Bill: Scout, Showman, Visionary*, Golden, CO: Fulcrum Publishing Inc., 2010.

Gard, Wayne, *The Great Buffalo Hunt*, New York, NY: Alfred A. Knopf, 1960.

Gilbert, Miles, *Getting a Stand*, Union City, TN: Pioneer Press, 1986.

Hutton, Paul Andrew, *The Apache Wars: The Hunt for Geronimo, the Apache Kid, and the Captive Boy Who Started the Longest War in American History*, New York, NY: Broadway Books, 2016.

Isenberg, Michael T., *John L. Sullivan and His America*, Chicago: University of Illinois Press, 1988.

Kazanjian, Howard, and Enss, Chris, *Thunder Over the Prairie: The True Story of a Murder and a Manhunt by The Greatest Posse of All Time*, Guilford, CT: Globe Pequot Press, 2009.

Lake, Stuart N., *Wyatt Earp: Frontier Marshal*, New York, NY: Pocket Books, 1994.

Lingenfelter, Richard E., *Western Lands and Waters Series XXVI, Bonanzas and Borrascas: Gold Lust & Silver Sharks, 1848-1889*, Norman, OK: University of Oklahoma Press, 2012.

Masterson, W. B. (Bat), *Famous Gunfighters of the Western Frontier: Wyatt Earp, Doc Holliday, Luke Short and Others*, Mineola, NY: Dover Publications Inc., 2009.

Miller, Nyle H., and Snell, Joseph W., *Why the West Was Wild: A Contemporary Look at the Antics of Some Highly Publicized Kansas Cowtown Personalities*, Norman: University of Oklahoma Press, 1963.

Monahan, Sherry, *Mrs. Earp: The Lives and Lovers of the Earp Brothers*, Guilford, CT: Globe Pequot Press, 2013.

Monahan, Sherry, *The Wicked West: Boozers, Cruisers, Gamblers, and More*, Tucson, AZ: Rio Nuevo Publishers, 2005.

Monahan, Sherry, *Tombstone's Treasure: Silver Mines and Golden Saloons*, Albuquerque: University of New Mexico Press, 2007.

O'Neal, Bill, *Encyclopedia of Western Gunfighters*, Norman: University of Oklahoma Press, 1979.

Silva, Lee A., *Wyatt Earp: A Biography of the Legend, Vol. 1: The Cowtown Years*, Santa Ana, CA: Graphic Publishers, 2002.

Silva, Lee A., and Silva, Susan Leiser, *Wyatt Earp: A Biography of the Legend, Vol. 2: Part 1: Tombstone before the Earps*, Santa Ana, CA: Graphic Publishers, 2010.

Siringo, Charles, *Riata and Spurs: The Story of a Lifetime Spent in the Saddle as Cowboy and Detective*, New York, NY: Cosimo Classics, 1927.

Spring, Agnes Wright, *The Cheyenne and Black Hills Stage and Express Routes*, Lincoln: University of Nebraska Press, 1948.

Sutton, Fred E., and MacDonald, A. B., *Hands Up! Stories of the Six-Gun Fighters of the Old Wild West*, Indianapolis, IN: The Bobbs-Merrill Company, 1926.

Tefertiller, Casey, Wyatt Earp: *The Life Behind the Legend*, New York, NY: John Wiley & Sons, Inc., 1997.

The Diagram Group, *The Way to Play: The Illustrated Encyclopedia of the Games of the World*, New York, NY: Paddington Press Ltd. 1975.

Turner, Alford E. (ed.) *The O. K. Corral Inquest*, College Station, TX: Creative Publishing Company, 1981.

Walton, W. M., annotated by Lisa Lach, *Life and Adventures of Ben Thompson Famous Texan*, Austin, TX: The Steck Company Publishers, 2016.

Williamson, G. R., *Frontier Gambling: The Games, The Gamblers & The Great Gambling Halls of the Old West*, CreateSpace Independent Publishing Platform, 2011.

PERIODICALS

Demattos, Jack, and Parsons, Chuck, "The Man Behind the Dodge City War: Luke Short's troubles brought about one of the American West's most famous photographs," *True West Magazine*, July 2015.

Hornung, Chuck, and Roberts, Gary L., "The Split: Did Doc & Wyatt Split Because of a Racial Slur?" *True West Magazine*, November 1, 2001.

Jay, Roger, "Wyatt Earp's Lost Year," *Wild West Magazine*, June 12, 2006.

Markley, Bill, "The Legendary West: 10 Destinations You Must Visit in a Lifetime," *True West Magazine*, July 2017.

INTERNET RESOURCES

Bill, Laurel Downing, "Tombstone temporarily transplanted in Alaska" *Senior Voice*, January 1, 2014. Accessed February 27, 2018. www.seniorvoicealaska .com/story/2014/01/01/columns/tombstone-temporarily-transplanted-in-alaska/344.html

City of San Bernardino, "Diary of the Earp Wagon Train to San Bernardino by Sarah Jane Rousseau." Accessed March 30, 2018. www.ci.san-bernardino .ca.us/about/history/pioneer_women/sarah_jane_rousseau.asp

City of San Bernardino, "Wyatt Earp in San Bernardino." Accessed March 4, 2018. www.ci.san-bernardino.ca.us/about/history/wyatt_earp.asp

Ford County Historical Society Accessed December 17, 2017 www.kansas history.us/fordco.

Ford County Historical Society Accessed January 7, 2018. www.kansashistory .us/fordco/dodgecity.html

Legends of America. Accessed January 11, 2018. www.legendsofamerica.com/ tx-fortgriffin/.

Lewis, Alfred Henry, *The Sunset Trail*, New York, NY: A.L Burt Company, 1905, Internet Archive. Accessed March 2, 2018. archive.org/details/sunsettrail00lewigoog.

National Bison Association. Accessed December 12, 2017, bisoncentral.com/general-info/bison-1-millionbison-1-million-2/bison-1-million/

Northern Cheyenne Tribe website. Accessed March 30, 2018. www.cheyenne nation.com

Rath, Ida Ellen, *Early Ford County*, Ford County Historical Society. Accessed January 5, 2018. www.kansashistory.us/fordco/rath2/05.html

Shillingberg, William B., "Wyatt Earp and the Buntline Special Myth" *Kansas Historical Quarterly* Summer 1996 Vol. 42, No. 2, Kansas Historical Society, 1976, 113-154. Accessed February 22, 2018. www.kshs.org/p/kansas-historical-quarterly%20 wyatt-earp-and-the-buntline-special-myth/13255

The Tombstone Epitaph, March 27, 1882. Library of Congress. Accessed March 30, 2018. chroniclingamerica.loc.gov/lccn/sn84021939/1882-03-27/ed-1/seq1/#date1=1882&index=1&rows=20&words=Earp+Earps&searchType= basic&sequence=0&state=Arizona&date2=1882&proxtext=Earp&y=11&x =10&dateFilterType=yearRange&page=1

The William F. Cody Archive: Documenting the life and times of Wild Bill, Col. Cody, Scout and Indian Fighter, W. B. (Bat) Masterson, "A Few Incidents in the Adventurous Career of the Famous Buffalo Bill that Have Passed Under My Personal Observation—His Early Days on the Frontier," Human Life Publishing Co., 1908. Accessed January 25, 2018. codyarchive.org/texts/wfc.nsp02038.html

Wikimedia Commons, 1870 Census, Masterson. Accessed March 30, 2018. upload.wikimedia.org/wikipedia/commons/3/35/1870_census_Masterson .jpg.

Wikipedia, "Bat Masterson." Accessed March 2, 2018. en.wikipedia.org/wiki/Bat_Masterson

Wikipedia, "Wyatt Earp." Accessed March 2, 2018. en.wikipedia.org/wiki/Wyatt_Earp

Wyatt Earp History Page. Accessed November 27, 2017, www.wyattearp.net.

INDEX

ACKNOWLEDGMENTS

First, thanks to Bat Masterson and Wyatt Earp for living extraordinary lives I could explore and tell about. Thanks to all the folks who recorded events during their lifetimes and those who preserve those records. Thank you, Erin Turner and the folks at TwoDot, for giving me the opportunity to write this book. Jim Hatzell, thank you for your outstanding illustrations.

I thank my fellow Most Intrepid Western Author Posse members for their help: Monty McCord for his assistance; Kellen Cutsforth for tracking down the document for Buffalo Bill Cody's involvement with Bat's rescue of Billy Thompson; Sherry Monahan for her help with understanding the game of faro; and Chris Enss for her support, guidance, and confirmation on Kate Elder's story. Thanks to the members of Western Writers of America; without them my writing career would not be where it is today.

Tom Clavin, author of *Dodge City*, thank you for your help. Hughes County Sheriff Mike Leidholt, thank you for your review. Longtime friend Phil "Theta" Bowden, thank you for your detailed critique. Mike Pellerzi, as always thanks for your cowboy point of view. Keep your powder dry and check your cinch. Historian Henry Crawford, thank you for your assistance with the buffalo hunting chapters. Thanks to Eric Forst, owner of Red Dog Saloon, Juneau, Alaska, for discussing Wyatt's pistol he left behind. A big thank you to freelance wordsmith Barry Keith Williams for an excellent job polishing the manuscript.

Thank you to my wife, Liz, for putting up with my long hours in the basement plunking away on the computer keyboard and shouting up the stairs, "How do you spell such-and-such word?!" and to the rest of my family for their support including son Chris's review of the first couple chapters. I thank all the critters who distracted me by occasionally peeking in my window to see what I was up to. Thanks to the Lord for giving me this opportunity and for the ability to think and write.

ABOUT THE AUTHOR

Bill Markley is a member of Western Writers of America (WWA) and is a staff writer for WWA's *Roundup* magazine. He also writes for *True West, Wild West,* and *South Dakota* magazines. His latest book, written with coauthor Kellen Cutsforth, *Old West Showdown: Two Authors Wrangle over the Truth about the Mythic Old West,* explores differing viewpoints on ten Old West characters and events. In addition, Bill has written three nonfiction books: *Dakota Epic: Experiences of a Reenactor During the Filming of* Dances with Wolves; *Up the Missouri River with Lewis and Clark;* and *American Pilgrim: A Post-September 11th Bus Trip and Other Tales of the Road.* His first historical novel, *Deadwood Dead Men,* was selected by Western Fictioneers as a finalist for its 2014 Peacemaker Award in the category Best First Western Novel. Bill wrote the "Military Establishment" chapter and thirty entries for the *Encyclopedia of Western Expansion.* He manages WWA's Facebook page as well as Old West and American History Facebook pages. He was a member of Toastmasters International for twenty years. He earned a bachelor's degree in Biology and a master's degree in Environmental Sciences and Engineering at Virginia Tech, worked on two Antarctic field teams, and worked forty years with the South Dakota Department of Environment and Natural Resources. Raised on a farm near Valley Forge, Pennsylvania, Bill has always loved history. He reenacts Civil War infantry and frontier cavalry and has participated in the films *Dances with Wolves, Son of the Morning Star, Far and Away, Gettysburg,* and *Crazy Horse.* Bill and his wife, Liz, live in Pierre, South Dakota, where they have raised two children, now grown.

ABOUT THE ILLUSTRATOR

Jim Hatzell is a graduate of the American Academy of Art in Chicago, Illinois, with a degree in Advertising and Design and in Illustration. Jim has also been in the motion picture business for nearly thirty years. Jim and Bill first met on the set of *Dances with Wolves* in 1989. Jim and his wife, Jacqui, make their home in Rapid City, South Dakota.